D1240835

A POLITICAL SCIENCE MANIFESTO
FOR THE AGE OF POPULISM

Populism and authoritarian-populist parties have surged throughout the world in the twenty-first century. In the United States, it's difficult to pinpoint the cause, yet Donald Trump appears to have become the poster president. David Ricci, in this call to arms, thinks Trump is symptomatic of a myriad of changes that have caused a crisis among Americans – namely, mass economic and creative destruction: automation, outsourcing, deindustrialization, globalization, privatization, financialization, digitalization, and the rise of temporary jobs – all breeding resentment, which then breeds populism.

Rather than dwelling on symptoms, Ricci focuses on the root of our nation's problems. Thus, creative destruction, aiming at perpetual economic growth, encouraged by neoliberalism, creates the economic inequality that fuels resentment and leads to increased populism, putting democracy at risk. In these circumstances, he urges political scientists to highlight this destruction in meaningful and substantive ways, that is, to use empirical realism to put human beings back into politics.

Ricci's straightforward argument conveys a sense of political urgency, grappling with real-world problems and working to transform abstract speculations into tangible, useful tools. The result is a deeply passionate book, important not only to political scientists, but to anyone who cares about public life.

David M. Ricci lives in Mevaseret, and is a former chair of the departments of American Studies and Political Science at the Hebrew University. He has been a fellow at the Woodrow Wilson International Center for Scholars in Washington, DC, the Institute for Advanced Study in Princeton, New Jersey, and the Brookings Institution. He is the author of seven books, including *The Tragedy of Political Science* (1984), *The Transformation of American Politics* (1993), *Good Citizenship in America* (2004), *Why Conservatives Tell Stories and Liberals Don't* (2011), and *Politics Without Stories* (2016).

A Political Science Manifesto for the Age of Populism

Challenging Growth, Markets, Inequality, and Resentment

DAVID M. RICCI
The Hebrew University

CAMBRIDGE
UNIVERSITY PRESS

CAMBRIDGE
UNIVERSITY PRESS

University Printing House, Cambridge CB2 8BS, United Kingdom

One Liberty Plaza, 20th Floor, New York, NY 10006, USA

477 Williamstown Road, Port Melbourne, VIC 3207, Australia

314–321, 3rd Floor, Plot 3, Splendor Forum, Jasola District Centre, New Delhi – 110025, India

79 Anson Road, #06-04/06, Singapore 079906

Cambridge University Press is part of the University of Cambridge.

It furthers the University's mission by disseminating knowledge in the pursuit of education, learning, and research at the highest international levels of excellence.

www.cambridge.org
Information on this title: www.cambridge.org/9781108479424
DOI: 10.1017/9781108785440

© David M. Ricci 2020

First published 2020

A catalogue record for this publication is available from the British Library.

ISBN 978-1-108-47942-4 Hardback
ISBN 978-1-108-74305-1 Paperback

Cambridge University Press has no responsibility for the persistence or accuracy of URLs for external or third-party internet websites referred to in this publication and does not guarantee that any content on such websites is, or will remain, accurate or appropriate.

CONTENTS

PREFACE*

Where is this book located in political thought today? In recent years, scholars, politicians, think tankers, journalists, and pundits have conducted an anxious debate about how democracy may succumb to what they call populism. Such thinkers do not fear a revival of late-nineteenth-century agrarian unrest in America, when Mary Pease told farmers they should raise less corn and more hell. But they have already published books such as John Judis, *The Populist Explosion* (2016),[1] Jan-Werner Muller, *What is Populism?* (2016),[2] Benjamin Page and Martin Gilens, *Democracy in America* (2017),[3] Edward Luce, *The Retreat of Western Liberalism* (2017),[4] Pankaj Mishra, *Age of Anger* (2017),[5] Mark Lilla, *The Once and Future Liberal* (2017),[6] David Runciman, *How Democracy Ends* (2018),[7] Steven Levitsky and Daniel Ziblatt, *How Democracies Die* (2018),[8] William Galston, *Anti-Pluralism* (2018),[9] Francis Fukuyama, *Identity* (2018),[10] Robert Kuttner, *Can Democracy Survive Global Capitalism?* (2018),[11] Barry Eichengreen, *The Populist Temptation* (2018),[12] Yascha Mounk, *The People vs. Democracy* (2018),[13] John Campbell, *American Discontent* (2018),[14] Paul Starr, *Entrenchment* (2019),[15] and Sophia Rosenfeld, *Democracy and Truth* (2019).[16]

The debate has examined many trends and events to explain the recent rise of populist governments and the success of populist candidates for public office in many countries. Opinions vary, but most of the debaters agree that an underlying cause

* This book cites, and quotes from, the presidential addresses of fourteen presidents of the American Political Science Association (APSA). I found that those addresses were especially relevant to my project because their authors stepped back from personal research to comment knowledgeably on their discipline – for example, on what it should investigate, and on how it should report its findings. D.R.

of contemporary populism is the resentment many people feel, with considerable justification, because of disruptive changes forced on their lives by the modern economy, which may be described as capitalism, free enterprise, neoliberalism, globalization, or a market-based society.[17]

Some of those changes – in working conditions, in the distribution of wealth, in the use of drastically new products such as smartphones, and more – are regarded by American Political Science Association president (2019) Rogers Smith as belittling beliefs that frame virtuous lives, as challenging traditional stations in society, and as deflating narratives that inspire important groups of citizens. If this goes on, some vital social bonds may vanish and some essential democratic institutions may collapse.[18]

In these circumstances, various parties to the debate have discussed what modern societies might do to avoid sinking into full-blown populism. Here is not the place to discuss their recommendations, which are diverse and not always compatible with one another.[19] Instead, *A Political Science Manifesto for the Age of Populism* proposes that, even while the debate continues in a general way, some scholars should target the overall crisis specifically in their research and teaching.

To that end, while the debaters continue to explore large-scale propositions about populism, what I will suggest is that some political scientists, in concert, should investigate and publicize cases of contemporary "resentment." I will further suggest that, to achieve an effective focus, this sort of research should highlight one particular source of resentment, which is the destructive side of what economists call the process of "creative destruction."

Such destruction, which I will discuss later, flows from economic innovations – such as automation, outsourcing, deindustrialization, globalization, privatization, financialization, digitalization, and temporary employment – that generate social disruptions, occupational dislocations, environmental damages, and personal injury to the point of breeding resentment, which fuels much of what happens, sometimes

undesirably, in American politics today.[20] People who analyze the nature of our times – in scholarly research, in news
broadcasts, on social media, in talk shows, in families, in party
forums, and among friends – often focus on issues that may not
seem immediately economic but cultural, such as rage against
immigrants or despair over waning family values.[21] Even those
issues, however, are usually fueled by elements of economic
change, such as when citizens fear that immigrants will take
from them good jobs that have not yet been outsourced to
globalization, or when parents (and children) who yearn for
closer relations at home are stressed out because many modern
mothers and fathers must work long hours to make ends meet.[22]

In this situation, drawing attention to the downsides of
creative destruction may encourage, or even inspire, elected
officials, journalists, campaign consultants, pundits, lobbyists,
political activists, and ordinary voters to try to mitigate the
damaging effects of economic change and therefore reduce
resentment and its populist consequences. As if to endorse this
strategy, President Emmanuel Macron, on December 10, 2018,
in a nationally televised speech, responded to intimations
of French populism by promising swift governmental action
designed to reduce resentment among demonstrators who,
he admitted, could not make a decent living in the modern
economy.[23] In their anger, before Macron's speech, thousands
of "yellow-vest" citizens took to French streets week after week
to protest, sometimes violently, against a combination of high
taxes and low wages that led them to conclude that politics as
usual was no longer acceptable.

As I write these lines, yellow-vest demonstrations are continuing and no one knows if the tax cuts and wage increases
that Macron promised will put the French populist genie back
in its bottle. But that the French president spoke out as he did
is an indication of seething passions waiting to be addressed.[24]

Mostly in reference to America, I will suggest, starting in
Chapter 1, a program of academic engagement with resentment, which I believe is the most powerful source of modern

populism. I seek in this book to enlist first of all political scientists, because they are my disciplinary colleagues. But I hope that what I write will also interest other scholars who care about public life, in disciplines such as sociology, anthropology, history, economics, geography, psychology, philosophy, religious studies, and more.

These men and women may rest assured professionally. Many of them rightly aspire to political neutrality, that is, to not taking sides between opposing sectors of society. However, academics need not shy away from the engagement I am about to recommend, because it violates no principles of responsible scholarship. That is so because to study resentment – why it arises, where it appears, and what it produces politically – is not a partisan project. Rather, from Republicans to Democrats, from the Tea Party to Occupy Wall Street, from Donald Trump to Bernie Sanders, from Senate Majority Leader Mitch McConnell to Speaker of the House Nancy Pelosi, from *The American Conservative* to *The Nation* magazines, from Hillsdale to Oberlin colleges, from MSNBC to Fox News, Americans agree that a good deal of resentment exists today and drives a large part of public life.[25]

In those circumstances, to investigate, to teach, and to write about *populism* via currents of *resentment* that emerge from *creative destruction* is not a matter of taking sides but an exercise in highlighting exceptionally important facts.[26] For example, some fact-finding along these lines took place in Washington, DC, at the American Political Science Association's 2019 Annual Meeting & Exhibition, which was dedicated to the theme of "Populism and Privilege."

1 THE AGE OF POPULISM

A number of preliminary matters must be dealt with before we can proceed to the central arguments of this book. So let us do that now, and then get down to business starting in Chapter 2: The Temple of Science.

A Compound Proposition

My first postulate is that we live in an Age of Populism. Like it or not, that is where we are. I will refer to populist president Donald Trump frequently as we move along. Indeed, as I write these lines, he so dominates America's public conversation that I am tempted to call the times we live in the Age of Trump. However, to name our era after Donald Trump would be to exaggerate his importance because this president is just a symptom of modern trends that have brought America to where it is today. These trends – in values, in expectations, in work, in information, in technology, in family relations, in international trade, in public manners, in finance, in politics, and more – will continue to shape the nation's life for many years to come, and not only in welcome ways.

Ergo, scholars and pundits have labeled the output of such trends populistic, not Trumpian. From that point of view, it is the overall condition, rather than the passing instance, which weighs most significantly on the country. Accordingly, I propose, while public life seems especially threatened and vulnerable these days, that some political scientists, whose profession is especially focused on that life, will address our political circumstances, in a populist age, by highlighting the disruptive results of what economists call "creative destruction."[27] Later, I will discuss creative destruction at some length.

But why highlight *economics* when our object is *politics*? Because, beyond the importance of this or that case of creative destruction, the overall exercise is a dynamic process of innovation in modern society that rewards some people – like Bill Gates, software engineers, accountants, Michael Bloomberg, hedge-fund managers, James Dyson, doctors, lawyers, investment bankers, Sam Walton – and penalizes others, like the workers sent home when General Motors closed its 4.8-million-square-foot assembly plant (larger than the Pentagon) in Janesville, Wisconsin in December, 2008.[28] Or, it rewards some high-tech communities, like New York and San Jose, while it punishes others in the Rust Belt, like Youngstown or Detroit. Therefore, in my view, this creative destruction, which is praised by most politicians for its ability to generate "economic growth," is extremely dangerous for upending millions of citizens' lives and thus powerfully challenging the basic institutions and practices of American democracy.

My proposition, then, is (1) that there is a national crisis, which I will call the Age of Populism; (2) that much of that crisis is caused by the results of creative destruction; and (3) that some scholars, but especially political scientists, should commit themselves, via research and teaching, to trying to mitigate those results. This is a compound proposition whose various elements, and the strategy I want to suggest for confronting them, will take some time, throughout this book, to explain.

What is Political Science For?

As for how my colleagues might relate to all this, we should begin by asking: What is political science for? Political scientists do not always ask that question explicitly.[29] They usually feel that what they are doing – which is studying politics – is so obviously important to society that they need not discuss its rationale at length. What they do instead, in political science departments from one college and university to another, is teach classes about their discipline's "scope and methods." In those classes, the professors discuss what sorts of people, events, procedures, and institutions should be subjects of political research. This is the matter of "scope." Additionally, they discuss how such things should be investigated. This is the matter of "methods."

This book extends those discussions, in that it explores a package of scope and methods that might be appropriate for some political scientists today. But for the moment, let us phrase the matter differently. Let us consider that, underneath talk about which subjects to study and how, there lies a large and sometimes unstated question, which is about what purposes political science should serve in a modern, democratic country.

I regard that question not as an invitation to theoretical speculation but as a call for immediate action. That is because "What is political science for?" is an urgent question that arises in a specific social, economic, and political environment that worries me greatly, and that is the Age of Populism. Are we not therefore somehow, at least somewhat, obliged to consider the nature and dynamics of that environment?

Now if, in the pages that follow, we will think along those lines, we will see that for some political scientists there may be, in all of this, a special role to play, an exceptional contribution of research, teaching, and publishing to offer students and colleagues, friends and neighbors, activists and pundits, a testimony, in some respects – in other words, a special vision of what at least part of political science is for. I will return to that possible project but, first, let us place it in perspective.

A Previous Political Era

Many of the trends that brought Donald Trump to power (such as political polarization, gerrymandering, globalization, automation, outsourcing, round-the-clock news, the gig economy, immigration, deindustrialization, too-big-to-fail banks, gated communities, silo thinking, click-bait journalism, digital addiction, platform capitalism, identity politics, media extremism, perpetual wars, educational elitism, and more) will remain after his administration and continue to shape public life. Therefore, although this president did not create the Age of Populism, it is epitomized in him, in the trends that brought him to power, and in the enthusiasm for, and the opposition to, what he says, does, and stands for.

That being the case, it is safe to predict that, in years to come, hundreds of books and thousands of articles, blogs, Facebook and Twitter posts, etc., will be written about Donald Trump. They will look back to analyze where he came from, and they will explore how his election and administration affected how Americans lived together. Anxiety will animate many of the people who will write those books, and they will divide, roughly speaking, between (1) those who believe that much in American life was appalling and therefore Trump's authenticity was the solution,[30] and (2) those who will feel that Trump himself was appalling, in which case the country had to undo much of what he said and did.[31]

Some such books have already been written. I won't take sides among them, but I want to note that the present wave of severe anxiety, fueled by conflicting fears and convictions, is not unique in the cycles of American public life.[32] For example, a similar upheaval struck America in the 1920s and 1930s, after an unspeakably horrible world war, when an old and largely aristocratic order was breaking down in many European countries, and when economic upheavals and hardships threatened America, most obviously in the Crash of 1929 and the ensuing Great Depression.

We should recall, then, that while America in those years experienced dangerous events at home and abroad, the interval between World War I and World War II was a time when, like today, some Americans went sharply right and others went sharply left.[33] This happened because many people worried that existing political institutions – from political parties to national elections, from federal agencies to judicial review – might fail to preserve democracy in the face of brutal alternatives such as fascism and communism. As challenges arose, Americans became aware of shocking circumstances, such as the 25-percent unemployment rate at home,[34] breadlines in the streets, inflation in Weimar Germany, famine in the Soviet Union, the Italian invasion of Ethiopia, pogroms against German Jews, the Moscow trials, the civil war in Spain,[35] the annexation of the Sudetenland, the Molotov-Ribbentrop Pact, and more. Most obviously, they saw that compelling ideologies took center stage in Europe, to the point where autocrats and dictators rose to power in Russia, Germany, Italy, Spain, Bulgaria, Romania, Greece, Turkey, Albania, Poland, Portugal, Yugoslavia, Austria, Lithuania, Latvia, and Estonia.

In those inter-war years, Americans agonized a great deal over matters of political principle. This was because, when challenged by right-wing and left-wing thinkers, who advocated dramatic and even charismatic leadership, democracy inspired by eighteenth-century Enlightenment ideals of moderate and sensible public behavior became difficult to defend. In a society increasingly committed to science and tangible metrics in industry, agriculture, commerce, transportation, education, and more, American faith in a higher law of natural rights, which via the Declaration of Independence and the Bill of Rights had historically justified the nation's constitutional and representative government,[36] seemed to many American thinkers a fragile inheritance, philosophically speaking, of well-intentioned but somewhat anachronistic Founders.[37]

In short, much of the inter-war anxiety called into question fundamental American institutions and practices. Accordingly, some fears in those days were almost apocalyptic, like some of the fears that fuel political anxiety today. Nevertheless, President Franklin D. Roosevelt and the New Deal devised a set of federal agencies and public policies – such as the Securities and Exchange Commission, the Social Security Commission, the National Labor Relations Board, farm subsidies, bank deposit insurance, rural electrification, public works, and more – to alleviate some of the Depression's major problems. Consequently, many Americans proceeded after World War II as if the systemic ruptures and failures that had alarmed them earlier had eventually been repaired.

Causes for post-war optimism abounded. Victory against Germany, Italy, and Japan inspired ideological confidence. The economy boomed and promised to continue growing via trade, science, and technology. The country enjoyed years of democratic progress, wherein McCarthyism was deplorable but injured relatively few people, while civil rights made considerable gains, though not large enough. From 1945 to the mid-1970s, many workers enjoyed industrial peace, while unions were strong and corporations were accommodating. Everyone knew that a nuclear war between the United States and the Soviet Union would be catastrophic, but most people assumed that it had been postponed indefinitely by the Cold War stalemate based on mutually assured destruction (MAD). And then, of course, in 1991, the Soviet Union collapsed, and democracy by American standards seemed poised to spread throughout the world.

Populism

We should recall these events not because they demonstrate that America solved its largest problems (we are still struggling with some of those). Rather, they indicate, in the Age of Populism, that we need not feel uniquely stressed because our culture and society are threatened by immensely powerful dislocations. In this sense, the lesson to be learned from earlier anxieties is not that solutions to large public problems are easy to achieve but that every generation, including our own, is entitled to confront even extremely difficult circumstances with some confidence that, in time, many of them can be overcome.[38]

And that, of course, is where we are now. Today, we confront massive and unprecedented troubles with little assurance that we can keep them from destroying the post-World War II mosaic of arrangements and understandings that for two generations kept most (but not all) Americans safe and prosperous. Post-war confidence in the "American Dream" has severely declined, for many reasons. Millions of urban and small-town manufacturing jobs have been automated away or outsourced to low-wage countries; rural families are increasingly in thrall to corporate giants like Cargill, Smithfield Foods, Monsanto, Archer Daniels Midland, Bayer, Tyson, and DuPont;[39] waves of recent immigrants are undermining the long-standing dominance of earlier immigrants and their descendants; the World Trade Center disaster on September 11, 2001 precipitated an interminable "War on Terror"; the Crash of 2008 destroyed prosperity for millions of "Main Street" families while "Wall Street" banks were bailed out by unfathomable billions of federal dollars; and the Electoral College victory of Donald Trump in 2016 led to what philosophers call a "category error" by transforming the White House into a stage for reality television.[40]

Intense efforts to understand current trends, and the costs they impose – such as crumbling infrastructure, bizarre income gaps, environmental deterioration, and plummeting social status – on many Americans in recent years have focused mainly on what scholars and journalists call "populism." This frame of mind they see as associated with the rise of Donald Trump, as generating the excitement of Bernie Sanders' primary campaign, as precipitating the election of Jeremy Corbyn to head the British Labour Party, as fueling the "Brexit" referendum on the United Kingdom leaving the European Union, and as underlying the growing power of right-wing leaders in France, Spain, Austria, Hungary, Poland, Brazil, and more.

Those who fear what they call populism accuse its enthusiasts of mistakenly preferring the principle of popular sovereignty over the complexities of actual government. Populists, they say, hope that what "the people" want will prevail in public affairs rather than that the totality of governmental institutions and instruments – a welter of legislatures, courts, commissions, elections, regulatory agencies, police forces, trade agreements, defense treaties, central banks, and more – will continue to shape public life.[41]

Thus, Barry Eichengreen suggests that "Populism... favors direct over representative democracy insofar as elites are disproportionately influential in the selection of representatives. It favors referenda over delegating power to office holders who can't be counted on to respect the will of the people."[42] And thus Yascha Mounk observes that leaders such as Donald Trump in America, Marine Le Pen in France, Nigel Farage in Great Britain, and Victor Orban in Hungary claim that "the most pressing problems of our time" are fairly simple and can be fully understood by "the great mass of ordinary people." Nevertheless, "the political establishment" has failed to resolve those problems, in which case populists believe that "the people" should take matters into their own hands by electing officials who, in the people's name, will do the job properly.[43]

Eichengreen in *The Populist Temptation* (2018), Mounk in *The People vs. Democracy* (2018), and William Galston in *Anti-Pluralism* (2018) for the most part regard populism as indifferent to democracy and hostile to liberal virtues such as compromise, coordination, and civility. I somewhat agree with those men and I will explain why later in this book. But some other writers argue that Donald Trump and his administration are rightly promoting an "America First" strategy by taking firm steps – such as withdrawing from international treaties on "free" trade, on nuclear proliferation, and on global warming[44] – to represent the interests and preferences of Americans who feel that Washington insiders, activist judges, liberal journalists, radical professors, corrupt labor unions, and arrogant minority leaders have for too long led the country astray.[45]

The second group of writers agree with the first that America is in danger.[46] In effect, however, they hold that those who threaten its tranquility and prosperity are people who they call *pluralists* rather than *populists*, that is, people who prefer "identity politics" to patriotism, and who endorse moral "relativism" rather than traditional virtues.[47] In which case, even though scholars and activists disagree on how to define what has gone wrong in the Age of Populism, we can conclude that both sides in this confrontation fear politics as usual because they feel that many politicians have abandoned them.[48] The result is mounting resentment in various quarters, to which I will return.

Three Responses

I believe that some political scientists should respond to such circumstances on three levels, all of which I will discuss more fully throughout this book. First, we should not so dwell on professional puzzles as to stand, unintentionally, aside from society's current needs.[49] To that end, political scientists should recall their forerunner David Easton. In his presidential address to the American Political Science Association (APSA) in 1969, Easton defined an earlier moment of crisis thus: "Mankind today is working under the pressure of time. Time is no longer on our side… An apocalyptic weapon, an equally devastating population explosion, dangerous pollution of the environment, and in the United States, severe internal dissension of racial and economic origin… move toward increasing social conflict and deepening fears and anxieties about the future, not of a generation or a nation, but of the human race itself."[50] Easton called on his colleagues for "relevance and action," which I believe, taking recent circumstances into account, should inspire some of us today.

Second, we should cast our net widely. On this score, we were admonished by another forerunner, Karl Deutsch. In his presidential address to the APSA in 1970, Deutsch stipulated that "The overwhelming fact of our time is change…" To deal with it, Deutsch insisted that political scientists should consult changes in "population, economic life, cultural and social practices … [in which case we must collect data] from economics, demography, sociology, psychology, and psychiatry.

Regardless of their disciplinary origin, such data are becoming crucial for political analysis … Not a marginal extension of political analysis … [but] inseparable from its core and essence."[51] Deutsch was right, I think, to call for widening our horizons. In later chapters, I will extend his plea for judgment based on far-flung data – i.e., casting a wide knowledge net – with a Temple of Science metaphor.

Third, political scientists should work hard to preserve whatever commendable principles and practices the country already enjoys. We cannot afford to believe that, in a dangerous era, those are safe and will take care of themselves. This point is made by Timothy Snyder, who warns against assuming that progress is "inevitable,"[52] as Francis Fukuyama did in 1989 when the Soviet Union was beginning to collapse, and when America seemed, to Fukuyama, the obvious precursor to worldwide liberalism and democracy.[53]

If progress is not inevitable, say modern sages, backsliding is entirely possible, as from democracy in the German Weimar Republic to dictatorship in the German Third Reich.[54] It follows that caution and conscious commitment should be our watchwords. As Mounk says, "… we retain the power to win a better future. But unlike fifteen or thirty years ago, we can no longer take that future for granted."[55]

Consulting Great Thinkers

Hollywood awards Oscars for best supporting actors and actresses. We should keep that in mind because, in times of great public stress, such as in the Age of Populism, great thinkers from the past can stand by our sides and offer large and useful political thoughts.[56] On this score, we should recall a somber message of the Nobel Prize winner (literature, 1980), Polish poet and diplomat Czeslaw Milosz. In *The Captive Mind* (1953), Milosz described how he lived through Nazi devastations in wartime Poland and experienced Communist brutality behind the Iron Curtain. Thereafter, he hoped that East Europeans would cope successfully with circumstances that had shattered conventional, traditional, and long-standing political assumptions, institutions, and practices.

What Milosz meant was that hard times call for inspiration from large political ideas – such as the concept of republican virtue, the principle of checks and balances, and the imperative of separating Church and State – many of which come down to us from previous ages of crisis, such as the Renaissance, the Reformation, and the Enlightenment. As the Cold War got under way, however, he assumed that American thinkers would little help their European counterparts on this score, because he judged that Americans, living in a fairly stable society, lacked the imagination to grasp what must be done when normal politics collapse.[57]

Times have changed since Milosz wrote, and many Americans now understand that life in their country has gone seriously awry. Therefore, although Milosz did not think that New Worlders had much to offer, I believe that American political scientists are capable of responding effectively to the current crisis, of turning to cardinal political issues, and of being mindful that standard academic concepts – animating a good deal of social science as usual – can sometimes fragment our experiences and deny big-picture inspiration.[58]

The bottom line to all this, which I will later explain more fully, is that at least some of us should go beyond routine political inquiry and regard first-order political ideas, such as those of thinkers like Plato, Aristotle, Machiavelli, Hobbes, Locke, Jefferson, Hamilton, Madison, Mill, Marx, Weber, Dewey, Orwell, Arendt, and Rawls, more as live issues than as, so often recently, mainly grist for academic exercises.[59]

The point is simple. Many first-order thinkers, in their times, dealt with change. They were surrounded by change, worried by change, buffeted by change, challenged by change. I don't suppose they got everything right. But they knew what their problems were, more or less. As William Butler Yeats observed after World War I, with perfect rhetorical pitch, "Things fall apart; the center cannot hold."[60] And that is where we are now, riveted by a unique president in the Age of Populism.

Neoliberalism

A final postulate is in order. I intend to propose a project for political scientists. To that end, I will later explain why I think some of my colleagues should have a special care for the destructive side of creative destruction. Various commentators, some of whom I noted earlier, agree that populism is generated by people suffering from change. What I will add to their view is that much of that suffering flows from economic destruction, which is sometimes regarded as inevitable but which, I believe, should not be accepted as such.

Along these lines, I will eventually insist that the chief danger to American politics and public life, the larger peril, is not populism but its source, which is a national commitment to unlimited change, sometimes called economic growth, via the process of creative destruction. That commitment appears in certain modern practices of free enterprise, or capitalism, often known as *neoliberalism*. In this sense, *populism* is the *effect*, but *neoliberalism* is the *cause*. Therefore, if the damages of neoliberalism can be mitigated, I believe that populism will subside at least somewhat. In which case, fortunately for all of us, its impact on modern politics will wane.

I will have much more to say about neoliberalism. For the moment, however, let us get underway by considering what is happening in political science nowadays, even before some members of that discipline will consider taking on a new professional responsibility.

2 THE TEMPLE OF SCIENCE

We live in a populist age; it threatens vital elements of American democracy; it encourages us to reconsider fundamental political principles; some scholars should relate to those principles in their work, and some political scientists should do that by focusing especially on the destructive side of creative destruction.

These are complex propositions, which we may begin to explicate by considering what political scientists are now doing, roughly speaking. What are we studying and teaching, and how does that reflect our present understanding of what political science is for, even in a populist age?

Scope and Methods

In truth, political scientists haven't decided exactly what political science is for. That is, they do not agree, except in very general terms, on what they together are doing, or should be doing. Therefore, when they discuss what are sometimes called "scope and methods" for their discipline, entire books may treat the subject of methods,[61] whereas matters of scope often warrant no more than a few pages. In those pages, colleagues usually focus on "politics," which involves "power," but they cannot define precisely either the term or its locus.[62]

So terminology is one problem for political science. Another is that when members of the discipline choose research topics and thereby demonstrate their preferences on scope, they divide up among themselves by investigating many different realms where people confront one another. Thus, they study a wide array of people who exercise many kinds of power (verbal, social, economic, physical, sexual, and more) in order to shape relationships in favor of this group or that.

Bewildering variety in research and teaching therefore shows up, for example, when the 2018 APSA's Annual Meeting in San Francisco scheduled over several days the presentation of papers, many simultaneously, in fifty-six "Divisions" of interest ranging from "Formal Political Theory" to "Comparative Politics," from "Legislative Studies" to "Race, Ethnicity, and Politics," from "Information Technology and Politics" to "Sexuality and Politics," from "Migration and Citizenship" to "American Political Thought."[63]

The same diversity emerged recently in an edited volume based on asking 100 political scientists which research questions should be raised in their fields and which earlier findings are especially noteworthy. Each colleague was invited to address these two questions in 1000 words or fewer. The answers, collected in *The Future of Political Science: 100 Perspectives* (2009), agreed neither on what should be done nor on what has already been done especially well.[64]

This situation – cacophony, really – is not new. Years ago, leading political scientists already threw in the towel on issues of scope. Thus Leon Epstein, in his 1979 presidential address to the APSA, admitted that "I find it difficult to offer general advice now that political scientists identify with increasingly specialized subjects and employ more disparate methods."[65] And thus Gabriel Almond, the APSA president in 1966, described various political science approaches in a 1988 essay entitled "Separate Tables: Schools and Sects in Political Science."[66]

For my purposes, pluralism within political science is useful because I propose that only *part* of the discipline, or only *some* political scientists, in effect only a *sector* within the many "Divisions" at the annual APSA meetings, should relate in a special way to events and circumstances in our populist times. There is no need to sweepingly revise current disciplinary interests and practices. Whatever most political scientists are doing – and many of them are doing it well, I believe – they will continue to do. There is the pluralism I just described. In my opinion it cannot, and should not, be discouraged.

Accordingly, some qualification is in order. In present circumstances, I propose a project of only partial extent, which flows from a realization that, as an adjunct to our talk about scope and methods, some of us should begin – professionally, voluntarily, rigorously, and responsibly – to become more involved politically than we used to be. This is, after all, an era more dangerous and frightening than the one which we, our students, and the public lived in previously.[67]

In short, I propose that a fraction of the total discipline should commit to a particular strategy and principle. Therefore, in this matter, unlike in some others, I will decline the advice of a distinguished forerunner. Lucien Pye, president of the APSA in 1989, recommended that his colleagues should pay special attention to a particular situation in his time, and which he described as a crisis undermining authoritarian regimes such as that in the Soviet Union.[68] I think, however, that such a collective commitment is neither necessary nor desirable. The American Political Science Association, within whose professional warrant our scholars work, is a big tent or, in sociological terms, a community rather than an organization, serving to collect colleagues rather than to point them in any particular direction.[69] I have no objection to it remaining so.

Procedure and Substance

Nevertheless – and here content is important – even though pluralism befits the discipline, many American political scientists come together in a practical rather than theoretical way, in that they direct much of their research and teaching to two cardinal subjects, which are "democracy" and "citizenship." Like other scholars, political scientists are active members of a society that values both of those matters highly, and they live in places where state and local governments encourage and may even mandate grade-school and college courses in "civics" and government.

It makes sense, then, that political scientists will participate in what amounts to a nation constantly renewing and improving itself along these two lines. To that end, colleagues talk to each other often about how to conduct their participation most effectively.[70] For example, Margaret Levi, APSA president in 2005, called upon her colleagues to fashion a new theory for government that should be democratic, representative, responsive, fair, and so forth.[71]

Democracy and citizenship are patently worthy ends, especially when times are fairly quiet and stable or, as economists might say, when *ceteris* is *paribus*. But in the Age of Populism *ceteris* is not *paribus*, and that is a situation which obliges us, I think, to consider that political science teachings on democracy and citizenship are mainly *procedural* rather than *substantive*.

These terms are straightforward. We may describe democracy as a set of techniques, such as national elections and town meetings, and we may think about citizenship as a matter of who belongs to the state – for example, who can carry its passport and enjoy the civil rights it grants. Together, such techniques (what citizens *do*) and matters of membership (what citizens *are*) generate procedural democracy.[72] That sort of democracy touches upon important affairs. But it also leaves open large questions about substance – that is, about what *should* be done with the powers of citizenship beyond just maintaining them, and about where the ship of state *should* sail rather than how it might just stay afloat.[73]

For example, Benjamin Page and Martin Gilens discuss democracy and citizenship in their *Democracy in America? What Has Gone Wrong and What We Can Do About It* (2017).[74] They describe democracy as "majority rule," and they insist that policy makers should serve voter preferences as expressed objectively in polls. To reach such a desirable state of affairs, they recommend public policies to provide citizens with more personal resources, education, and information than they possess today, all of which can challenge, and perhaps even reduce, the influence of money, advertising, and lobbying over American politics.[75]

This view of American democracy amounts to strengthening its procedures, to enabling "the people" to express fully their opinions, and then to hoping for the best.[76] It is a commendable but incomplete vision, because in difficult times we need – I think very urgently – to supplement procedural arrangements with at least some acts of substance. On this score, present circumstances call for recommendations that will go beyond even an admirable concern for democratic machinery.

Happily, scholars can be not just specific but also patriotic to this end. Therefore, in line with my recommendation that some of us will engage with large political ideals promoted by great thinkers, let us note what gets slighted when we concentrate, even commendably, on repairing democratic *practices*. At that point, what can get overlooked are the *purposes* for which such practices can be used. And those purposes include the *public goods* envisioned – but not in modern terminology – when the Founders, in their electrifying Preamble to the Constitution, declared that "the People of the United States, in order to establish a more perfect Union," created the Constitution "to provide" for "justice," for "domestic tranquility," for "the common defense," for "the general welfare," and for "the blessings of liberty."

With such goals in mind, it seems to me that, in hard times, the bottom line is that America needs not just excellent trappings of procedural democracy but also, on occasion, constructive acts of substantive citizenship.[77] That is why I will propose, in later chapters, that some scholarly research and teachings will recommend such acts designed explicitly to mitigate the social and economic damage caused by creative destruction.

Universities

Meanwhile, let us return to what political scientists are doing now, even before they might consider my proposition. I have suggested that, lacking clear agreement on *scope*, my colleagues do not know exactly *what* they are doing together. But they know *where* they are, which is mainly in American universities. And that is a context worth considering here at some length.

Universities are modern America's intellectual lynchpin. They are where most formal knowledge is generated, where it accumulates, where it is discussed, and where it is promoted for use elsewhere. In America, millions of people who want to become engineers, doctors, lawyers, architects, chemists, ministers, journalists, programmers, psychologists, teachers, managers, nurses, pollsters, accountants, physicists, advertisers, meteorologists, biologists, bankers, brokers, and more pass through universities to become skilled thinkers and workers. In short, men and women in many realms of American life are affected by how they are informed and trained in the country's system of higher education.[78]

In that system before the Civil War, America built colleges, and those had fairly narrow philosophical schemes of organization. That is, the founders who ran the colleges – who were usually devout – adhered to mission statements which indicated what was to be studied, and which often aimed at renewing the supply of ministers needed in the New World. For instance, Harvard turned out Puritan ministers, Rhode Island College (later Brown University) educated Baptist ministers, the College of William and Mary produced Anglican ministers, and the College of New Jersey (later Princeton University) trained Presbyterian ministers. Elective courses were rare and, in these small institutions, with no more than hundreds of students, if politics was studied at all it likely appeared in the guise of "Moral Philosophy." This was an Enlightenment compendium of moderate theological and secular maxims, fit for the Age of Reason, designed to promote a decent social contract, and usually taught in the senior year of studies by someone of wide horizons, such as the president of the college.[79]

After the Civil War, while an industrial revolution unfolded in America, science rather than theology gradually became the rule in higher education, and some colleges expanded into, or were superseded by, private and public universities crowned by professional schools and going beyond bachelor degrees to offer master and doctoral studies. In these new entities, it became common for professors – as experts in their fields – rather than founders to shape the curriculum, so that academic disciplines rather than mission statements set the tone. The result, after 1900, was to turn growing universities into intellectual smorgasbords, bringing together "departments" and institutes, with greatly diversified scholars and research centers, where "the sum of the parts added up to a nominal whole joined by no organizational principle or rationale other than administrative and financial convenience."[80]

Multiversities

In 1963, Clark Kerr, Chancellor of the University of California, called these conglomerations "multiversities."[81] Because such entities aspired to promote expertise in many fields, professors had much to do with deciding what was investigated and taught. However, as years passed, all this became increasingly expensive, to the point where financial officers became a dominant feature of university life.[82] Then, more than ever, each university president became less a leader of the whole institution – which in the post-college era anyway no longer had a preconceived aim – than a competent broker, smoothing out balances of power among professors, students, parents, alumni, townspeople, grant agencies, corporate sponsors, foundations, sport fans, and other interested parties.[83]

Generation after generation, critics have called for Kerr's kind of universities to emphasize education more and training less, and to promote humane values along with valuable skills.[84] Their voices have not reduced the influence of money in higher education – after all, one cannot run a school without substantial budgets – but they do indicate that important questions can be raised about the purposes that universities serve in a complex world. And those questions, in turn, bear on what we have been asking, which is what political science is for, in that same world.

As Kerr pointed out, apart from dormitories, stadiums, shuttle buses, alumni reunions, and the like, but in relation to what people know about the world and our place in it, modern universities are collections of departments (plus institutes containing related departments and scholars)[85] where professors, divided more or less into academic disciplines, investigate various parts of nature and our lives, after which those professors teach students whatever it is, practical or theoretical, that their disciplines manage to discover. This means that one department teaches economics, another teaches physics, one teaches history, another teaches mechanics, one teaches statistics, another teaches accounting, one teaches entomology, and so forth. In those circumstances, universities will occasionally establish new departments dealing with new knowledge – say, with conflict resolution or nanotechnology. On that score, universities are admirably flexible instruments, able to create new workspaces for intellectual pioneers who seek breakthroughs in modern knowledge.[86]

In Kerr's world, all that is clear. In a nutshell, modern universities are congeries of departments, first investigating and then teaching. What is not clear is who decides on the distribution of departments, or fields of knowledge, in each university. For example, who decides which professors will address what? That is, who decides that there will be a department treating this subject but not that one? Or, who decides that this department is doing its job but that one is not? Or, who decides when a new department is needed while another would be superfluous? Or, in the final analysis, who in the university decides if its sum total of existing departments is adequate, in the sense that they cover all the ground that should be covered so that the nation's citizens will learn, from this great knowledge institution, what they need to know in order to live well?

That is, (1) who decides on the institution's overall mission, in the service of which a compendium of academic disciplines work simultaneously, and (2) who decides whether or not a particular department, or all of them together, are serving that mission faithfully? Who, in short, in this very large entity where each department is doing its own thing, is in charge of holding all this activity together or, in effect, herding these cats?

To rephrase these questions in social science terms, we might ask where is the standard "model" that, more or less, explains the shape and character of the university as a singular institution in modern society – which it certainly is – at a time when scholars have, roughly speaking, fashioned models for other singular institutions such as churches, towns, tribes, armies, factories, nations, big box stores, and platform companies? And if there is no standard model, can it be that the eminent university where I studied years ago, where I stood one afternoon before Widener Library while bells tolled to mark the passing of President John F. Kennedy, where in hundreds of classrooms today, thousands of professors teach 20,000 students – can that institution have no plan or organizing principle at all?

Clark Kerr wrote about universities more than fifty years ago. Since then, many of the schools he described have grown and innovated, and most of them, large and small, while serving a diverse population, are led by officers who feel they must respond to budgetary imperatives and marketplace considerations. In practice, this means that American universities are constantly evolving, sometimes adding new programs and departments, sometimes cancelling others, occasionally going online, looking for and relying heavily on adjunct teachers, offering practical training in many fields, and providing space and staff for groundbreaking research.

Despite this increasing complexity, Kerr's concept of a "multiversity" is still useful, because it can still serve to denote an institution that has no particular shape or inherent goal. Consequently, many thinkers, for or against Kerr but not always explicitly so, raise questions about universities and how they work, about where the money for higher education comes from and who will spend it, about what resources should be allocated to this end or that – often to more or less liberal arts or business administration – and why. To make a long story short, we may conclude that the conversation about such things is interesting but inconclusive, because a signifi-cant reconstruction of universities, away from their present muddle, is unlikely to occur for so long as parties to the conver-sation have material and ideological interests that they prefer not to compromise.[87]

On the other hand, for political science to deal with problems that arise in a populist era, it does not matter if modern uni-versities will or will not change their line-up of departments, institutes, and schools. That is, we don't need to fight to recon-struct Kerr's universities. We need simply to think about them in a new way, and especially about how their departments are distributed and what they do. That question we can address without reference to whether or not the present configur-ation of academic interests and resources is satisfactory in a general sense. We need only to observe that political science departments, in every university, are already equipped to per-form a special function, directed at the Age of Populism, which scholars in other departments are not now performing consist-ently and effectively.

This point is worth repeating. There are excellent fields of interest in Kerr's multiversity, and various departments there house disciplines that are commendably expanding the avail-able sum of knowledge about many things and creatures – about what Lewis Carroll called "cabbages and kings."[88] Nevertheless, something very important is missing from Kerr's schools. And political science, as I will explain later on, is in a position to compensate for that.

The Temple of Science

To portray the missing element clearly, I want to suggest a higher-education model that resembles, metaphorically, a Grecian Temple of Science, where the term *science* is used in the European sense as a field of knowledge, as in the French *sciences politiques*, the Spanish *ciencias politicas*, and the German *politologie*. We can think of this model, which is only suggestive and not precise at all – I repeat, only suggestive and not precise – as a sort of Athenian Parthenon, with fluted columns marching around a rectangular sanctuary, and above those an architrave, frieze, and pediments linking the columns to support the temple's roof.[89]

If we use this Temple model to stand for an intellectual edifice representing the world of academic knowledge,[90] we can see, in our mind's eye, many scholarly columns, located figuratively in universities today and housing various "sciences," such as physics, history, biology, philosophy, political science, and electrical engineering. The model says nothing about how big or important its various columns are. But that they are physically separate helps us to understand immediately that, in the real world, most professors work only in their columns and know little or nothing about what people study and teach in other columns.[91]

This isolation is obvious with regard to subjects, from sociology to chemistry, from immunology to accounting, and so forth. But it is not just subjects that inhabit different columns, because many scholars in those columns use research methods that are little understood by their neighbors. For example, in the economics department, scholars may deploy statistics; in area studies, they must use foreign languages; in astronomy, mathematics is a necessary tool; and in anthropology, some practitioners will become embedded observers.

To continue the metaphor, if the Temple of Science's columns were to stand only by themselves, they might fall down. But they are capped and held together by architraves and friezes which, by analogy, we can regard as the academic world's management sector consisting of deans, provosts, chancellors, trustees, and the like.[92] In most cases, these people are not directly involved in the creation and dissemination of knowledge. But the administration they provide – a sort of centripetal force – enables the university to generate that scholarship which is, after all, the Temple's signature function.

The Temple's Roof

There remains, in this modern Parthenon, a roof supported by pediments. And there, as Hamlet said, is the rub. Because the striking thing about the roof is that, unlike in the Temple of Science's columns, there are no scholars there. That is, no modern scholars are sitting on the Temple of Science's roof collectively, distilling there lessons derived from various Temple columns together and teaching, for example, that climate change (in meteorology's column) has something to do with marine extinctions (in biology's column), with hurricane damages (in the accountancy column), with community breakdowns (in anthropology's column), and with populist politics (in political science's column).

The bottom line here is that, by displaying an empty roof, the Temple of Science model shows us graphically that modern universities are missing a very important capacity. This occurs because, while departments are producing *experts* in this field or that, and while administrators are helping them to do so, the same departments are usually unable or unwilling to produce *generalists* who will integrate expert knowledge from different realms (columns) and provide wide-ranging advice to students and the public at large.

Let us restate that point. In the Temple of Science, there are departments that, as we saw, reside in columns that stand pretty much alone. But there is no department that consists of professors whose task it is to sit, figuratively, not in a column but on the Temple's roof, to study from there what is known in many columns, combine the available facts and insights, and pass on teachings that will help us all live together.

In other words, America finds itself in the Age of Populism, where events and inclinations investigated in many columns threaten to destroy exactly that sensible democracy and moderate citizenship that, in theory at least, embellish American exceptionalism. But universities do not squarely confront this situation, because they do not provide a department or discipline – again, figuratively on the roof – that would collect what we know from wherever knowledge resides, distill this information, and explain to students and the public how it shows the way to progress and prosperity.

Thus in the Temple mode, the Age of Populism as a whole is not on the scholarly agenda, although parts of it may be. And this is because what we call populism, and even its obvious avatar Donald Trump, represents a *general* calamity, flowing from many trends interacting with one another, rather than a *specific* issue of one dimension, to be analyzed and resolved comfortably – academics as usual – within a particular Temple of Science column.

Limitations

Yet many scholars are outraged by Trump. Why, then, are there no teachers on the Temple's roof? One reason is difficult to name, but we may regard it as "cultural" because, since the late nineteenth century – after Darwin's theory of evolution appeared – Western societies essentially decided that *the scientific method* can produce knowledge more useful and valuable than any other sort of knowledge, bringing great improvements in medicine, agriculture, industry, transportation, communications, commerce, and so forth.

The result was that many scholars came to believe that science is the main or only road to progress. And since professors, each in his or her own field, first investigate and only afterwards teach, it followed that their work at universities, discipline after discipline, came increasingly to emulate science. In department after department, professors fashioned hypotheses, searched for evidence, and hoped to find law-like regularities. Therefore, what they knew and taught appeared to be more certain than what was being done less scientifically, say by professors of philosophy or by theologians at divinity schools. Consequently, when fields were compared, knowledge that could not be cast as scientific was widely regarded as somehow imperfect, somehow dubious, somehow less reputable than science, i.e., the real thing.[93]

So here is the first reason why few professors aspire to sit on the Temple of Science's roof, handing out general advice based on various disciplines simultaneously and therefore not possibly clear and exact enough to warrant respect for being "scientific."[94] But there is a second reason why the roof is empty, and that is the fact that the Temple's columns are so full of information that most human beings, including professors, cannot get a grip on all that is known in any one column and certainly not all that is known in two or more columns.[95]

In other words, no one can sit on the roof and reasonably claim that she knows what is going on below, when the sheer amount of stuff in several columns is so great that she cannot conclusively argue that she knows enough to connect all the available "facts" (which she cannot entirely assimilate) to any sort of definitive advice. A professor who would try that could easily be challenged by sceptics who might ask: "Sure! But have you read the articles relating to that subject by Professors Smith, Chang, Khouri, Cohen, Lombardi, Patel, and Gesundheit?"

Economics

From the metaphorical Temple of Science, then, a paradoxical syllogism emerges. (1) We see that, with no scholars on the roof, the university is not adequately confronting our populist era.[96] (2) We see also why the Temple's professors, including political scientists, for quantitative and qualitative reasons, cannot expect that they will sound persuasive if they will offer general advice about that era or any other. Accordingly, (3) we understand that little or nothing would be gained from their trying.[97]

On the other hand, this story most definitely should not end here. In a sense, it is true that modern people do not seek advice from the Temple's roof. But that does not mean that political scientists should continue doing only what they have done until now. Instead, in my opinion, they should consider a paramount aspect of learning in universities that we have not examined yet, but which is an open secret, and which is this: Regardless of what appears in the Temple of Science model, in the real world of American sciences there is one discipline – that of economics – which frequently and confidently dispenses advice about how Americans should live together.

Therefore, although they do not use our terms, it is as if economists believe that their discipline is capable of analyzing and assessing what other Temple columns study, to the point where, *in effect*, economists can sit on the Temple's roof and explain to everyone else how to get along efficiently and prosperously. Furthermore, as we shall see in a moment, this advice, especially about the desirability of perpetual economic growth, is accepted by many people.

So here is an oddity. In the Temple of Science, in theory, no one can successfully sit on the roof. But in practice, the economists seem to be up there anyway. What does that mean? Does it mean that, in the real world, there is a blip in the Temple model?

If there were a blip, we could ignore it as a technical trifle if we were convinced that the advice that economists offer to society is satisfactory. But what many economists recommend as social policy – on how we should live together now, and on how we should get through the coming years – is nowhere near satisfactory. Indeed, as we shall see, it fosters dangerous trends that are at least partly responsible for the Age of Populism.

In which case, we have reached a turning point for what I have been proposing all along, which is that some political scientists should begin to criticize part of what economists recommend, which politicians promote, which business people celebrate, and which many ordinary Americans praise but which, for example, has recently automated millions of good jobs out of existence, has destroyed hundreds, if not thousands, of Main Streets in favor of Walmart, Target, Walgreens, Kroger, and Home Depot, has strip-mined and fracked many vulnerable citizens, has increasingly privatized public services, has neglected enormous swaths of national infrastructure, has addicted millions of citizens to smart phones and fast food,[98] and has hollowed out the middle class.

That is the situation we will turn to now.

3 MAINSTREAM ECONOMICS

We have arrived at *economics*, even though this is a book about *politics*. Therefore, lest we forget, here again is the overall objective. In our populist age, some political scientists should start paying special attention to a matter that I have not yet explicated, but which I have already described several times as the *destruction* caused by what economists call creative destruction.

To get closer to understanding that mission and why it is essential, we need now to consider two faces of economics. In this chapter, I will discuss how economists persuasively define themselves as social scientists with a distinctive and effective way of looking at human affairs. In the next chapter, I will explore the central recommendation, in favor of ceaseless economic growth via creative destruction, that economists offer to their students and the public, which those people generally accept, but which is so unsatisfactory as to contribute substantially to why we are now enduring populist difficulties.

Mainstream Economics

We may start with the nature of economics as a scholarly enterprise. This is a complicated business, so please bear with me while I begin by considering "mainstream economics."

The first thing we need to understand is that the term "mainstream economics" refers to what most professors of economics believe and is therefore used to describe conventional thinking in their Temple of Science column. Specifically, what mainstream economics projects is a persuasive set of *assumptions*

that are used to justify powerful *teachings*. Most American
economists endorse at least the assumptions I will describe in
a moment. Furthermore, many endorse a certain collection of
teachings that they regard as flowing from those assumptions,
and that we will eventually see are usually more in favor of
competitive capitalism than of democratic socialism.[99]

The vocabulary here is problematic. Thus "mainstream
economics" is a term used by many writers to describe what
they consider to be the central thrust of economics. This they
do, for example, in books by journalists like Jeff Madrick and
economists like Juliet Schor.[100] However, in other sources,
mainstream economics is named differently. Thus economists
Avner Offer and Gabriel Soderberg refer to "core doctrines of
economics,[101] economists Joe Earle, Cahal Moran, and Zach
Ward-Perkins reject what they call "neoclassical" economics,[102]
think-tanker Dean Baker criticizes "standard economics,"[103]
and political scientist Jonas Pontusson postulates an "economic
orthodoxy" that he calls "the market-liberal view."[104]

Now, if mainstream economics is conventional – that is,
inside the box of economics overall[105] – how many economists
belong or do not belong to the mainstream? Knowledgeable
sources dodge this question and speak approximately, which
is not surprising because there are around 20,000 members of
the American Economic Association and they are not formally
bound by a professional template. Thus, Nobel Prize winner
(economics, 2001) Joseph Stiglitz writes that, "As we peel back
the layers of 'what went wrong' [in the Crash of 2008], we
cannot escape looking at the economics profession. Of course,
not all economists joined in the jubilation of free market economics; not all were disciples of Milton Friedman – a surprisingly large fraction, though, leaned in that direction."[106]

Furthermore, if there really is a "mainstream" in economics,
how can that be so when there is no mainstream in other
social sciences such as sociology or political science where, in
those disciplines, instead of promoting a conventional wisdom,
various "schools of thought" and "methodological approaches"
compete with one another? Oceans of ink have been spilled

on that question or its cognates. Either you believe that the mainstream economic view represents truth and therefore is refined and promulgated as a demonstrable certainty from one generation to the next, or you believe that mainstream economics serves powerful commercial forces in modern society and therefore gets subsidized and rewarded to the point where, because most economists promote it unswervingly, many people come to believe it is true.[107]

Whichever, aside from those who conform, are there economists who reject only some assumptions and teachings of the mainstream? That is, are there economists who reject not *all* of the mainstream but only *some* of its shared understandings? Yes, there are, including but not limited to figures such as Amartya Sen, Juliet Shor, Joseph Stiglitz, Thomas Piketty, Emmanuel Saez, Gabriel Zucman, Robert Skidelsky, and Robert Frank. Their works, which have much to say about economic injustice and inefficiency, provide a wealth of empirical evidence for social critics like Edward Luttwak, Timothy Noah, Hedrick Smith, George Packer, Robert Reich, John Ehrenreich, and Chris Hedges.[108]

Mainstream Assumptions

The next thing we need to understand – to avoid fruitless recriminations – is that *mainstream economics* is not a blanket term invented by some writers so they can use it to criticize prevailing economic ideas because they, the writers, favor increasing government regulation of business, a more egalitarian distribution of income, stricter environmental protection, higher taxes on the rich, and so forth. The term itself is neutral and its purpose is to identify something that really exists, in and around, say, a certain range of economic models, axioms, functions, and theorems. This is clear because mainstreamers, including tenured professors at leading universities, themselves often talk, and talk proudly, about standard ideas in their field. Thus, Nobel Prize winner (economics, 2017) Richard Thaler observes that "economics has a unified, core theory from which everything else follows. If you say the phrase 'economic theory,' people know what you mean."[109]

Not surprisingly, there are differences of opinion about how exactly to describe this core theory, about which disciplinary assumptions and teachings to emphasize more and less.[110] I have my favorites among scholars who participate in this debate. I won't name them here, though, so as not to unfairly attribute to them opinions that I may imperfectly represent because the subject is inherently contestable. That said, and basing myself on writers who are, I think, thoroughly knowledgeable about this issue, the following assumptions seem to me to describe the sort of economic thinking that features prominently in American economics departments.[111]

Methodological Individualism
First, there is an assumption of "methodological individualism." Mainstream economists assume that the most important economic actors are individuals, who decide what is important to themselves, and who act so as to gain, acquire, or achieve it. This assumption draws the attention of mainstream scholars toward individual behavior, or abstract models of individual behavior, and therefore pays little or no attention to the way groups act, as if groups – from families to churches, from corporations to governments, from labor unions to banks – are simply collections of individuals among whom each is out chiefly for herself or himself.[112] Thus sociologists and anthropologists often "do" groups, whereas economists usually "do" individuals.[113]

Rational Calculations
A second assumption is that people, when engaged or not in economic activity, are animated by rational calculations. Rational in this sense is not a synonym for "reasonable," which might be a cogent notion of what is good or healthy or fitting for human beings. Rather, rational in the economic sense pertains to the technical matching of means to ends. A person decides that he or she wants something and then seeks to

apply the most effective available means to that end.[114] In this sense, saint or sadist, one acts "rationally." Economists leave it to philosophers and theologians to say otherwise.[115]

Utility

A third assumption is that the driving force behind rational behavior is the hope of acquiring not a particular thing but the quality of "utility" that someone can enjoy from that thing. Each person decides what will make himself happy or prosperous, then sets out to gain it. The point here is that, for economists, utility is a subjective quality so that, as Jeremy Bentham said, in terms of utility defined as happiness there is no difference between reading poetry and playing the game of push-pin. As a purely descriptive matter, in economic theory each person seeks out whatever will produce utility in his or her own eyes.[116]

Self-Interest

A fourth assumption is that, because economics assumes that individuals seek utility, it is clear that workers, on behalf of wages, and employers, on behalf of profits, are driven chiefly to satisfy their personal desires. But by extension economists can also claim that people in other social realms do the same, in which case in governmental matters – a very important realm for political scientists – some economists advise us to assume that voters, activists, elected officials, and bureaucrats act mainly out of self-interest. This sort of reasoning underlies "public choice theory"[117] and helped James Buchanan win a 1986 Nobel Prize in economics.[118]

Prices

A fifth assumption is that individuals trying to obtain utility are guided in their calculations by prices, which economists claim are linked to marginal production costs and which, in ideal markets, present themselves as equal to whoever intends making a sale or purchase. Marginal pricing is important because, among other reasons, it contributes to an ideal market situation where, unless government interferes, buyers and sellers presumably interact solely on the basis of price information, which is objective and therefore fair to all participants.[119]

The Invisible Hand

A sixth assumption is that when individuals go to market, some to sell and others to buy, within a framework of prices known to all, an "invisible hand" brings together all of their preferences and priorities into a configuration of deals that can be considered "efficient." This assumption of a benevolent, invisible hand that assures that, for a fee, people like butchers and bakers will supply our needs was postulated during the eighteenth-century Enlightenment by Adam Smith.[120] It was an elegant way of keeping a just, but also non-denominational, God at our side when various philosophers were no longer sure that Providence cared.[121]

Equilibrium

A seventh assumption is that if the invisible hand is permitted to operate more or less freely, the sum total of all deals made between individual actors will generate a benign balance, which economists call "equilibrium" or "general equilibrium." Associated with the work of economists such as Leon Walrus, Vilfredo Pareto, Kenneth Arrow, and Gerard Debreau, the notion of a society-wide equilibrium of voluntary exchanges, providing utility to both buyers and sellers, suggests that leaving people free to make deals among themselves will maximize the utility that can be attained by the amount of economic resources available at any particular time.[122]

Mainstream Teachings

Mainstream economics contains more than seven assumptions and we will meet some of the additional ones later. I will also have more to say about the original seven. For the moment, though, what I have described is enough for me to offer a generalization about what the conventional, standard, neo-classical, core, modern, central, signature thrust of economics is about.

According to this generalization, economics as a "discipline" – or, as a column in the Temple of Science – aims at explaining how natural and human resources can be used "efficiently," or how "factors of production" can be combined fruitfully, in trading situations that economists call "markets," with "innovation" helping us to generate the maximum amount of "utility" that those factors can provide. Oddly enough, if all of this works well – that is, if government will just let people alone to get on with their economic propensities – there is no need for society, or, as Offer and Soderberg write, "if the model is true, then society is redundant."[123] The United Kingdom's Prime Minister Margaret Thatcher may have had something like that in mind when she declared that "there is no such thing as society. There are individual men and women and there are families."[124]

Gross Domestic Product and Welfare

At least three very large teachings flow from this sort of economics. The first concerns the fact that when individuals buy and sell goods or services in order to acquire or achieve utility, they pay for what they get. As a result, their transactions can be registered as expenditures, after which those expenditures can be added up, in dollar terms, so that the totality of transactions can be represented by a monetary aggregate that denotes what economists call the gross domestic product (GDP).[125]

Most importantly, that sum, in any particular country, in whatever currency, represents the amount of utility that individuals in that country have generated in consequence of buying and selling. It follows that GDP may be regarded as a collective index of happiness and satisfaction. And therefore, because in every exchange each side either buys or sells in order to become better off, the sum of their exchanges is a measure of what economists call "welfare."[126]

Markets and Value

The second teaching is related to the first. If the sum of exchanges, in money terms, tracks the quests of many individuals for utility and therefore registers the welfare of all economically active individuals in a country, then the mechanism that facilitates exchanges is a necessary part of that country's economic equipment. And that mechanism, according to mainstream economics, is the "market," to which each individual comes to sell what he has and buy what he wants. In that sense, markets create "value," because that quality appears when an exchange takes place and both sides emerge from it happier and more prosperous than before they traded.[127] And if markets are the field where value is created, then markets should be permitted to function freely so as to continue to produce that value.[128]

Economic Growth

The third teaching – and this is really the capstone, the flagship, the epitome, the *ne plus ultra* of mainstream economic teachings – builds on the first two. If (1) GDP (which economists promote) is an index of welfare, and if (2) markets (which economists recommend protecting) are where the exchanges that add up to GDP are created, then (3) the purpose of economic action is to generate well-being and prosperity, from one year to the next. In other words, the third mainstream teaching is that economists, (a) by studying the factors of production, and (b) by analyzing how those can be combined and peddled effectively in markets, more or less (c) show us how to generate welfare. Even more specifically, what economists show us is that, (d) if markets are carefully fashioned and reliably maintained, (e) they will facilitate so much productivity that, as time passes, increasing amounts of utility will be created for the country.

Let's rephrase this. In effect, economists teach us that the main purpose of economics, as a Temple column, is to help everyone understand how to maintain and increase productivity or, in a word, to promote "economic growth." GDP is nominally (in America) a dollar index. Therefore, if it rises from one year to the next, the later and higher sum only shows that more dollars are circulating in the country. However, appropriately interpreted, GDP shows much more, because the assumption of mainstream economics is that when GDP goes up (subtracting for inflation) it is composed of more things (and/or services) than previously, which themselves embody more utility and are therefore, when taken together, desirable.

Three Propositions

The implications of promoting economic growth are cardinally important, and very complicated, and we will come back to some of them. For the moment, let us only confirm that it is truly a representative teaching of the mainstream. For example, the great importance of economic growth underlies what economist Alan Blinder offers as three "noncontroversial propositions" that, for Blinder, sum up what he calls "the economic way of thinking."[129] These three propositions stipulate that: (1) "For most goods and services produced and sold in a market economy, more is better than less." (2) "Resources are scarce." And (3) "Higher productivity is better than lower productivity."

The first proposition, that more is better, certainly justifies economic growth. It is, however, nowhere near being "noncontroversial" (although mainstream economists may regard it as obvious).[130] In fact, it only seems sensible to say "more is better" if we ignore a great many specific cases of where it is not. Therefore, as one critic observed, "More is not enough. Often, it's not even better. Sometimes it's decidedly worse."[131] This would be true, for example, of making more teakwood tables (cutting down jungle habitats), doing more dental work (required because people eat too much sugar), raising more shrimps in ponds (causing downstream pollution), buying more SUVs (burning up more gasoline than smaller cars), and installing more self-service supermarket checkout machines (increasing unemployment among former and potential cashiers).[132]

The second proposition, about scarcity, connects to the third, about productivity. The sequence is as follows. If resources are scarce, people feel constrained by not having as many things as they want to consume; therefore, we need rising productivity at work to more effectively turn resources into more things than we have today; after which, when there will be more things, we will consume more of them than previously and thereby reduce our unpleasant sense of being constrained. That is, more things generate more happiness or, in economic terminology, more utility. We will return to this notion.

The Salience of Economics

In America, collecting national economic statistics became a federal project in the 1930s whereupon, after World War II, because GDP figures had become available, politicians moved quickly to declare that the national government should promote economic growth that would, hopefully, prevent a relapse into the terrible idleness and poverty that plagued many Americans during the Great Depression.[133] In those circumstances, because economists were present to explain to students, the public, and elected officials how to generate economic growth, and because that growth was widely considered to be America's main public policy goal, economics became, in the intellectual world, what Lorenzo Fioramonti has called "the most powerful of all disciplines."[134]

This salience of economics we should try to understand, although it cannot be measured precisely.[135] In general, the power of economics as compared to other disciplines – the perceived importance of one Temple column as opposed to others dealing with human affairs – comes in many parts. But the bottom line is this: When economists talk about how to achieve economic growth, they sound especially credible because, to many people, economists sound like what they know is "scientific."

What happens here is that in a society where, since Darwin, scientific work - meaning empirical or experimental work - enjoys great prestige, economists define the target of their research as activities that can be tracked by the expenditures they entail.[136] That is, economists work with reference to dollars (or other currencies), which exist in exact quantities and are not the sort of intangible items that other disciplines deal with - for example, "love" in psychology, "conservatism" in political science, and "holiness" in theology. Economists take this simple metric, collect relevant examples of it - wages, profits, loans, sales, taxes, production costs, debts, and more - which presumably reflect economic activity, and then, in lectures and writings, they analyze those examples mathematically, as if scientifically.[137]

When enough mathematical formulations about expenditures are available, some economists claim that the regularities of behavior they reveal, if any, are similar to natural laws like those discovered by physicists.[138] They may even suggest that economic laws of behavior are as regular and predictable as those which govern the solar system.[139] And all this the discipline as a whole discusses within a complex web of metaphors - like "curves," "thought experiments," "game theory," "marginal productivity," "equilibrium," "countervailing power," and "consumption function" - which seem scientific even when, like all metaphors, they aren't.[140] Because other social science disciplines do not, or cannot, persuasively make similar claims, economics seems, by comparison, singularly impressive.

Methodological Individualism

The bottom line here is that a general reputation for being scientific generates great prestige for economics. But a more specific factor, somewhat technical, is the "methodological individualism" assumption we noted earlier. Focusing on individuals - from consumers to CEOs, rather than groups or organizations – as prime economic actors, economists argue that each individual behaves in the special way that economists describe as "rational" for seeking "utility." So many people behave this way, economists tend to say,[141] that when such people go about making voluntary economic deals with other people, the result is an equilibrium that can be interpreted, in theory at least, as an optimal condition in social affairs.

That is, if economic exchanges are made freely – and there is one implication of the term "*free* enterprise" – each party to an exchange enjoys more utility after the exchange than she did before, else why make the exchange at all? As Nobel Prize winner (economics, 1976) Milton Friedman says, "both parties to an economic transaction benefit from it provided the transaction is bi-laterally voluntary and informed."[142]

To buttress this proposition, economists draw "indifference curves" (as if on graph paper), in seemingly scientific fashion, to show how exchanges between two individuals can be regarded as satisfactory. Thus, in the Edgeworth Box diagram, one person (a consumer) has a curve representing what quantities of, and at what prices, she is willing to *buy* X (when there is a lower price for X, she will buy more of it; when there is a higher price for X, she will buy less of it). At the same time, another person (a producer) has a curve representing what quantities of, and at what prices, she is willing to *sell* X (where there is a higher price for X, she will sell more of it; when there is a lower price for X, she will sell less of it). Where those two curves meet, the price of the buyer and the price of the seller are the same, in which case, when both sides agree to trade at that meeting point, both sides will benefit.

I will say more about Milton Friedman's informed voluntarism and the a-historical Edgeworth Box, both of which are, in fact, painfully unrealistic. Meanwhile, let us note that, in theory at least, if all parties to "voluntary" economic exchanges are better off than before, this is surely an admirable result, and perhaps even optimal for America if millions of such exchanges every day are facilitated, or unimpeded, by government policies.

Voluntary Exchanges

Ergo, starting from individualist assumptions, economists suggest to non-economists that if they, as political leaders and followers, will heed economic advice and direct government to maintain markets that will enable voluntary exchanges, the country will grow increasingly prosperous and happy. On this point, economics seems praiseworthy to many people for aiming America in the right direction. However, the concept of "voluntary" in such matters is complicated by the fact that, in real life as opposed to theory, people are exposed to powerful practices such as commercial advertising, which encourage them to act *not* voluntarily but in line with sometimes subtle and sometimes obvious nudges.[143] In other words, what if economists are *mistaken* for suggesting that markets, suitably maintained, will increase well-being because, in those markets, *voluntary* trading is conducted?

Mainstream economics deal with the likelihood of *involuntary* trading – which would confound their theory – very successfully by mostly assuming that it doesn't exist.[144] By definition, it cannot exist if people make decisions based on "rational calculations," because if those decisions are rational, they arise from within individuals and not from what surrounds them, such as advertisements. The key concept here is "consumer sovereignty," which suggests that consumers – who exercise purchasing power when they shop – are stronger than producers, because consumers cannot be compelled, but can only be enticed, by producers (or stores) to buy what is on sale.[145]

The fallacy of downplaying ads was pointed out long ago by economist John Kenneth Galbraith, who observed that manufacturers and stores (i.e., "producers") spend billions of dollars on advertising,[146] much of which is not truthful, to persuade (but not force) ordinary people (i.e., "consumers") to buy not what they independently desire but what producers want to sell to them. He called this order of influence "the revised sequence," by which he meant that conventional economic thought assumes that consumers control producers whereas, in fact, the reverse is true.[147] To make a long story short, it is as if Galbraith agreed that consumers cannot be *forced* but added that they can be *duped*.

Galbraith's argument has little influenced mainstream economists, who devote almost no research or teaching to advertising, and this for three reasons that are not registered formally. The first is that economists mainly ignore non-monetary impulses – say, tradition, envy, custom, love, class sentiments, charisma, and institutional solidarity – because admitting the influence of those factors on all of us would refute the marginal utility, rational-calculations model of billiard-ball-like consumers just buying what they want at prices they are willing to pay.[148] In other words, the abstract, rational individual model – the basis for "methodological individualism" – is so useful for generating fame and fortune in the discipline of economics that most economists try to preserve it even though psychologist Daniel Kahneman received the 2002 Nobel Prize in economics for demonstrating that many consumers miscalculate probabilities and therefore cannot make accurate choices or rational trades.[149]

The second reason why mainstream economists stay away from advertising and its power is that many American corporations, like General Motors or Amazon or Walmart or Apple, are very large compared to John Q. Public or Joe the Plumber. In that situation, which cannot be hidden, a power imbalance threatens American principles of democratic equality. As Andrew Hacker said, the world of real economic life is like elephants (corporations) dancing in the barnyard among chickens (the rest of us).[150] It is therefore comforting to believe that, if the concept of consumer sovereignty is accurate, the chickens will not get crushed, i.e., that little consumers are actually stronger than big corporations.

Third, for more than 100 years now, public relations and advertising talk have infected discourse in modern society, where some people are paid to deceive other people, or, in the polite phrases that describe such deception, to "spin" perceptions into comfortable beliefs or to "frame" reality so as to make it look like something else.[151] If the scholars who write about this sort of manipulation are correct,[152] what they know challenges the mainstream economic notion that most people make their decisions "rationally," that is, as a deliberate reflection of desires that they sense in themselves and that they seek to fulfill without reference to signals from other people. In truth, if one has *needs*, that is one thing. But if one has *wants*, they can spring from outside manipulation rather than inner conviction.[153]

Academic Imperialism

At the outset of this chapter, I said we should consider two faces of economics. The first face relates to how economists come to seem especially persuasive among social scientists by displaying a distinctive way of looking at human affairs. Along these lines, we have seen that mainstream economics seems objective for looking scientific, with mathematics and models; it seems effective for measuring life exactly, in money terms; it seems useful for showing how the country can increase welfare, via economic growth; it seems virtuous for showing that trades can achieve a fair equilibrium if they are voluntary; it preserves a reputation for realism by downplaying causes of irrationality in economic behavior; it comforts us by affirming that we control large corporations instead of them manipulating us. The list is long and impressive.

Let us add one more factor to this list and then move on to considering the second face of economics, which is its signature advice in favor of economic growth. This final factor we may regard as a kind of academic "imperialism," in that some economists enjoy great prestige because they have leveraged their view of "rational" human behavior into a claim that whoever studies economics will best understand how individuals make (or should make) decisions in fields as diverse as political campaigning, nuclear strategy, global warming, buying cars, and choosing marriage partners.[154] Moreover, to understand economic thinking is, or so economists say, to find answers to questions such as who wins in sumo wrestling? Why do many drug dealers live with their mothers? Why are seatbelts deadly? Who should pay for oil spills? Why are some people against abortions? Why do capitalist employers ignore race when hiring? Why are brown eggs more expensive than white ones? Why do people vote? and more.

In short, in addition to its presumably effective research and teaching having to do with money and money matters – and who among us cannot use advice on that important subject? – economics as a discipline tells Americans that it is more useful than other columns in the Temple of Science even in realms where those columns have traditionally ruled.[155] This far-reaching claim appears repeatedly. For example, Gary S. Becker and Guity Nashat Becker, *The Economics of Life: From Baseball to Affirmative Action to Immigration, How Real-World Issues Affect our Everyday Life.*[156] For example, Steven D. Levitt and Stephen J. Dubner, *Freakonomics: A Rogue Economist Explores the Hidden Side of Everything.*[157] For example, Robert H. Frank, *The Economic Naturalist: In Search of Explanations for Everyday Enigmas.*[158] For example, Dan Ariely, *Predictably Irrational: The Hidden Forces That Shape Our Decisions.*[159] For example, Steven E. Landsburg, *The Armchair Economist: Economics and Everyday Life.*[160] For example, Tim Harford, *The Logic of Life: Uncovering the New Economics of Everything.*[161] The blurbs for such books strengthen their claim that economic wisdom trumps (excuse me) much of what other columns in the Temple might offer.[162]

4 CREATIVE DESTRUCTION

I have discussed so far why, for general reasons, economics today enjoys special prestige compared to other social science disciplines. Let us now consider, more specifically, that the discipline of economics is held in great regard in America because its mainstream recommends very powerfully to citizens and politicians that the central policy goal of government at local, state, and federal levels should be perpetual economic growth. Consequently, we will see that admiration for economic growth brings economists to praise the process of "creative destruction," and we will then see how that praise inspired my original proposal, that in the Age of Populism, some political scientists should take up arms against the *downsides* of economic creativity, which have become terribly dangerous to public life.

Promoting Growth

As we noted in Chapter 3, economic growth as registered in GDP statistics became a national goal after World War II. Pent-up wartime demand for civilian goods and the conversion of wartime factories to civilian production fueled a consumer boom, which assured Americans that their country would not retreat into another Great Depression. Moreover, journalists, academics, business people, public intellectuals, and elected officials praised growing affluence because, among other reasons, they thought it proved America's moral superiority when compared to lesser prosperity in the Soviet Union during the Cold War.[163] Furthermore, economists insisted that, in their professional opinion, growth was inherently virtuous, because it would create a bigger pie that could be divided among everyone, or because it would generate a rising tide that would lift all boats.[164] Even liberals who worried about trends in, say, environmental pollution and habitat destruction, admonished other liberals to commit themselves to economic growth, albeit "fairer" and "faster" than existing growth.[165]

For whoever seeks a precise description of growth, economists offer a reassuring formula: GDP = C+I+G+(X–M), or, in plain English, Gross Domestic Product equals private Consumption plus gross Investment plus Government spending plus (Exports minus Imports).[166] Technically speaking, within this formula most economists suggested, and most politicians agreed, that government should foster growth by encouraging consumer "demand."

The emphasis on demand meant making sure that consumers would have enough money to buy what they needed and wanted, where wants were constantly evoked and amplified by modern advertising. Most notably, it was John Maynard Keynes who stressed that government should maintain "demand," if necessary with infrastructure projects such as during the Great Depression. The emphasis here was on "fiscal policy." Later, however, even critics of Keynes such as Milton Friedman called for government to maintain demand, although to that end Friedman recommended mainly manipulating the nation's quantity of money by changing interest rates. The emphasis there was on "monetary policy." Between the followers of Keynes and those of Friedman, some points of analysis were different. But the main point was clear: Maintaining "demand" would stimulate production, and when more products were made they would, when sold, drive up indices of growth.[167]

Within growth as the settled goal, a few economists called for stimulating GDP by pumping up the "supply" of products. Here, the thesis was that manufacturing more products, by hiring and paying more suppliers and workers, would stimulate consumer demand, would promote sales, would raise profits, and would thereafter increase public revenues, when those profits would be taxed at even moderate rates.[168]

Mainstream economists regarded this "supply-side" view, which required reducing taxes for the well-to-do – that is, for people most likely to invest in creating more supply – as "trickle-down" economics.[169] In that theory, major benefits (lower taxes) *would surely* go to the top of society, while other benefits (jobs, good wages) *might* trickle down to those at the bottom. In plain language, the rich would certainly gain, from tax cuts, whereas the poor, if things worked out, might get something later, or might not. John Kenneth Galbraith, who grew up on a Canadian farm, described such a theory as "… the less than elegant metaphor that if one feeds the horse enough oats, some will pass through on the road for the sparrows."[170]

Controversies broke out between people who favored demand-side or supply-side prescriptions for economic growth. We cannot resolve those controversies and they need not concern us here.[171] It is enough to note, for the record, that presidents Ronald Reagan, George W. Bush, and Donald Trump, all Republicans, encouraged Congress to enact supply-side tax cuts.[172]

What is more relevant to our purposes, however, is the ubiquitous presence of talk about economic growth, no matter how it is promoted, from the right and the left. In fact, talk about economic growth, and how to achieve it, and who will most likely do that, and have they succeeded in generating it or not, infuses America's public conversation at every hour of every day, now reported with mind-numbing repetition in twenty-four-hour news stations that broadcast, for example, "Quest Means Business," "MoneyWatch," and "After the Bell." Therefore, space here permits us only to note briefly some reasons why the footprint of economic thought appears so prominently in the landscape of public policy talk.

Success for Economics

First of all, the discipline's basic definitions and goals are promoted enthusiastically in talk about public affairs because they validate important parts of what pundits call "the American Dream." Historians trace this ideal back to the Puritans and the Protestant Ethic, to Benjamin Franklin's autobiography, to Ralph Waldo Emerson on "self-reliance," to *The McGuffey Reader* on work ethics, to Horatio Alger's stories of young men who get ahead mainly on pluck, to Andrew Carnegie on the gospel of wealth, to Bruce Barton on the entrepreneurship of Jesus, and so forth.[173] The point of the story is that if individuals will make strenuous efforts and offer unusual contributions to society, those will be so appreciated as to reap outstanding rewards.

And this, after all, is exactly what mainstream economics teaches, that people who freely make deals with other people – as in Edgeworth Boxes – provide utility and therefore deserve to receive utility in return. In which case, if a person becomes rich by lawful means, economic theory shows that that person's success is deserved.[174] So there is a sense in which, among social sciences, economics stands out for certifying – presumably scientifically – the validity of the national story.

Cognitive Capture
Second, because many economic ideas mesh fully with long-standing promises in American life, economists and their ideas are widely discussed and cited, thereby generating what is called "cognitive capture." This term suggests that, for many people, the vocabulary of economics appears in a familiar range of concepts when public affairs are discussed. In radio, newspapers, television, and social media, for example, there are endless references to economic indicators such as "the natural rate of unemployment," "efficient markets," "assets and liabilities," "austerity," "bailout," "balance of payments," "the bond market," "buyback," "stock options," "cost-benefit analysis," "credit default swap," "externalities," "high-speed trading," "too big to fail," "long and short," "moral hazard," "opportunity costs," "positional goods," "privatization," "restructuring," "synergy," "venture capital," and "yield."[175]

To speak of the totality of such terms as an expression of cognitive capture is *not* to claim that people who use, or who are familiar with, this vocabulary are in thrall to any particular economic view of the world – say, that they are disciples of John Maynard Keynes or Friedrich Hayek. It is to suggest, however, that to the extent those terms are common in chattering about circumstances that we share, the people who use or recognize that vocabulary are thinking that public affairs can best be understood in economic terms rather than, say, ethical, or spiritual, or artistic, or communal, or cultural terms.

That is one reason, apparently, why the economists, bankers, former bankers, and future bankers – men such as Hank Paulson, Ben Bernanke, Timothy Geithner, and Laurence Summers – who handled Washington's response to the Crash of 2008 while thinking in economic terms, bailed out the big banks (Wall Street) with trillions of federal dollars but, by leaving out of their calculations compassion and empathy,[176] did almost nothing to help millions of small homeowners (Main Street) who defaulted on their mortgages and lost their homes.[177]

Of course, not everyone thinks about life in economic terms, because many people work at part-time, precarious, and/or dead-end jobs that may provide (barely) a living wage but do not really permit economic creativity.[178] However, there are many who do think in those terms, therefore I will return to cognitive capture, in effect, when I discuss the neoliberalism that rules America's public conversation in the Age of Populism and is very economically minded.[179]

An Extra-Scholarly Role

Third, a great many economists, and people who studied chiefly economics (or business administration) in colleges and universities, are employed outside of American higher education, in think tanks, in media circles, in research institutes, in trade associations, in banks and insurance companies, and as consultants to corporations and investors. In such places – and in policy conferences and media interviews – they constantly project their views, speaking to the public, to foundations, to legislators, to lobbyists, to bureaucrats, to reporters, to financiers, and more.

In doing so, they generate and bolster cognitive capture with their language. But they may also, while guided by principles incorporated into that language, personally influence specific decisions relating to important economic matters, for instance, by working at Federal Reserve banks or for the International Monetary Fund. The same principles may also animate them while holding key Washington jobs – say, in the Treasury Department or the Council of Economic Advisors – where, together with the president, they sanctioned multi-billion-dollar federal bailout loans after the Crash of 2008. No other social science discipline is so directly linked to centers of power in government and commerce, and certainly one result of this massive extra-scholarly role is to promote, and not just from ivory towers, an economic rather than, say, political view of the world.[180]

Creative Destruction

In Chapter 3, I highlighted reasons why economics is especially admired in America for its intrinsic qualities – embodied in assumptions, principles, methods, and so forth – in comparison to other fields of knowledge. In Chapter 4, so far, I have explained something of how these qualities, expressed in economic teachings, came to play an outsized role in America's conversation about public life. Plus, I have emphasized how all this is capped by the goal of economic growth, which economists recommend and politicians endorse.

Accordingly, to this point we have seen that the subject of economic principles and teachings is large and complicated. Nevertheless, we have progressed to where the final part of my original proposal – that some political scientists should take a special interest in the downsides of "creative destruction" – is approaching. To arrive there, however, we have first to simplify a bit. To that end, we must begin to think of economics as a discipline, or a Temple of Science column, that regards itself as being principally about creative destruction.

Creative destruction is a phrase, coined by economist Joseph Schumpeter,[181] which describes the process by which new technologies and products are designed and brought to market, gaining for their owners and promoters success while replacing old technologies and old products. A new item, like a transistor, becomes profitable, and the people who produce and sell it prosper; simultaneously, the old item, like a vacuum tube, becomes obsolete, whereupon the skills and machinery that went into making it lose value and may even become worthless.

Actually, I should qualify what I just said. I am *not suggesting* that introductory economics textbooks declare explicitly and repeatedly that economics is all about creative destruction. But I *am observing* that those books, which are used for instruction in economics departments across the land, are about how to combine factors of production effectively, and that they are about how to generate more production wherever possible, and that they are about encouraging innovation as the key to getting *more* out of the resources that are available (remember Alan Blinder stipulating that "Higher productivity is better than lower productivity").[182]

Moreover, when innovation does come along – embodied in new knowledge, new technology, new design, new products, new marketing techniques, new business models, and more – economics textbooks say that, at that moment, while consumers make their choices, creative destruction unfolds, when new devices and arrangements defeat the old in a marketplace of voluntary transactions. When that happens, some employers, owners, and workers will fall behind and suffer. But their distress, in economic theory, is simply the price we pay as a society for getting GDP to go up, which is what prosperity is all about.[183]

Therefore, as shorthand for many details, let us regard economics as the science of creative destruction, or as the steady promotion of constant innovation. After all, this is how economists regard their own work, with adjustments to be made here and there around the edges, and with increasingly sophisticated mathematical formulations fashioned to show how, in fact, this is the best way forward.[184]

The Cost Side

The fly in the ointment is this: Political scientists and ordinary citizens – that is, people who are especially concerned for the health of American democracy – should regard this recipe for perpetual creative destruction as extremely problematical. For example, the concept itself amounts to an enormously powerful "frame," in the sense that, when used in conversation, it "frames" what is happening in such a way as to (1) highlight creation – of trains, cars, planes, antibiotics, polio vaccine, miracle rice, computers, barcodes, smartphones, GPS, etc. – and (2) downplay destruction whereby, for example, social dislocations, as we saw in Chapter 1, can produce resentment and therefore populism.[185]

Yet destruction, like creation, is everywhere. Thus automobiles are prized and coachmen are forgotten. Thus automatic elevators become routine and elevator operators disappear. Thus Instagram is celebrated and Kodak workers are gone.[186] Thus Walmart prospers and Main Street languishes. Thus television prices drop and television repairmen must retrain. Thus FedEx goes up and Post Office workers go down. Thus Netflix has over 50 million American subscribers and Blockbuster stores have vanished.[187]

In other words, and without mincing words, the phrase "creative destruction" gently "spins" an occasionally brutal process that, in plain English, is analogous in some respects to war, with winners and losers. In other words, in both creative destruction and war, one sets out to demolish other people's incomes and lifestyles; one plans surprise attacks backed up by, say, great financial power; one unapologetically ruins individuals, families, neighborhoods, firms, unions, family farms, towns, and cities; one deliberately transfers wealth and livelihood from this actor to that; and one without remorse fosters in other people anxiety and feelings of insecurity over what might happen next in their lives.[188]

Of course, people who advocate creative destruction do not describe what they recommend as "war," which most of us regard as an unattractive way of living together.[189] But, like business professor Clayton Christensen, they do plan deliberately for "disruption," and they analyze not "aggression" but "innovation."[190] Moreover, they talk not about "belligerents" but about "entrepreneurs." And they discuss the clever devastation of one's "competitors," who they do not call "victims," as a process whose consequences, in the long run, are benign rather than merciless.[191]

Unfortunately, reality is not so mild.[192] Thus, in the 1930s, Germany's generals *cleverly* decided to put radios into tanks. It was a great innovation. As a result, the Wehrmacht rolled over the French Army in 1940. This was not exactly what France and England wanted. Moreover, during World War II, Allied scientists *cleverly* worked to invent an atomic bomb. This, too, was a great innovation. They succeeded and dropped two of those on Japan. The world has lived fearfully ever since.

That was war. But in the civilian world, Jeff Bezos in 1994 *cleverly* created an online book store that did not pay most state and local taxes. Consequently, Amazon sold books more cheaply than traditional bookstores could and eventually drove many of those stores, such as the Borders and B. Dalton chains, out of business. More recently, Uber and Airbnb are *cleverly* using a business model – based on subcontractors – that avoids many taxes and insurance premiums. As a result, they are ruining cab drivers and hotel operators who are obliged to pay those costs in full.

Many "creators" know that their economic environment is warlike.[193] They also know that, in the marketplace treadmill of fierce competition leading to economic growth, additional damages are in store. Thus, if a modern, sophisticated, and well-funded start-up laboratory were to create a cheap

but excellent artificial coffee, putting it on the international
market would devastate the economies of Brazil, Vietnam,
Columbia, Indonesia, and Ethiopia.[194]

No one expects that to happen soon, but economic history is
not reassuring. For example, German scientists around 1900,
led by future Nobel Prize winner (chemistry, 1905) Adolf von
Baeyer, invented a profitable artificial indigo dye and thereby
destroyed most of India's indigo horticulture.[195] Closer to home
in America, 3D printers and driverless vehicles are expected to
wreak havoc in industry and commerce, within a decade or
two displacing millions of employers and employees, engineers and craftsmen, in manufacturing, construction, transportation, maintenance, and more.[196]

Luddites

Economists who favor economic growth tend not to spend
much time discussing its costs, and we will come back to that
in a moment. They often insist, though, that those who complain about destruction are like Luddites. The reference is to
the Luddite movement of textile workers who, in England
between 1811 and 1816, vandalized textile factory equipment
in an attempt to persuade creative factory owners not to lower
wages paid to skilled workers.[197]

In other words, modern Luddites are defined as being people
who stand in the way of progress, as being pessimists who do
not sufficiently appreciate the way economic growth has, over
centuries, lifted millions and even billions of people all over the
world out of poverty and poor health, isolation and ignorance,
provincialism and prejudice.[198] As a graphic example, just consider that streets in the world's great cities, before automobiles
appeared, were strewn with fly-blown horse manure that children were hired to collect.[199]

From all this we should conclude that criticism of Luddites is
not exactly fair but not exactly misplaced either. We all know
that, in life rather than theory, it is good to be ethical but worthwhile to be realistic. So on behalf of realism, we should recognize that the concept of creative destruction is not something

economists invented to make themselves look shrewd. Rather, it is an existing practice within society which they simply recognize, describe, analyze, and facilitate. Moreover, we should agree that prosperity is desirable. That does not mean, though, that it is free, and some of its costs may be distributed inequitably. Furthermore, it is a fact of life that some people are more economically effective than others and therefore more likely to innovate or benefit from works by people who innovate. The question is, what do we owe, ethically, to those who, through no fault of their own, are *not* especially effective?[200]

Who is Getting What?

This question brings us back to my proposal about what some political scientists should do in our troubled times. In academic life today, the discipline of economics, as one column in the Temple of Science, focuses in particular, via individual transactions and national aggregations, on economic growth and its process of creative destruction. There is nothing delinquent or irresponsible in that emphasis. And we should commend economists who perform their disciplinary mission well, on behalf of students, clients, and the public.

It is also true, however, that while economists are performing their professional task more or less competently, their discipline is dealing almost entirely with the creative side of creative destruction. I can't prove this proposition about little analyzing of destruction because I cannot give examples of what isn't there.[201] But it really isn't much there, as if economists are so busy with the positive side of creative destruction that they mainly leave its negative results – say, gig employment, silo media, global warming, habitat destruction, social envy, community deterioration, smartphone addiction and more – to people in other disciplines, in other columns of the Temple of Science.

Those people might be sociologists, psychologists, political scientists, demographers, historians, philosophers, and so forth. What is important for us is that, unlike economists

who work in a discipline that mostly considers economic productivity and innovation, those other scholars work in disciplines that are not collectively dedicated (as members of Temple
columns) to investigating cases of economic damage, disloca-
tion, destruction, and despair. Some people in those disciplines, as concerned individuals, investigate such cases, and we
are indebted to them for much of the information we possess
on those subjects. But there is no collective commitment on
their part to do this work, and that is where I believe that some
political scientists can now play a special scholarly role in the
Age of Populism.

The technical stake here we can infer from Robert Reich's
observation that the "meritocracy claim, that people are paid
what they are worth in the market, is a tautology that begs
the question of how the market is organized and whether
that organization is morally and economically defensible."[202]
Translated into terms we have already noted, Reich is saying
that people who promote economic growth tend to assume
that the supposedly "voluntary" trades that enter into GDP are
fair, as charted in the Edgeworth Box (which Reich does not
mention) projecting supply and demand curves to show where
buyers and sellers find prices at which they agree to trade. But
then Reich adds that we do not know (unless we have checked
via direct investigations) how the buyers and sellers in any
real Edgeworth Box (again, that is not his term) reached their
current positions in society, in which case some people may, by
force of circumstances, be short on bargaining power in their
box and therefore unable to *reject* the "voluntary" trades being
offered to them.[203]

Let's put this another way, again within the routine vocabulary of economics. Marginal utility theory, based on rational
calculations, and focused on individual actors, assumes that
both sides to a trade are satisfied with it. That is, in trading
both sides gain.[204] But other scholars may insist on asking
who *real* (not theoretical) traders are and how sizable are their
real resources of power, of wealth, or education, or status, or
health, or location, and more. In such cases, some trades may

result in losses, which people like Milton Friedman more or less assume, *a priori*, cannot be incurred for so long as trades are defined as "voluntary."[205]

Consider, though, whether or not the trades accepted by suppliers offered price P for shirts by Walmart – an international behemoth that in 2018 ran almost 12,000 stores, employed 2,300,000 workers, and collected $500 billion in revenues – are truly "voluntary." If the price P is terribly low, how can a small shirt factory in Bangladesh afford *not* to accept Walmart's proposal?[206]

But it is not only behemoths that illustrate the need for checking to see who is who and who is getting what. After all, even Adam Smith, who postulated the invisible hand, suspected before national economic statistics were collected that "masters" who have some wealth can hold out longer than "workmen" when bargaining over wages.[207]

The Road Not Taken

So here is the crux of the matter. Society needs economists because they study economic *creativity*, which is an important matter. But if they won't highlight economic *destruction*, someone else should, because that is *also* an important matter, especially when some things are getting out of hand in our times. Therefore, I propose, and I will in Chapter 5 explain further, that political scientists are likely candidates for the job.

First, however, let us note a final reason for feeling that economics is too important to be left entirely to economists. As a matter of conventional wisdom since the end of World War II, most American economists and their disciples in non-academic life have been steadily pro-capitalist, which is historically understandable because they live in a society that promotes that point of view. However, they have also, and also understandably, expressed their support of capitalism by being anti-communist or, in scholarly terms, anti-Marxist. Accordingly, they don't use, or rarely use, Marxian concepts to understand the world. And there, something is seriously and significantly absent, like when the dog did not bark for Sherlock Holmes.[208] I want to be very clear on this point. America does not need Marxian calls for armed revolution. Even in hard economic times, democracy is preferable to civil war and fortunately, unlike when Marx wrote, it (democracy) is widely available to ordinary people who want to elect new leaders to make new laws and public policies.[209] That much is patently clear. But we might benefit from using some Marxian concepts – which most economists do not – for the sake of intellectual analysis because, as a critic of capitalism, Marx powerfully highlighted what he thought were its downsides, even unto describing the process of creative destruction without using that term (which was later invented by Joseph Schumpeter).[210]

To begin with, Marx welcomed capitalism as a progressive social and economic force that would demolish the stifling practices of feudalism. (There is the creativity.) This he maintained in his theory of history, which praised capitalism for its ability to improve upon and supersede feudalism's constraints at home and at work. On the other hand, Marx pointed out that, while it was welcome to begin with, capitalism was not a flawless society but one that imposed severe social, economic, and emotional costs upon many of its citizens. (There is the destruction.) That is, for Marx, who did not use our vocabulary, capitalism in effect entailed certain measures of creativity followed by some of destruction.

Americans scholars don't need to become Marxists to know this. But their scholarly teachings might acquire a heightened sense of urgency if they would occasionally note some dramatic Marxian concepts and phrases that, in a sociological sense, say something about where capitalism is likely to go unless someone heads it off at the pass. For example, there is the Marxian notion of how, during the reign of capitalism, "all that is solid melts into air." That notion is certainly relevant to how many Americans – some of them conservatives and some of them liberals – today feel that their principles and traditions are under constant assault, are constantly "melting," in the ever-churning modern economy.[211]

Marxism also suggests a notion of "class war," which might shed light on what is happening between the One Percent (one class) and the Ninety-Nine Percent (other classes) in America. Furthermore, that confrontation might be considered via the Marxian concept of "exploitation," where one group (or individual) takes advantage of another's weaknesses. Then there is the Marxian concept of an "industrial reserve army," which might illuminate the modern situation where many good jobs are either automated away or sent overseas, leaving behind a pool ("army") of impoverished and desperate workers who live precariously while more effective Americans take home a lion's share of the nation's GDP. In these circumstances, Marxists have decried what they call the "immiserization of the working class," which is a phrase that might sensitize us into understanding some of the convictions that led many people in, say, the American Midwest – depressed and deindustrialized – to vote for Donald Trump and Bernie Sanders.[212]

Moreover, some aspects of the present consumer society, where baubles are being purchased privately rather than infrastructure being funded publicly, might seem more understandable if we were to focus on what Marxists call "the fetishism of commodities," which leads people to value private over public goods. And while we are on the subject of cultural manipulations, general suspicion of mass media nowadays might be regarded as one consequence of what Marxists call "false consciousness," where advertisements that are *very* cleverly designed to entice people into buying things they don't need wind up encouraging many voters to believe that no one in public now speaks to them truthfully.

A final realm of possible "disinformation" – a Russian/Marxist term – may shed light on America's horrendously costly wars in Iraq and Afghanistan.[213] Iraq had no weapons of mass destruction. Why, really, did President George W. Bush insist that it did? Bin Laden is gone. Why, really, is Washington still making war in Afghanistan? Beyond invoking unreliable conspiracy theories, some plausible answers to such questions might emerge if the subject of Middle East oil and Great Power politics were linked to what Marxists have for more than a century called "imperialism."

"All that is solid melts into air," "class war," "exploitation," "industrial reserve army," "immiserization of the working class," "fetishism of commodities," "false consciousness," "disinformation," and "imperialism." The point is not that American scholars should become Marxists. But political stories powerfully influence the way we see the world, which is a matter to which I will return. Therefore, we should bear in mind that mainstream economists are closing off some of our analytic options by, in effect, telling an un-Marxian or even anti-Marxian story.[214] For the record, they are also ignoring or neglecting the democratic-socialism story, but there is no room here to dwell on that.[215]

5 TARGETING NEOLIBERALISM

Here is the sequence so far. Much of the search for knowledge takes place in Kerr's multiversity. The Temple of Science model suggests that that institution is excellent in some ways but lacks a *general* commitment to confront the populist age in which we live. While such a commitment is absent, modern society has nevertheless accorded unusual authority to the Temple's economics column, as if scholars there possess especially useful knowledge as compared to what is discovered by other disciplines (columns) dealing with people.

Within what economists say, mainstream economics is regarded as particularly incisive. It recommends that government should above all promote economic growth, which is generated by creative destruction. The recommendation in favor of growth is accepted by many Americans, from politicians to industrialists, from workers to corporations, from farmers to doctors, from ministers to talk show hosts. In the light of this intense interest in, and support for, economic growth, the downsides of creative destruction, some of which fuel populism, receive much less attention.

Karl Polanyi

I believe that some political scientists should fill in some of what is missing. But before we move on to consider where and how they might do that, let us note an insight on this subject from one of the great thinkers worth engaging in our times. Thus Karl Polanyi observed in *The Great Transformation* (1944): "Nowhere has liberal [that is, Enlightenment] philosophy failed so conspicuously as in its understanding of the problem of change. Fired by an emotional faith in spontaneity, the common-sense attitude toward change was discarded [in the nineteenth century, after the Enlightenment] in favor of a mystical readiness to accept the social consequences of economic improvement, whatever they might be. The elementary truths of political science and statecraft were first discredited, then forgotten. It should need no elaboration that a process of undirected change, the pace of which is deemed too fast, should be slowed down, if possible, so as to safeguard the welfare of the community."[216]

In effect, Polanyi declares that change – political, economic, social, and technological – is not compelled by some fixed rule like the law of gravity, something which, for the religious among us, constitutes an immutable act of God and which, for secular people, is something to which they must adapt rather than something they are allowed to control.[217] Instead, Polanyi reminds us that statesmen and educated people were once wary, and for good reason, of permitting change to go forward without consideration for how it might be limited for "the welfare of the community." This is, I believe, a common-sense observation that we should keep in mind as we begin now to address what many of today's opinion leaders, in and out of the academy, are powerfully hawking.[218]

Targeting Neoliberalism

Polanyi suggests that it is reasonable to "slow down" some effects of creative destruction. But he does not say *how* scholars, or anyone else, should promote such a slowdown. Therefore, I want to recommend that we should direct our thoughts and efforts to that end by targeting the late-stage capitalist belief system that social scientists and historians call neoliberalism. *Neoliberalism* is the practical and ideological force that inspires *creative destruction*, in which case challenging the former may help us soften the impact of the latter.

So the first reason for targeting neoliberalism, which relentlessly advocates creative destruction, is, for me, a matter of principle, because I believe it endangers our society.[219] On that score, in my opinion, taking the measure of neoliberalism's imperfections is a matter of conscience.

The second reason for targeting neoliberalism is practical. Political scientists (as a class) do not legislate, and we vote only in small numbers. But we do study, we do teach, we do publish for one another, we join our neighbors in acts of good citizenship, and we have a presence in the mass media. In all these realms, targeting neoliberalism would be a practical strategy for at least part of our discipline.

Thus, (1) to be practical would be to specify a common adversary and, by aiming at it, assemble otherwise scattered pieces of research about various instances of social and environmental destruction. Furthermore, (2) to be practical would be to explore where a dangerous force comes from in history and how the costs it imposes are likely to continue if no one checks them. And finally, (3) to be practical would be to maximize impact, would be to unite around a visible target and offer nonpolitical scientists accessible and riveting information about exceptionally important events and trends. It follows that if, say, journalists would pay attention to our findings along these lines, politicians and voters would hear from media sources more than they do today about what political scientists are together criticizing and why.

What is Neoliberalism?

So what exactly is "neoliberalism"? The term refers to a *new* (modern) liberalism that in some respects resembles the *old* (classical) liberalism that Polanyi criticized and that arose in the nineteenth century. At that time, the term "liberalism" referred to a set of ideas that, roughly speaking, condemned the economic arrangements of late-stage feudalism, and that admired a wave of enterprise galvanized especially by middle-class creativity (which could not fully flower under feudalism) in realms such as science, commerce, manufacturing, agriculture, banking, education, transportation, communication, international trade, and more.

Many years later, the ideas and practices of neoliberalism came to constitute an updated version of this former liberalism that, as we saw, Karl Marx first praised and then criticized. The later liberalism is therefore equal, in another vocabulary, to contemporary "capitalism," which, sanctified by mainstream economics, endorses repeated acts of creative destruction and is therefore a source of both prosperity and devastation.

In a sense, then, neoliberalism is the pro-creative-destruction ecology of American social life that we should investigate in the Age of Populism. However, it is also something around which there already exists a lively public conversation. Therefore – and this is an ethical matter of no small importance – if some of us will participate professionally in that conversation, our presence there will be directly relevant to the society in which we live.

Commitment to that last point, in effect, was proposed by Robert Putnam, APSA president in 2002, who declared that "My argument is that an important underappreciated part of our professional responsibility is to engage with our fellow citizens in deliberation about their political concerns, broadly defined." Putnam went on to argue that public alienation and disengagement from government have grown, therefore political scientists should debate them more than they have. He said the same about globalization and social justice. And he affirmed that "I believe that attending to the concerns of our fellow citizens is not just an optional add-on for the profession of political science, but an obligation as fundamental as our pursuit of scientific truth."[220]

Unfortunately, to study neoliberalism and its effects is easier said than done, because neoliberalism is not a *thing*, like a dog, which can be scientifically described in specific ways as different from other things, like bananas or granite.

Neoliberalism is, instead, a *concept*, relating to the social world like many other concepts such as justice, power, authority, rights, charisma, democracy, and more. That being the case, scholars and pundits who talk about neoliberalism don't always agree on exactly what they are talking about when they use that term. Moreover, in the Temple of Science, different sorts of professors, from different columns, approach research subjects differently, to the point where many books and articles address, but not always consistently or compatibly, aspects of modern life that they ascribe to neoliberalism.[221]

Accordingly, there are complicated interpretive controversies in all this that we cannot resolve here. But what happened – that is, the historical record – is fairly straightforward. The Crash of 1929 and the Great Depression challenged American faith in capitalism,[222] while John Maynard Keynes insisted that private markets would not automatically balance themselves in a socially beneficial way. Consequently, government intervention in economic activity seemed to many voters warranted, whereupon, in 1932, they elected Franklin Roosevelt president with a Democratic majority in both the Senate and the House of Representatives. Roosevelt and his Democratic colleagues enacted New Deal measures, such as the Securities and Exchange Act, the Glass-Steagall Act, and the National Labor Relations Act, which placed some capitalist institutions under government supervision. Later, Washington in the 1960s and 1970s continued to keep some capitalist creativity in check, for example, initiating programs to improve workers' safety and increase environmental protection.

Then, as voter impressions of damage caused by the Crash and the Depression faded, the conservative Ronald Reagan was elected and began to restore to capitalism, now called "free enterprise," some of its earlier powers. Thus "neoliberalism" began to "take off" in the 1980s, when large tax cuts, mainly for the well-to-do, fueled an expansion of prosperity financed by massive federal spending deficits. Consequently, supported by most Republicans and many Clinton Democrats, leading up to the Crash of 2008, labor unions were weakened, public services were privatized, interest rates were unleashed, social services were reduced, welfare became "workfare," home mortgages were "securitized," commercial and investment banks were permitted to engage in brokerage and insurance,[223] corporate and private political contributions were uncapped, "globalization" led to "deindustrialization," "downsizing" encouraged "outsourcing," disparities of income and wealth separated the One Percent and the rest, while conservative think tanks (such as the Cato Institute and the Heritage Foundation) and conservative media outlets (such as Encounter Books, *The Washington Times*, and Fox News) were established to promote neoliberal ideas and policies.[224]

Homo Politicus

These were some elements of *what* happened in recent American history. That such things transpired is not much in dispute. What is more complicated and controversial is *why* they happened. That is, to ask why neoliberalism appeared, and why it now dominates American life, is to engage in inexact interpretations of what the facts imply, is to argue over which intangible ideas and concepts drove the establishment and evolution of those facts.

On this score, scholars agree that neoliberalism, as an extension of capitalism, entails a very fundamental mental switch away from the concept of *homo politicus* to the concept of *homo economicus*.[225] Starting with Aristotle, great thinkers long considered people to be political animals (*homo politicus*), who are naturally intended (as opposed to how Greeks assessed neighbors who they called "barbarians") to live together consciously in a well-organized community (or *polis*). In that community, people could exercise their capacities for self-rule, for defending home and hearth, for making moral judgments, for legislating rules of conduct, for creating art and commerce, and for pursuing a good life. In the same community, a person of central importance was the citizen, who was endowed with a potential for reason, with the right to hold office, and with the power to participate in (some) community decisions.

Assuming that they were in the category of *homo politicus*, citizens eventually came to be regarded, say by Locke, Montesquieu, Jefferson, and Madison, as naturally competent to fashion social contracts that would empower them to exercise sovereignty (political power) together, thereby maintaining institutions and practices – such as religious tolerance – by which their communities (states) would stand or fall. By extension, the aim of achieving social contracts fostered democracy in the modern world, where in the nineteenth and twentieth centuries more and more people became citizens, protected by constitutions and other legal arrangements that afforded them opportunities for maximizing their natural talents for public expression and political action.

Homo Economicus

While all this unfolded, disciples of Aristotle suspected, as he did, that people who lived mainly by and for commerce – the so-called *homo economicus* – were dangerous to society. The problem was that, driven by an acquisitive instinct, such people might so resolve to accumulate money and riches, rather than just reasonable sustenance, that their passion for piling up wealth might generate social conflicts and thereby undermine the community's ability to foster moderation, reciprocity, respect, balance, and civility.

Nevertheless, when fairly static feudal classes in Europe began to disintegrate, some people – a growing middle class – began to enlarge industry and trade in European society. In those circumstances, acquisitive behavior – in banking, in manufacturing, in timber, in mining, in large-scale buying and selling of slaves, cotton, sugar, wool, tobacco, pottery, textiles, spices, and coffee – became more acceptable than formerly, and thinkers like Adam Smith began to talk about the "natural propensity" of all people "to truck, barter, and exchange one thing for another."[226]

Accordingly, thinking positively about the sort of people summed up in the phrase *homo economicus* (although not using that term) became more common than previously.[227] Simultaneously, a new science of economics, from Smith to Ricardo to Jevons to Pareto to Schumpeter and further, arose to analyze what happens when people are measured less by their rank in society (feudalism) and more by their contribution to economic efficiency (capitalism).

In philosophical terms, it was as if men and women were no longer born to seek a good life (for example, in Aristotelian or Christian virtue) but to make themselves useful in a natural system of voluntary market exchanges, which no one created or controlled. In economic terms, which annoyed Polanyi, it was as if people were expected to welcome lives marked by constant flux, as if creative destruction were sacrosanct and citizens had no choice but to accept its dislocations. In social terms, it was as if residents would not be regarded chiefly as *political citizens* in the state – for example, enacting laws to control constant change – but as *economic actors* competing in implacable markets. In Kantian terms, although neoliberals are not disciples of Kant, it was as if everyone were destined to risk becoming a means to someone else's end.[228]

Economic Consequences

Because it assumes that people are *homo economicus*, neoliberalism promotes distinctive beliefs about the nature of (1) individuals, who animate the modern economy. Then it promotes distinctive beliefs about the nature of (2) markets, where *homo economicus* individuals presumably come together to trade. And then it promotes distinctive beliefs about the nature of (3) commercial corporations, which arise from the way in which economically minded people sometimes aggregate their resources and ambitions in order to produce and to profit.

From these and related beliefs, various consequences follow. Limited space here permits us to consider only a few of them. They cannot be explained in straight-line fashion, as if they flow from a single theory or syllogism, with one proposition leading to the next, and after that another and another. But neoliberal propositions do hang together, based on shared and interlocking concepts. So let us first consider those that are mainly economic, and then we will consider those that are mainly political.

The Market-Based Society

For example, when neoliberals assume that people belong to the category of *homo economicus* – which is another way of describing the mainstream economic concept of utility-seeking people calculating rationally – they sanction a predominantly "market-based" society. In that society, every adult is expected to cultivate his or her own worthiness "to compete" against others,[229] even though neoliberals do not think of this society as a Hobbesian war "of every man, against every man."[230] That is, each person is evaluated by how much marginal utility he or she can contribute to the market; many individuals must turn themselves into commodities for sale to others; each worker is regarded as an animated machine enabling production; young people are advised not to seek moderation and stability but to adapt and evolve ceaselessly according to changing market needs;[231] education for life and citizenship is transformed by globalization imperatives into a national commitment to job training;[232] and so forth.

Some people, naturally ambitious and competitive, probably enjoy these circumstances. Many others are constantly anxious and "lead lives of quiet desperation."[233] Yet all this seems reasonable to neoliberals even though no one can really be sure why some people succeed economically and others, who may be reasonably energetic and conscientious, do not. After all, in capitalist thought, everyone is supposed to earn in proportion to his or her contribution to output and prosperity. But, in truth, no one – not economists, not employers, and not workers – has ever measured the market system's basic building block, which is, according to neoliberals, the marginal utility of any person's contribution (that of owner or renter,

supervisor or secretary, hotelier or bellhop, Steven Spielberg or
Julia Roberts, and so forth) to economic activity.[234] So we don't
really know, according to marginal utility theory, why some
full-time, hard-working people are mired in poverty.[235]

Natural Markets

Neoliberal faith in economic growth works through an
assumption that markets are natural. Citing opinions
expressed by former CEO of the Goldman Sachs Group and
then Secretary of the Treasury Henry Paulson (2006–2009),
Larry Bartels describes this faith as a "general tendency to
think of the economy as a natural system existing prior to, and
largely separate from, the political sphere."[236]

Now, if markets are natural (economic) and separate
from governments (political), one can argue that in markets
successful people deservedly acquire money and property,
which they can use to resist government power.[237] In which
case, in a way, efficient markets, by sustaining economically
secure citizens, are what keeps governments from becoming
tyrannical.

In addition, however, to assume the existence of natural
markets is to ascribe to them natural consequences, such as
inequality. In which case voters, and government officials,
need not inquire too closely into where those consequences
come from. Inequality, for example, is painful to some people,
therefore some of them seek government help. But political
decisions, say neoliberals, are artificial, selfish, and inherently
fallible, whereas market decisions are genuine, flow from
impartial confluences, and are simply the price that we (actually, the losers) must pay for progress.[238]

In fact, to insist that "capitalism" or "free enterprise" works
through "the market" is a slight-of-hand trick, because natural markets don't exist.[239] David Graeber has pointed out
that, despite Adam Smith's supposition that markets arise
naturally from the division of labor and the propensity to
barter, the history of primitive societies reveals only contrived
markets fashioned differently by various tribes, cities, and

governments.[240] Nevertheless, neoliberals not only assume that markets are natural and precede government, they also believe that, on behalf of economic "efficiency," the chief obligation of governments is to protect unremitting competition and creative destruction in those markets even if that requires criticizing politicians and voters who might want, on behalf of society, to regulate such churning.[241]

Entrepreneurs

Neoliberals argue that "entrepreneurs" generate creativity and prosperity, but that claim is only part of a wider neoliberal notion that "capitalism" (or "free enterprise") and its special characters, such as entrepreneurs, produce economic growth and progress.[242] The argument here is that governments, everywhere in the world, should establish the wherewithal for ceaseless economic competition, including conditions such as "law and order, the foundations of secure property rights, and an inclusive market economy." Where those conditions have obtained, as during the Industrial Revolution in England, "The engine of technological breakthroughs throughout the economy was innovation, spearheaded by new entrepreneurs and businessmen eager to apply their new ideas."[243]

On the one hand, at home this thesis justifies using government to legislate in favor of a fraction of the class of *homo economicus* as if they are the movers and shakers of national prosperity. On this score, tax breaks and subsidies for commerce are enacted, and the theory of supply-side economics is commended.[244] On the other hand, the same thesis promotes globalization abroad, which extends domestic practices into the international arena – assuring profitable access for American managers and investors – by insisting that each country should act in the spirit of competitive capitalism in order to avoid economic "failure." Resistance is scorned, as summed up with rhetorical brilliance by Thomas Friedman's praise for "the golden straitjacket"[245] – unpleasant but effective – which consists of economic practices fashioned and enforced by globalization champions such as the World

Bank, the International Monetary Fund, and the World Trade Organization.[246]

What is neglected in this scenario for going forward are people who are not remarkable, who are nevertheless virtuous, and who contribute greatly to progress and prosperity. For example, there are scientists and engineers who discover things like antibiotics and Lipitor, who understand why glaciers are melting, who learn to grow two blades of grass where one grew before, who invent transistors and turn them into computers, who place satellites in orbit and broadcast from them signals for GPS systems. Some of these people may aspire to profit greatly from their work, as neoliberals claim. But others may act from a sense of vocation, for instance, from the challenge of discovering something new.[247] And they may be willing to do that as government employees, which would cost society much less than when, in the name of promoting innovation, neoliberals insist that discoveries paid for by government research grants should be turned over to capitalists for development.[248]

A second loss relates to fairness. To the extent that innovative businessmen succeed, they do not produce prosperity by themselves. Other people have a hand in their success and may deserve to be treated more generously than they are today. Philosophers have made this point by insisting that science, technology, education, and good health surround successful entrepreneurs, who get ahead by standing on the shoulders of giants, by working with earlier discoveries, and by reaping gains from government spending on research and infrastructure.[249]

Furthermore, praise for entrepreneurial creativity usually discounts how it may profit from the occasional indecencies of historical forces, and especially from those associated with war.[250] For example, while British capitalism flourished along with colonial exploitation, Hilaire Belloc described as follows England's major cultural advantage during the battle of Omdurman (1898) against Arab tribes in the Sudan: "Whatever happens, we have got / the Maxim gun and they have not."[251] Moreover, American capitalism thrived greatly after 1945 because, protected by the Atlantic and Pacific oceans, it emerged from World War II unscathed compared to Germany, France, the United Kingdom, the Soviet Union, China, and Japan.[252]

Free Trade

Underlying neoliberal support for globalization is enthusiasm for "free trade." Free trade justifications go back to nineteenth-century economist David Ricardo and his principle of "comparative advantage," which says that any country can benefit from *exporting* what it can produce most efficiently and *importing* what its trading partners can produce most efficiently. That is, exploit your comparative advantage and let your trading partners exploit theirs. Later economists would draw the same conclusion in terms of marginal utility theory, where producing efficiently (using few or cheap resources) generates inexpensive utility, to be exchanged for someone else's inexpensive utility (based on using few or cheap resources) in return.

Thus Nobel Prize winner (economics, 2008) Paul Krugman declared to his readers that "If you had taken the time to understand the story about England trading cloth for Portuguese wine that we teach to every freshman in Econ. I, [then]… you know more about the nature of the global economy than the current U. S. Trade Representative (or most of his predecessors)."[253] With that kind of confidence emanating from economists, the conservative pundit Charles Krauthammer, perhaps recalling what he studied in college, agreed with Krugman by declaring: "That free trade is advantageous to both sides is the rarest of political propositions – provable, indeed mathematically."[254]

Well, not exactly. There are serious problems with this abstract model, to the point where using it as a basis for making real-world decisions may cause enough local resentment to propel some voters into populism. One is that, as understood by neoliberals, the model suggests that, under conditions of free trade, economic boats everywhere are rising, to the point where hundreds of millions of people worldwide are no longer as poor as they used to be.[255] Here is an accomplishment that little impresses many American workers, some of whom lost their jobs when American factories outsourced many of those jobs to Mexico after the North American Free Trade Agreement (1994) was proposed by Republicans in Congress, supported by more Republicans than Democrats in both Houses,[256] and signed into law by the neoliberal President Bill Clinton.[257]

A second problem with the free-trade model is that it deals with average gains. That is, neoliberals argue that "America" and "China" are better off, in GDP terms, from massive trading between them. This may be true, if GDP is a test of national welfare. But it is also a barometer of creative destruction, in which competitive innovation produces local winners and losers. In which case, many Americans may feel that, even if "America" is better off, they themselves lost ground.[258]

Or, in a powerful political story of recent years, it turns out that in a national economy driven largely by creative destruction working through free trade and globalization, the richest One Percent of Americans now own 40 percent of the country's wealth,[259] while the average family in the top One Percent of income receivers took in more than twenty-six times the average family income of the other 99 percent of income receivers.[260]

Shareholders and Stakeholders

Free trade is dominated by large actors, which are often business corporations, and those are regarded by neoliberals as best administered according to "the theory of shareholder value." Milton Friedman explained this theory as early as in 1970, but did not name it at the time, when he argued that the sole responsibility of corporate managers, within whatever legal guidelines the state may determine, is to maximize profits.[261]

In other words, because shareholders own the corporation, its officers are obliged, by their terms of employment, to serve those shareholders by earning for them as much profit as the law permits. In theory, at least, the notion of managers serving shareholders even justifies the practice of "venture capitalists" buying enough shares to take over a corporation, selling off parts of the enterprise, loading up what remains with debt, but all the while paying substantial dividends and/or creating for the new owners other financial benefits (such as buying back the corporation's stock in order to boost its market price).[262]

In short, the shareholder theory is an elaboration of Alfred Sloan's aphorism, from the 1920s, that General Motors, which Sloan led, existed to make money rather than motor cars.[263] The problem there, for social thought, is that the theory of shareholder value clashes with older notions, familiar to political thinkers, which may be used to assess corporations that operate, after all, under public authorizations. Joint-stock corporations, such as the eighteenth-century Charles River Bridge Company in Massachusetts, which enjoy limited liability and other valuable privileges by law, were invented by Western societies to serve public needs, such as building a bridge over a particular river.[264] In the realm of such corporations, profit was an expected by-product, but public service was the larger goal.

Accordingly, even when in the early nineteenth century the flexible practice of general incorporation (without a specific legislative charter and with no designated purpose) was authorized in America by state laws, there remained some sentiment in favor of regarding corporations as artificial persons, licensed and charged with serving not just *shareholders* but also other citizens. These might include corporate clients, consumers, tenants, workers, neighbors, taxpayers who pay for public education and infrastructure, governments that protect corporations from foreign enemies, and more.[265]

This view, which is in effect a *stakeholder theory* of corporate management, harks back to a time when Populists and Progressives feared that capitalism was run mainly for the benefit of bankers and industrialists – that is, shareholders – who critics regarded as serving themselves and exploiting the public.[266] That suspicion lasted well into the New Deal, but it has been challenged by neoliberal thinkers ever since.[267]

Scarcity

Homo economicus, natural markets, entrepreneurs, free markets, shareholder values: All these terms, framing neoliberalism, rest on a supposition that economic activity is about "scarcity," much like psychology is about personality. Neoliberalism adopts this concept from mainstream economics. As Nicholas Gregory Mankiw says in his bestselling textbook *Principles of Economics*, "Economics is the study of how society manages its scarce resources."[268] Or, as we saw Alan Blinder saying, there are three "noncontroversial propositions" in "the economic way of thinking," and the second of these is that "Resources are scarce."[269] That point may seem obvious when people have in mind, say, the limited amount of gold worldwide, or the shortage of curbside parking spaces downtown.

Nevertheless, economic scarcity is not simple. One difficulty has to do with how resources are distributed and allocated within the existing economy. For economists, "resources" in this sense are the items – from coal, to clean water, to antibiotics, to wood, to aluminum, to oil, to computers, and many other things – that get combined in families, in factories, in farms, in schools, in laboratories, and more, to produce goods that people want. It follows that, because such resources are not endlessly and easily available, there is at any moment a finite supply of them. In which case, a market mechanism is needed to enable citizens to compete against one another, voluntarily of course, and to receive, each according to his or her utility contribution, more or less from the stock of goods that scarce resources, in combination, are capable of producing.

Well, again, not exactly. One problem is that, on scarcity, neoliberalism draws no distinction between "needs" and "wants." Needs are, roughly speaking, what we require to get along as normal, ordinary, moderate, balanced, and civilized people. On that score, it is obvious that the world's population today, if organized to that end, could easily make enough, for example, tables, chairs, shirts, pants, bread, jam, dwellings, and medicines to supply what everyone really needs.[270] So satisfying *needs* is not prevented by scarcity. Add to the needs list some luxury items based on cravings and idiosyncrasies, and the necessary productive capacity still exists.[271]

Wants, however, are an entirely different matter. Wants have to do with what we "desire" rather than what we "need."[272] And our desires are constantly enlarged by social norms, by advertisements, by fashion, and by keeping up with the Coopers who are themselves straining to stay ahead of the Smiths.[273] In a way, then, desires are innumerable and insatiable. It follows that satisfying wants/desires completely is impossible. There is simply not enough stuff to go around.[274]

In these circumstances, the axiom of scarcity fits into a neoliberal endorsement of "consumer sovereignty," where presumably it is consumers who rule the economy and corporations that merely seek, obediently, to satisfy their demanding customers.[275] That consumer desires are created day after day by ubiquitous advertising, that store shelves can be cleared only if we will buy things that we don't need, that planned obsolescence is built into cars, appliances, furniture, and other items, that many children and adults have more toys and clothing than they can play with or wear: All these are common-sense observations that must be ignored by neo-liberalism because they might validate the critics who claim that large corporations actually dominate small consumers rather than the other way around.

Economic Growth

If perpetual scarcity exists, one way to deal with it is to generate endless economic growth. More growth equals more things equals more acquisitions equals more happiness... until one decides to pursue the next new thing. Apart from the treadmill quality of this proposition, it may sound plausible until one considers that when neoliberals borrow their analysis of economic growth from mainstream economists, and when they boundlessly admire that project, they usually overlook or discount the inevitable adjunct of growth, which is what economists call "externalities."

A useful item, say a home air conditioner in 1950, may be produced where it did not previously exist and may therefore be considered a welcome multiplier of economic growth. But beyond its market price, making that product and many others may impose on society "external costs," some personal and some social, for example, environmental pollution and ecological disorder.[276] Which means that "more" is not necessarily "better."

In our day, the worst of externalities is global warming, driven by burning fossil fuels purchased at market prices.[277] Global warming is catastrophic, but you would not know that from buying affordable gallons of gasoline. The problem is that market prices, which add up to GDP and therefore indicate economic growth, do not necessarily include external costs, because they register only the *marginal utility value* (short-term) of items that are exchanged. And the problem there is that the marginal utility prices of items like gasoline, used on a daily basis in the modern economy, mostly do not take into account either the *long-run fate* of humanity, or the *absolute value* of the Earth – its soil, its forests, its water, its air, and more – which supports us all. So we keep driving, all too often in gas guzzlers.

Some neoliberals claim that when we will become richer, we will be able to afford to solve ecological problems; that is, they say we can continue to do what we are doing now, to boost GDP, and we can at the same time safely assume that, somewhere later on, people who will be less vulnerable to scarcity will create the efficiencies and substitutions we need to prevent disastrous externalities.[278] They might also explain, along these lines, that because economic growth is *required* for progress and prosperity, there is a growth versus climate "tradeoff" for which we must seek "an optimal path that puts the benefits and costs of each into balance."[279]

Nowadays, that optimum path, in strictly economic terms, might entail enacting a carbon tax.[280] Its proponents assume that if carbon emitters will have to pay more for what they are doing, they will stop emitting.[281] What would happen to the Earth if they would just frown and pay up (as comfortable people do when the price of gasoline for their SUV rises) is discussed nowhere in neoliberal writings that I know of. For, as Naomi Klein says, "To admit that the climate crisis is real is to admit the end of the neoliberal project."[282]

Ideology

Another difficulty with the notion of scarcity relates to its role in neoliberal "ideology." Ideology is a term sometimes used by scholars in reference to what are called "catechisms" or "creeds" in religion, where some authoritative source, such as the Bible, is distilled into a collection of principles and propositions, such as the Nicene Creed of 325 AD, which tell us what life is about and what we should do with it. On the secular front, Marxism is sometimes seen as this sort of ideology, composed of various linked principles and propositions derived mainly from the writings of Marx, Engels, Lenin, and Stalin.

Neoliberalism is *not* an ideology in this sense. It has no leaders like the Pope, and it has no authoritative scriptures like those of Marxism.[283] However, "ideology" is also a term with sociological dimensions. It can be used to describe a compendium of principles and concepts, which are not based on formally authoritative sources, which are not written down anywhere systematically, but that indicate what some people do together in society and why what they do justifies their collective status, perhaps conferring on them wealth, prestige, and political power.[284]

In this sense, the assumption of perpetual scarcity, borrowed from mainstream economics, is part of a powerful complex of ideas that add up to an ideology that is commended by, and that is promoted by, many of the more successful people in America today. In this sense, it is a middle-class, or bourgeois, ideology – as opposed to an aristocratic, or proletarian ideology – because, to deal effectively with what they call scarcity, neoliberals praise and applaud people who generate growth (there are the entrepreneurs), who encourage growth, who justify growth, who admire globalization (there is the free trade project), who support privatization (there is the marketplace), who injure or eliminate jobs, traditions, small towns, unions, bowling leagues, and more, all in the name of progress (there is the creative destruction).[285]

For example, Edward Conard explains that capital is chronically scarce because "workers" or "voters" won't cut back on consumption.[286] There is the scarcity assumption. In his view, it justifies lowering taxes on entrepreneurs so that those people, when successful, will retain enough money to invest – that is, to pay for taking "risks" that only they, among workers and voters, will incur but that society requires in order to stimulate innovation (economic growth), to the benefit of all.

But what is the context? Conard identifies himself as a "former managing director of Bain Capital, LLC."[287] We should note, then, that his contention, on behalf of investors like himself, is a long-standing thesis, going back to the 1830s when classical economists such as Nassau Senior justified (bourgeois) profits by arguing that capitalists practice "abstinence," whereas workers provide "labor."[288] That is, capitalists refrain from a measure of consumption, accumulate savings, then use that money to build productive enterprises, and therefore deserve to profit when those enterprises generate goods for the benefit of society at large. In other words, what Conard says today is, in effect, more or less what industrialists and business people have long claimed. But he makes the case for capitalist privileges and power in terms of "innovation" rather than "abstinence," probably because we don't usually believe that abstinence is characteristic of people like Jeff Bezos, Bill Gates, George Soros, Mark Zuckerberg, or Michael Bloomberg, to say nothing of President Donald Trump.

Political Consequences

So far, we have looked at neoliberal ideas that relate mainly to economic practices. In the real world, though, even small economic practices can have large political consequences.[289] So let us consider some of those now, even though they are so large that we can explore them here only briefly. Like neoliberal economic ideas, these political consequences cannot be depicted in straight-line fashion, as if they express the orderly unfolding of a formal theory. They do connect, however, via shared concepts, and they are worth noting here, even unsystematically, because they are especially relevant to political scientists who, in the Temple of Science, might commit themselves professionally to analyzing America's political condition in the Age of Populism.

Public Goods

Let us start by noting that neoliberalism is very weak on "public goods," which in any society provide a large part of social well-being. The Constitution says that "the People of the United States, in order to ... establish justice, insure domestic tranquility, provide for the common defence, promote the general welfare, and secure the blessings of liberty to ourselves and our posterity, do ordain and establish" constitutional government in America. Thus, in its Preamble, the Constitution describes the new government as responsible for facilitating the achievement of several public goods that will benefit all citizens.[290]

The reason why neoliberals are weak on public goods is that they are strong on markets, as opposed to governments.[291] That markets fail to provide public goods (such as fresh air, clean water, and national defense) is obvious, but it was also demonstrated logically by economist Mancur Olson, who argued that, because everyone can enjoy a public good once it is created, rational (self-centered) individuals will decide not to pay for it voluntarily.[292] If it is there, they will use it; if it is not there, they will wait for someone else to pay to create it; once that other person, or persons, has paid, *then* rational individuals will use it, thus acting as "free riders."

Technically speaking, markets do not provide public goods because such goods cannot be priced, like cars and breakfast cereals, for separate and voluntary purchase. For example, weapons are necessary for the creation of a public good called national security. However, it is not likely that customers would be willing to pay separately, say in Home Depot, for missile fins or tank treads, and then send those parts to the Pentagon so that soldiers could assemble them into weapons to defend the country. Therefore, public goods will only appear if government will tax (force) citizens enough to pay for them. But neoliberals recommend enacting the lowest taxes possible, in order, presumably, to leave money in private hands so that profit-seeking entrepreneurs will be able to innovate. In which case, the neoliberal prescription for how to maintain government services while not raising enough tax money to support them thoroughly is that individuals should mainly pay government for what they use, such as water, parks, libraries, roads, trash removal, sewage, education, and more. As one privatization enthusiast says, "We must scale government benefits to economic contributions. Charge users for the [government] services they consume."[293]

There is a philosophic issue here. Which goods will be regarded as *public goods* depends on which goods a society decides, on the basis of ethical considerations, to regard as publicly valuable or not, after which it will provide them or not on the basis of taxation for the general welfare of society's members. Thus, when Barack Obama was president and there were Democratic majorities in both Houses of Congress, they decided together that health services should be available to all citizens, to which end they enacted the Affordable Health Care Act of 2010. The argument was that many millions of Americans could not afford existing private health insurance policies but that the community as a whole would benefit from paying for everyone to be as healthy as possible.[294]

In response, neoliberal politicians and intellectuals, who preferred that health care would remain private, within the realm of competitive market practices, argued that Democratic politicians wanted to enact a public health care law so that the receipt of affordable health services would cause poor people, previously uninsured, to become loyal members of the Democratic Party. In other words, beyond law, order, and national defense, all of which protect markets and private enterprise, neoliberals are apt to regard proposing, and then providing, additional public goods as designed to achieve political gain rather than social well-being.[295]

Democracy

As it is weak on public goods, neoliberalism is also weak on democracy, again because it focuses mainly on the market economy. That economy encourages creative destruction, pursues endless growth, and generates the One Percent outcome, sometimes called the "Winner-Take-All Society."[296] In that society, the top One Percent of citizens receive more than 20 percent of the nation's yearly income and own more wealth than the nation's bottom 90 percent.[297] This striking inequality of economic rewards and resources was the central theme of Bernie Sanders' 2016 campaign for the Democratic presidential nomination.[298]

Against critics like Sanders, neoliberal thinkers insist that, according to the economic model of marginal utility, people who have large incomes deserve what they earn because they make corresponding contributions to national prosperity. A large gap in personal incomes is therefore justified. What this economic approach to rewards does not explain is that small incomes are spent mostly on *needs*,[299] whereas large incomes cover *needs and savings*, in which case the savings (wealth) can be used, via lobbying and campaign contributions, to project power in politics.[300]

In other words, when unequal *incomes* turn into unequal *wealth*, which they inevitably do, the democratic principle of one person, one vote is endangered because some (moneyed) people have, in effect, more *power* than that conveyed by a single vote.[301] In recent years, that power in politics has been enormously boosted by two Supreme Court decisions, where the justices voted 5–4 in *Citizens United v. Federal Elections Commission* (2010) to permit virtually unlimited group political contributions and again 5–4 in *McCutcheon v. Federal Elections Commission* (2014) to permit virtually unlimited individual political contributions.

Is this money crucial? Because ballots are cast secretly, we never know exactly which citizens vote for one policy rather than another, or why one candidate rather than another wins an election. Therefore, when scholars compare whatever campaign spending figures are available, they disagree on whether or not money *by itself* can assure electoral success to whoever spends more. Nevertheless, there are clear indications that, as the saying goes, money talks.[302] Indeed, the Supreme Court inadvertently endorsed that notion when it ruled that, by expressing the opinions and preferences of those who give, campaign contributions are no more nor less than a form of free speech, which is guaranteed by the Constitution.

In effect, the Court considered the *legality* of money-backed talk but did not take that talk's *impact* into account. Yet candidates pay special attention to people who are likely to contribute, and elected officials are reluctant to act against the interests of people whose money they will need to cover campaign expenses next time around.[303] In such circumstances, democracy becomes, to some extent, a neoliberal marketplace, a political form of "consumer sovereignty" whereby some citizens figuratively "buy" candidates with their single votes, and whereby other citizens figuratively "buy" candidates with thousands or millions of dollars' worth of campaign donations and lobbying.[304] Officially, all citizens are equal. But, as George Orwell explained in *Animal Farm* (1945), when some animals (the pigs) gain control of the farm's resources, all the farm's animals may remain *equal* in a formal sense, even while some of them (the dominant pigs) are in fact *more* equal than others.[305]

The Middle Class

As we have seen, neoliberals prefer the market-centered economy. Consequently, again, they are weak on something very important politically, and that is the *middle class*. This weakness suggests a glitch in their economic theory because, if they expect supply-side innovations to generate economic growth, it is not clear from where they expect that consumers will earn enough money to buy what innovators are going to offer/supply to them.[306]

In the One Percent economy, attention focuses on *what is there*, in the sense that a great many modern resources and power have been captured by One Percent of Americans. The problem of the middle class, on the other hand, is *what is not there*; among the remaining 99 percent of Americans, ever fewer people possess the resources and therefore the power that had once belonged to a vibrant middle class that thrived in America between the end of World War II and the mid-1970s.[307] Those were the days when, as Robert Reich points out, "the income of a single schoolteacher or baker or salesman or mechanic was enough to buy a home, have two cars, and raise a family."[308]

What happened is not that technological productivity declined or that formerly middle-class people stopped working hard and responsibly but that, in later years, the rules of the economic game – determining who will win and who will lose – changed around them. For one thing, banks, credit card companies, brokers, and insurance agencies benefited from new legal arrangements that permitted them to consolidate and charge higher fees than before, to the point where the financial sector (which employs relatively few people and generates more paperwork than it makes commodities) began to take in more of America's national GDP than the people who manufacture things, from food to medical instruments to clothing to home appliances and to machine tools.[309]

Moreover, people who did manufacture things were, as a class, unable to hold out for a greater share of the nation's productivity gains because private-sector labor unions shrank. It was a classic Edgeworth Box situation, where workers (who were selling labor) had little bargaining power against employers (who were buying labor) because, for example, many of their jobs could be outsourced to low-wage countries, many other jobs could be eliminated by increasing automation, many workplaces could be flooded with temporary personnel,[310] many illegal immigrants could undercut wages for *bona fide* citizens, and many factories could be closed down because free-trade agreements permitted easy importation of cheap goods made in countries where unions did not exist. Furthermore, while neoliberals pushed for reduction or privatization of public services, an economy emerged where in many families two people must work to make ends meet even minimally. In those cases, some people have been squeezed out of the middle class by their inability to pay for things they formerly had obtained free or inexpensively.[311] This is the story, for example, told by Alissa Quart, about how millions of ordinary Americans, conscientious and reliable, working for low wages and sometimes on several jobs, cannot afford pregnancy expenses, cannot afford child care, cannot afford college tuition, cannot afford health insurance, cannot afford home mortgages, and cannot afford retirement plans that were formerly subsidized by employers.[312]

The decline of the middle class is an issue where consulting with great thinkers is patently worthwhile. For example, Ganesh Sitaraman notes recent decades of increasingly unequal incomes in America, leading to a severe shrinking of the middle class to the point where, in 2015, for the first time in generations, middle-class Americans no longer constituted a majority of the population.[313] But when the country lacks a moderate, middle-class anchor, he says, growing class differences, pitting poor against rich, threaten the republican values and civic constraints that, starting with Aristotle, Polybius, Cicero, Machiavelli, Harrington, and Montesquieu, eventually inspired the Constitution.

Thus, from where we are today, Sitaraman recalls first-order political thinkers and their ideas. Whereupon, while engaging those thinkers, he cites and analyzes the anti-tyrannical constitutional balance among groups and classes that some of them, such as John Adams, Thomas Jefferson, and James Madison, fashioned for America. He then explains, by drawing on recent empirical studies, how, because the middle class is in decline, that vital balance is being lost today. And, finally, he recommends public policies, in education, banking, and employment compensation, by which it can be restored.[314]

Populism
I will again sound repetitive for proposing that neoliberalism's enthusiasm for markets is implicated in a further political problem, which is the rise of populism. A mainly market-based economy may not be the *only* cause of populism, but it is certainly *one* major reason why populism has grown in recent years.

The sequence is as follows. While GDP rises, and while it is regarded as demonstrating that the country enjoys more prosperity than ever, then the decline of the middle class is an indicator that prosperity is not reaching many Americans. As Nobel Prize winner (economics, 2001) Joseph Stiglitz declared point-blank: "The American economy no longer works for most people in the United States."[315]

The problem here is that rewards for hard work in America are being distributed unevenly within a worldwide matrix of globalization, including free trade and financialization, which can only be resisted if America's government will be strong enough to confront numerous and powerful corporations that profit from existing economic arrangements and oppose all political inclinations to change them. But the state apparatus in America is weaker than it used to be because, when neo-liberal principles are translated into practices, "the state" gets weakened in favor of "the market," as we have seen. This even though, when the state is weak, it cannot make adjustments that might be necessary to provide, beyond present market-based outcomes, well-being and prosperity for all its citizens.[316]

Many Americans therefore feel, increasingly since the 1970s, that they have been treated badly by markets and that no one is doing anything about it.[317] In the circumstances – and here are the grounds for populism – resentment is turned against conventional political leaders who, for years, were nominally in charge but produced only more of the same. Surely this resentment in 2016 worked against Hillary Clinton because, as a candidate for president then, she looked like a former office holder who, while taking home millions of dollars in speaking fees, had done little to compensate "losers" in the war of all against all.[318]

At the same time, Donald Trump benefited from resentment when his slogan, "America First," encouraged many ordinary Americans to feel that he would stand up for them against a corporate world whose leaders cared more for globalization, deindustrialization, creative destruction, automation, free trade, and international finance than for the well-being of most neighbors at home.[319] That Trump was, objectively speaking, a member of the global elite did not deter his supporters.

The Death of Truth

To round out this review of some neoliberal political consequences, we should note what may be called "the death of truth."[320] America's market economy, which neoliberals praise and promote, is not based on scarcity, no matter what neoliberals claim, because, for at least a century, American factories and workers have been able to produce everything that everyone *needs*. There is no scarcity to overcome, then, except in the unevenness of distribution. In fact, flowing from modern science and technology, overproduction – which is the exact opposite of scarcity – is a constant threat.

Accordingly, the real imperative underlying modern commerce and technology is to convince people to buy what they do *not* need, and for this purpose advertising has evolved into a complex and sophisticated form of incessant persuasion where *truth*, if it exists at all, is secondary to provoking *wants*.[321] In ads, young and beautiful people dash about, alone or together, accompanied by snappy music, wearing new clothes, driving flashy cars, using famous toothpaste, tennis rackets, and smartphones, promoting Calvin Klein, Toyota, Nike, Apple, American Express, Tide, and, via Chipotle, McDonald's, and Applebee's, and happily eating their way through life.[322] In the circumstances, as Stephen Colbert put it, metaphorically speaking, *truth* is something we *think* with our heads, by ourselves, whereas *desire*, aroused by nonstop ads, is something we *know* in our hearts.[323] In other words, truth is beleaguered and desire is boundless.

Now this is, not surprisingly, analogous to the way in which neoliberals, via their enthusiasm for mainstream economics, make no judgment about what people prefer and why they buy anything.[324] For so long as something on sale gives people pleasure (utility), it is commendable for contributing (via GDP) to their well-being and that of society. If apparently frivolous goods are going viral, so be it. After all, value is not what *is true* across the board but what people *feel is true* for themselves. As Bentham said, pushpin or poetry, it's all the same.[325]

Of course the language of persuasion, refined and elaborated in commercial advertising, quickly spread via exercises in public relations to other realms of life, to wherever people could gain an advantage by making something look more attractive than it really is.[326] It was inevitable, then, that advertising techniques would powerfully influence politics, especially in lobbying and campaigning, where a great many things – such as taxes and war, and some candidates for public office – have always had to be made more attractive than they really are.[327]

The problem here is that, in public life, and especially in democratic societies, truth is not something we can easily do without. In fact, it is a vital *public good* for, without truth, how can democratic citizens think accurately about the condition of their society and how they might vote and speak up to improve it? In that sense truth is a public good because, when it exists, it is available to all citizens, and their access to it serves to make them all better off.[328]

More specifically, without truth, people cannot talk to each other constructively, cannot understand each other's interests, and cannot adjust together successfully to real-world conditions.[329] Yet truthful talk is not a default setting in the Age of Populism, personified by a president who runs the White House like a soap opera and often sounds like a

walking advertisement for himself and his branded proper-
ties.[330] Indeed, when confronted by adversaries or journalists
wielding the truth, the president accuses them of promoting
"fake news," and his spokespeople claim that Trumpian declar-
ations, even when patently false, are justified by "alternative
facts."[331]

History teaches stern lessons about the importance of
truth.[332] For example, Hannah Arendt, who fled to America
from Nazism, warned, in *The Origins of Totalitarianism* (1951),
that fascist and communist regimes erased the difference
between fact and fiction, true and false, to the point where
their citizens would willingly endorse and commit extraor-
dinary brutalities.[333] And George Orwell, after serving unhap-
pily as a British propagandist during World War II, in *1984*
(1948) darkly portrayed fictitious but plausible societies whose
leaders, such as Big Brother (who Orwell invented and named),
promote public policies based entirely on lies. Thus Orwell's
protagonist Winston Smith, living in Oceania (including
mainly North and South America, Britain, and Australia), and
working in the Ministry of Truth, where official explanations
and justifications changed daily, warned that there can be
no freedom without truth. As Smith said: "Freedom is the
freedom to say [the truth] that two plus two makes four. If that
is granted all else follows."[334]

John Stuart Mill

To sum up, creative destruction is promoted ceaselessly by
neoliberalism, therefore some political scientists should frame
their concern for destruction within the public conversation
on neoliberalism. I will return to all that in a moment. But first,
let us illuminate the neoliberal propositions I have discussed so
far by citing a great thinker who was seriously worried about
change and prosperity.

Thus John Stuart Mill, in his *Principles of Political Economy* (1848),
commented as follows: "I confess that I am not charmed with
the ideal of life held out by those who think that the normal

state of human beings is that of struggling to get on; that the trampling, crushing, elbowing, and treading on each other's heels, which form the existing type of social life, are the most desirable lot of human kind, or anything but the disagreeable symptoms of one of the phases of industrial progress."[335]

Clearly, Mill would oppose neoliberalism were he alive today. Therefore, he continued: "It [the trampling, crushing, etc.] may be a necessary stage in the progress of civilization ... But the best state for human nature is that in which, while no one is poor, no one desires to be richer, nor has any reason to fear being thrust back by the efforts of others to push themselves forward." Mill called this "best state" the "stationary state," in the sense that it would not pursue endless economic growth but would rest content to make here and there small scientific and technical adjustments that would improve people's lives.[336]

In the Age of Populism, while we are beset by severe personal, social, cultural, ethical, commercial, and ecological strains, I believe that hoping for less struggle, for less trampling, for less pushing forward, and for less of a human footprint on the Earth – that is, hoping to mitigate creative destruction in neoliberal times – is a reasonable aspiration. Perhaps that is what Polanyi had in mind when he warned that not all *change* amounts to *progress*.[337]

However, to transition to such a state of affairs in America would require far-reaching *political* decisions, which economists don't typically study and which neoliberals, who prefer market outcomes, disdain. So let us turn now to the study of politics, to see where political scientists might take a stand against the perpetual-growth optimists.

6 HUMANISM

What have we seen so far? (1) That we live in the Age of Populism, which is an era of dangerous trends and forces. (2) That public life in that era is churned by painful conflicts and polarizations, some of them generated by a market-based economy that creates winners and losers who are not necessarily more or less meritorious than each other. (3) That on the advice of economists in the (metaphorical) Temple of Science, politicians, opinion leaders, and ordinary citizens are strongly committed to economic growth, which emerges from creative destruction, which entails constantly changing social and economic practices leading to pockets of prosperity but also to the One Percent problem of inequality. (4) That, among other consequences, inequality gives rise to political contributions that, in the name of free speech, confer political power on dollars along with voters, to the point where, in effect, a marketplace based partly on moneyed activism has come to influence all branches of government.[338] (5) That, in that marketplace, many people increasingly believe that institutions and other people are not telling them the truth. (6) That, against a backdrop of all these factors, resentment grows and encourages populism. And so forth and so on.

In those circumstances, which I think are extremely worrisome, how might political scientists proceed? Because the truth is that, so far, like many other scholars, and of course like most ordinary citizens, they have not responded collectively to what I just described.

Many political scientists are followers of Aristotle in that they assume that most people are *homo politicus*, naturally intended to live in communities, which in the modern world have become states. Because politics in those states entail a wide range of relationships, some personal and some social, between many people and to various ends, the political science discipline is pluralistic and embraces a wide array of different sub-fields – from "Information Technology and Politics" to "Legislative Studies," from "Formal Political Theory" to "Women and Politics."

In practice, however, in whatever their sub-fields, most political scientists tend to investigate, teach, and publish about democracy (say, institutions and techniques) and about citizenship (say, political rights and participation). Moreover, when they talk about such subjects, they are most likely to highlight what many colleagues have regarded as procedural rather than substantive matters, that is, how things *get done* (or not), rather than which things *should be done* (or not).

The Default Setting

Professionally speaking, then, the default setting for many political scientists is an abiding interest in democracy – what it is (and is not), where it is (and is not), who its citizens are (and are not), how it is working for them (or not), whether it needs repair (or not), and more. That being the case, if some of us will want to focus on large trends that plague our times, we can easily remain within our professional vocabulary and research techniques, where many of us are anyway working on subjects, including stubborn conundrums, related to democracy. So our first step in the direction of analyzing the Age of Populism, if we choose to go down that road, is not even a step: We are already there.

We should be aware, however, that there is an auxiliary dimension to political science's default setting, and that is our commitment, as scholars, to work scientifically wherever that is possible. On this score, most political scientists are post-Darwinians because, in our world of knowledge, scientific (empirical) research and analysis are more highly regarded than the (value-laden) suppositions that are sometimes called "qualitative research."[339]

In a moment, along with Ian Shapiro, I will commend the practice of empirical research. But I want first to warn that, on the subject of democracy, such research tends not to support and may even cast doubts on democracy.[340] A good many empirical studies, including some of the best, suggest that American democracy is attenuated and imperfect. Sometimes scholars point out (1) that *average voters* fail democracy, that many of them are polarized, that many of them ignore electoral issues, that many of them refuse to learn about candidates, that many of them neglect public interests, and more. And sometimes scholars point out (2) that *powerful players* – individuals and groups – deliberately distort the system, for example, via intense partisanship, gerrymandering, large campaign contributions, lobbying, sponsored punditry, social media manipulations, and more.

The point here is that, if we want to serve a democratic society, it is not enough to study democracy and then prove that it doesn't work. We must do more than highlight dreary instances of ineptitude and irrationality.[341] We must go beyond concluding that American politics is dysfunctional,[342] or that the modern state cannot make decisions and stick with them,[343] or that, as time goes by, democratic nations create such a gridlock of conflicting groups that political standoffs and stalemates are the rule of the day,[344] or that because, nowadays, many citizens are politically incompetent, we should replace them with an "epistocracy" of people who "know" rather than just entertain "opinions."[345]

Humanism

We should, in a word, make some of our work contribute to what has historically been called *humanism*. Humanism was the informal creed of many intellectuals during the Enlightenment, who believed that ordinary people are competent enough to overthrow social restrictions and discriminations on the road to fashioning more equitable practices and making them work well.[346] Humanism was the faith of thinkers like Thomas Paine, with his appeal in *Common Sense* to colonial Americans for an insurrection against King George III.[347] It was what inspired James Madison, Alexander Hamilton, and John Jay, in *The Federalist*, to insist that representatives of the people were capable of hammering out a constitution that would defend and protect all (white male) Americans.[348] It was Ralph Waldo Emerson identifying with the "party of hope." It was Abraham Lincoln calling on Americans to ensure that government of the people would not perish from the Earth. It was William Jennings Bryan refusing to let his compatriots be crucified on a British cross of gold. It was Woodrow Wilson going to war to make the world safe for democracy. It was Franklin D. Roosevelt proclaiming that Americans have nothing to fear but fear itself.[349] It was Rosa Parks taking her seat on the bus. It was Martin Luther King maintaining his belief in a dream. And, for the academic world, it was Richard Rorty telling us that, if a scholar is to serve her society, "You have to be loyal to a dream country rather than the one to which you wake up every morning."[350]

Rorty did not mean that we should be unrealistic about our social aspirations. We need empiricism to know what is happening. And when populism is promoted by truth-challenged leaders like Donald Trump, which Rorty did not live to see, we need empiricism more than ever. What Rorty had in mind, though, was that sometimes people can be inspired to go beyond the facts, to change the facts, to do what is right rather than what is routine. What he insisted, therefore, was that we should be optimistic about the chances of achieving even unlikely goals.[351]

In other words, what Rorty really believed was that we should do scholarship with *passion*, about things that are important to us and to our society, regardless of short-term forecasts. Coincidentally, that is what Theodore Lowi, APSA president for 1991, called for in his presidential address. Lowi argued that many works of modern political science are "dismal" and lacking in "passion" because, while accepting the present bureaucratic state's parameters, they use that state's economic yardsticks to shape research in fields like public opinion, public policy, and public choice. The dispassionate results show up in political science journals like the *American Political Science Review*, which Lowi criticized for publishing few articles that "transcend their analysis to join a more inclusive level of discourse."[352]

To restate the matter, we should be passionately committed to things we *know* are true, even though current circumstances might seem indifferent or even hostile to them. In that sense, and to learn from a great thinker, we should recall that James Madison rejected Thomas Jefferson's suggestion of rewriting the Constitution in every generation. Madison believed that such constant change would undermine habits, emotions, traditions, and trust in government.[353]

It was not, I think, a matter of proof; it was something that Madison felt he simply knew. In our day, it would not be fanciful to apply the same insight, against constant change, when economists and neoliberals encourage us to generate the serial disruptions of creative destruction. Paradoxically, to insist every morning that the downsides of creative destruction are our target would not be utopian because it would be conservative in the best sense, according to, say, the standards of Edmund Burke, who praised social stability, moderation, small group solidarity, habits, and traditions.[354]

That a liberal like me can align with a conservative like Burke suggests that, in the matter of trying to mitigate the damage, destruction, and dislocations of economic growth, we can be passionate without slipping into partisanship.[355] To that end, various sensible sources encourage us. Thus journalist Evgeny Mozorov says that "The overriding question, 'What might we build tomorrow?' blinds us to questions of our ongoing responsibilities for what we built yesterday."[356] And conservationist

John Sawhill declares that "In the end, we will be defined not only by what we create but by what we refuse to destroy."[357] And World Health Organization director Gro Brundtland warns that "We must consider our planet to be on loan from our children, rather than being a gift from our ancestors."[358]

Along these lines, the Hippocratic Oath has long enjoined doctors to do no harm. For political scientists, Samuel Huntington, president of the APSA in 1987, in effect suggested a corollary to Hippocratus when he observed that "by and large, political scientists want to do good … [with regard to] social goals or public purposes … [where these include] enhancement of liberty, justice, equality, democracy, and responsibility in politics. The impetus to do good … is … embedded in our profession."[359] To extend Huntington's sentiments, political scientists can promote the "good" in different ways within their pluralistic profession. But surely one of those ways could be to focus on indiscriminate economic destruction, innocent losers, and subsequent political resentment.

A New Role

The default setting of political science encourages practitioners to consider many aspects of democracy. But that central theme does not stand alone. Get the facts straight, but believe that they can evolve. Study politics quantitatively, but add qualitative considerations. Study representative governments, but compare them to authoritarian regimes. Study the politics of individuals, but see what groups do politically. Study the majority, but keep an eye on minorities. Study the rich, but don't forget the poor. Study leaders, but also track followers.

As I said earlier, this pluralism in political science, but with an emphasis on democracy, gives us room to maneuver if we will want to direct some of our attention to the downsides of creative destruction. To rephrase that, we need not aspire to overthrow current disciplinary interests and practices but to add something to them. What most political scientists are doing, in the Big Tent of their Temple of Science column (to mix metaphors), most of them are doing well. So I am not suggesting that they stop.

What I am proposing, instead, is a project that flows from a recommendation that, as an adjunct to our occasional talk about what we together should be doing (scope and methods), some of us should become – professionally, voluntarily, rigorously, and responsibly – more involved politically than we used to be.[360] And I suggest that strategy because, in populist times, some circumstances – which will not all fix themselves – are more dangerous than those that we, our students, and the public, lived with previously.

Yes, some scholars should go up on the Temple of Science's roof. From there, they should study, teach, and publish about how to arrange our lives more successfully than living conditions are presently ordered in the Age of Populism. The roof-sitters will not all agree among themselves, and we will not all agree with all of them. The point, though, is that they will talk about what they think they know from their own and other Temple columns as if, in an Aristotelian sense, their enterprise endeavors to understand what bears upon *homo politicus* seeking a good life in a good community.[361]

Here is a bottom line because, I think, modern political science is the academic discipline most suited for this work. First, because when we consider scope and methods, we agree that it is our scholarly job to investigate degrees of power, which affect who prospers more and who prospers less in many realms of life treated by various disciplines in the Temple of Science. APSA president (1956) Harold Lasswell made this point when he described power struggles authoritatively in his canonical *Politics: Who Gets What, When, How* (1935).[362]

Lasswell's formulation of "who gets what, when, how" has been quoted innumerable times by later political scientists.[363] Moreover, it was extended analytically by Peter Bachrach and Morton Baratz to cover almost every sort of power relationship, that is, not just what *does* happen (and why) but what *does not* happen (and why), that is, not just *decisions* but also *non-decisions.*[364] Therefore, we have a warrant to study power in many realms, where it creates both winners and losers. And, of course, we have good examples of power research along these lines, such as Larry Bartels, *Unequal Democracy* (2008),[365] and Jacob Hacker and Paul Pierson, *Winner-Take-All Politics* (2010).[366]

Furthermore, we are heirs to humanistic thinking, such as during the Constitutional Convention, about how to make a system that will work well or, at least, not badly.[367] On this point, we were advised to think constructively by Austin Ranney, APSA president in 1975, when he advocated what he called "political engineering." On political engineering, Ranney said, "I mean the application of empirically derived general principles of individual and institutional behavior to fashion institutions intended to solve practical political problems."[368]

Some colleagues will say that advice from the Temple's roof, on how to live together better, will gain little or no traction in a modern society that favors scientific analysis and definitive conclusions. In which case, we should stick to that analysis and those conclusions. I, too, fear that traction from the roof is hard to come by. But, following Richard Rorty, I hope it will sometimes appear.

And besides, because I am not sure what sort of good society, ideal in every respect, I could ever suggest – I will come back to that difficulty in a moment, with Judith Shklar – what I am really proposing for roof-sitters is something less ambitious. What I am proposing is that, with a bird's-eye view from above, some political scientists will highlight destruction and damage, that is, will highlight the social and ecological costs of unmitigated creative destruction. If we will do that, we will keep on public display conditions and consequences that, if enough citizens will notice them, may be taken into account when, in the spirit of humanism, voters and legislators may consider moving on from where we are now.

It is a question of taking up intellectual slack. Mainstream economists, politicians, business people, journalists, think tankers, and others in favor of growth via creative destruction know that some destruction occurs. But they tend not to worry much about it. They will continue to assume that the system is basically effective, in which case we need mainly to fix not the system but the people in it.[369] What the winners believe, then, is that destruction may be inevitable but also positive, because it creates an ever-growing number of things to buy and sell, thus driving up GDP and the community's welfare. Therefore, in a neoliberal world, people should adjust to the system rather than vice-versa.[370] In a word, so much for the Luddites.

Against Tyranny

For what I propose, inspiration surrounds us, because strange and dangerous trends vex the Age of Populism and broadcast urgency. However, whoever wants to highlight the downsides of creative destruction must consider *how* to proceed.

To that end, we should start by reflecting on a thesis proposed by Judith Shklar, who was president of the APSA in 1990.[371] In her 1989 essay, "The Liberalism of Fear," Shklar stood with those people in modern history – she called them liberals – who, since the Enlightenment, have advocated overthrowing various forms of what they regard as tyranny against freedom.[372] These manifestations of tyranny differ from generation to generation, from witch trials to slavery, to colonialism, to lynchings, to concentration camps, to misogyny, and more. And therefore liberals of one era, say John Locke, do not necessarily highlight the evils that shock another, say Isaiah Berlin.[373] But to Shklar the main point was that tyrannical practices stimulate *all* liberals to criticize the existing order and work to improve it. In her opinion, that is what the *philosophes* did, that is what the American Founders did, that is what Abraham Lincoln did, and that is what Franklin Roosevelt did.

Most importantly, Shklar did not describe liberals as promoting an ideal society, complete with philosophical theories that pinpoint the meaning of life and justify specific institutions and practices.[374] What unites liberals, she thought, was their fear of terrible acts, of coercion, of oppression, of discrimination, of confinement, of domination, and of other appalling conditions that citizens should condemn. In other words, what unites liberals is not what they are *for* but what they are *against*. As Shklar said, liberalism does not "offer a *summum bonum* toward which all political agents should strive, but it certainly does ... begin with a *summum malum*, which all of us know and would avoid if only we could."[375]

Without intending to do so, Shklar in effect suggested what some political scientists might do by way of offering advice from the Temple of Science's roof. Hers was, after all, a common-sense view of social responsibility, as if, when some situation seems sufficiently tyrannical, sufficiently dangerous, sufficiently painful, and sufficiently unfair, it should be publicly criticized and condemned. That is, we do not need to formulate a theory or a philosophy of what exactly must be censured and what exactly should come next. We need, though, to focus on acts and circumstances that are obviously cruel.[376]

Let's put all this another way. There are many good people in America who praise economic growth, and some of them know that the creative destruction that fuels such growth can damage Americans who, for one reason or another, cannot keep up. But much of this awareness is abstract, is a matter of theory, is a fleeting idea, is an occasional twinge rather than a persistent foreboding that arises from direct and distressing confrontation with the painful dislocations of economic growth.[377]

In these circumstances, there is room for a rooftop project, for some scholars to highlight what actually happens, and to whom, as a result of economic creativity. If, when conditions will be sufficiently known, voters and journalists and politicians will enlist to mitigate them, then perhaps some of the powerful resentment that met the Sanders and Trump campaigns in 2016 will abate.[378]

For Realism

Ergo, we don't need to practice epochal political philosophy from the roof. Even in its absence, a sensible and pragmatic emphasis on the facts can make large and commendable contributions to social improvement.[379] Nevertheless, we must still ask ourselves, in professional terms, how to proceed *methodologically*.

On this score, we can follow the lead of political theorists like Ian Shapiro. For Shapiro, objectivity and professionalism, and rigorous investigatory procedures, must guide our research and teachings. But we must beware, he says, of using methodologies that are fashionable among colleagues but do not necessarily explain events accurately. Instead, we should embrace what Shapiro calls *realism*, where it is the questions we ask rather than our methodologies that are likely to direct us to facts that will lead to useful findings.[380] Or, in a variation of the same thesis, we should choose our research topics not according to the *methodology* at hand but depending on the nature of the *problem* we wish to explore.[381]

If that is so, and here I extrapolate, we have arrived at an in-house formula for framing the anti-tyranny issues that Shklar recommended we study. If it is *problems* that we aim to analyze, we should not shrink from investigating many unjust *situations* – for example, much of creativity's destruction – that now plague American life. In short, among political scientists, even as it is respectable to invest time and energy to use and refine various research procedures, including rational choice theory and functionalism, it is also respectable to examine circumstances that appear to constitute a problem. Thus, it is problem-driven research that appears in books such as Jacob Hacker, *The Great Risk Shift: The New Economic Insecurity and the Decline of the American Dream* (2006),[382] and Suzanne Mettler, *The Submerged State: How Invisible Government Policies Undermine American Democracy* (2011).[383]

What Should We Challenge?

In the Age of Populism, some political scientists should participate, as democrats and Enlightenment liberals, in the already lively public conversation about neoliberalism. By itself, an inclination to participate there does not tell us exactly how to proceed. Nevertheless, we have considered two parts of what I think is a reasonable response to that question of how. In Shklar's terms, we should be especially motivated by what we regard as obvious instances of *tyranny*. And in Shapiro's terms, we should frame our research projects more to address urgent *problems* than to extend methodological *projects*.

There is, however, a third part to the issue of how political scholars might join the public conversation on neoliberalism in populist circumstances, and it is this: *Which* problematic conditions should we explore? There is no simple answer to this question, because acts of creative destruction take place in many realms of life, therefore we must direct our attention depending on which of those acts seem most destructive and/ or most damaging. On that score, however, there are two areas of inquiry in which findings will be useful at least for contradicting the calm assurances of neoliberals who say that present conditions in America are what we should expect and also beneficial to society as a whole. A few words about these, and we will move on in Chapter 7 to consider how political scientists might confront the Age of Populism effectively within an appropriate *narrative*.

Real People

The first area to be investigated pertains to the *individual* in modern society. Neoliberalism assumes that *homo economicus* is the typical modern person, calculating rationally and pursuing subjective utility. Such people are driven, by circumstances and expert advice, to define themselves in terms of what the market will bear.[384] Outstanding actors among them, according to mainstream economics, will take the lead, as entrepreneurs, in creating new practices and products, to spur economic growth and thrive by competition.

Is this a realistic description of the people who live in America, or anywhere? "Not really, but who cares?" – I am paraphrasing Milton Friedman, Nobel Prize winner (economics, 1976). A scholarly model's assumptions don't have to be accurate, Friedman claimed, if its predictions are useful.[385]

However, the matter is a great deal more complicated than that if one asks, useful for *what*? And also, useful to *whom*? Surely much of the modern economy – producing climate change, producing massive employment shifts, producing undemocratic surveillance, producing the *precariat*,[386] producing click-bait politics, producing "epistemic rot,"[387] undermining cherished traditions, shrinking the middle class – is far from useful for many citizens. In those circumstances, to *really* prosper together, we are entitled to *realistic* descriptions of *real* people, some of them winning and some of them losing, but all of them, nowadays, playing in a game recommended to us by people who, unlike Aristotle, think we all are, and should be, *homo economicus*.

So one area of inquiry for some political scientists who are worried by downsides of creative destruction, and who want to mitigate that destruction, is the age-old question of human nature. What do we know about *real* people as opposed to those *postulated* in the neoliberal vision of modern society, with its abstract formulas that assure us that this is the best of all possible worlds?[388]

Here is where political science's wide-ranging warrant for studying all sorts of *power* can send us to learn from other columns in the Temple of Science, from columns such as sociology, anthropology, business administration, philosophy, history, psychology, and literature. From those columns we can see that scholars and scientists have already discovered a great deal about what real people are like, and therefore much informed thinking may bear on what treatment they deserve from other people.

For example, who are the real people who make everyday life possible? Given the work they perform, do some of us owe them, ethically speaking, more than what we currently pay them?[389] How do real people behave? For example, how do they deal with the constant pressures of economic competition?[390] What are their motivations? For example, is profit their only reason for working or are some of them driven by a sense of vocation to serve others?[391] How do real people handle modern complexity? For example, how do they deal with the huge variety of goods now offered in stores and online?[392] And what are the talents of real people? Obviously, some of us are naturally good at making money while others are naturally good at producing art and literature. But if the latter are paid poorly or not at all, who will beautify our surroundings and inspire our souls?[393]

Furthermore, if we are already talking about real people, what does it mean to say that they are rational or not, more or less? In the neoliberal world, some people look like they choose to behave irrationally, in which case perhaps they deserve to become losers.[394] But is that a fair assessment, or is it simply to measure their behavior by what economists say rationality is? After all, most people have an understandable rationale for what they do in their own circumstances, whereas the "rationality" that mainstream economists promote, adding up to GDP, may sanction circumstances entailing harsh efficiency (including temporary work without paid social benefits, such as driving for Uber), which exist in the modern economy and confront many hapless citizens.[395]

Real Markets

The second area to be investigated pertains to *markets*. Many shortcomings of neoliberalism, which recommends creative destruction, flow from assuming that existing markets are actually natural markets, from which progress, prosperity, and well-being emerge as if all that government has to provide is, roughly speaking, law and order to maintain contracts voluntarily entered. In truth, though, markets in the *real* world do not naturally exist. They flow from tax laws, traditions, personal habits, political pressures, court decisions, budgets, government regulation, and more, which shape what goes into them and what comes out of them.[396] Therefore, together with what we know of *real individuals*, some of us should study how *real markets*, rather than theoretical markets, can be improved.

On the one hand, talk about real markets can start from what they are not. That is, they are *not* markets as described in paper-and-pencil models of economic competition. If American markets worked the way those models assume that markets do, they might allocate gains and losses equitably. But real markets don't work that way, as if the deserving succeed, economic growth climbs, and all boats rise (everyone wins).[397] Real markets don't always have many buyers, they don't always have many sellers, they don't always have identical products, they don't always have mobility for all factors of production (labor, capital, data, technology, etc.), they don't always have easy entry and exit, and they don't always have complete information.[398]

In other words, in the world we live in, which can be studied and challenged, fairness and neutrality may be postulated but there are always real people who possess, or strive to achieve, economic advantages. For example, sometimes they are born to effective parents, who send them to private schools, and sometimes they grow up not in slums but in suburbs full of soccer moms. Sometimes they exercise more mobility than other people can, and sometimes they acquire more information than other people have. Sometimes they buy out other sellers, sometimes they use patents to prevent competitors from arising, sometimes they expensively advertise their wares, and so forth.

Furthermore, in many cases, winners may succeed in building advantages into the way their market-centered society operates, say with low inheritance taxes, with buybacks to increase the value of their stocks,[399] with a Federal Reserve Bank that favors creditors over debtors,[400] and with no government supervision of derivatives. After which they will prosper greatly, and their children will be "born on third base."[401]

On the other hand, talk about real markets can start not from what an abstract model says they are, which they *are not*, but from what they actually *are*, which means looking at the advantages they may be conferring, day after day, on some people as opposed to others.[402] From this perspective, neo-liberalism entails government decisions about what Robert Reich calls five "building blocks" of capitalism. These are *property*, that is, what can be owned or not; *monopoly*, that is, how much market power is permissible or not; *contract*, that is, what can be bought and sold, and how; *bankruptcy*, that is, what to do when purchasers don't pay; and *enforcement*, that is, making sure that everyone observes the rules laid down by these government decisions.[403] What decisions have already been made in these areas, we should ask, and who do they favor?

Driverless Cars

To study those five building blocks of real markets diligently is to encounter many of the downsides of creative destruction. I will leave those for my colleagues to catalogue, but just one example may suffice here to illustrate the importance of keeping track of such downsides and investigating them constantly so that, hopefully, they will be widely discussed and their effects mitigated.

"Autonomous vehicles" are being developed by the wealthiest high-tech and car companies, including Google, Apple, Amazon, Tesla, Mercedes, General Motors, and Ford.[404] There is little or no popular demand for this product.[405] Nevertheless, to justify their intent to supply us with autonomous vehicles whether we want them or not, entrepreneurial corporations with deep pockets claim that their new product, when it will become feasible, will avoid mistakes made by human drivers. If that is the case, we are told that – if workable vehicles are successfully developed, and if society will tax itself to pay for the expensive infrastructure needed to guide them electronically along America's roads – these vehicles of the future will save a significant number of lives by preventing traffic accidents.[406]

In truth, this is mainly an argument of convenience. Large corporations do not have consciences but are designed to seek profits.[407] To that end, workable driverless vehicles have the potential for generating *stupendous* profits – actually, not just stupendous but *colossal* – because, in the process of installing those vehicles, *tens of millions* of American car and truck owners will be compelled, like it or not, to pay to replace what they are now driving.[408] The costs of this creativity will spread to the support system for cars and trucks, entailing closure of gasoline stations, neighborhood garages, parking lots, and accessory stores, and forcing the reconfiguration of roads, houses, factories, stores, and offices.[409] It is hard to estimate how much consumers will have to spend on the driverless replacement vehicles; it is hard to estimate how many workers will have to find new jobs (some servicing and deploying the new machines); and it is hard to estimate how much society will have to pay to refashion its present patterns of rural, suburban, and urban life.

That horseless carriages (especially cars and tractors) replaced transportation and farm horses was an earlier case of creative destruction. At that time, millions of American blacksmiths, hackneymen, harness makers, footmen, farriers, carriage makers, hostlers, saddlers, wheelwrights, draymen, grooms, stable owners, breeders, knackers, and auctioneers gave way to people who worked for car manufacturers and auxiliary services.

Some progress was surely achieved.[410] But what was the price in personal stress, anxiety, and despair? No one knows. As decades passed, it is probable that most of these displaced people found other jobs, many in manufacturing. Thus over time, we usually assume that they substituted one sort of employment for another.

But how long did that substitution take? And how much suffering did the people who participated in substitution endure while it unfolded?[411] And how many years will substitution require this time around? And will that happen completely, with everyone finding new employment even though many good American jobs are being outsourced and, in factories and offices, automated out of existence?

Some pundits nowadays suggest that permanently unemployed or underemployed citizens might be allocated some kind of guaranteed income, although not much.[412] But will that provide recipients with meaning in life? That question deserves to be asked plainly and repeatedly. To put the matter in terms we have already considered, why is America permitting the "autonomous vehicles" project to go forward for the benefit of *shareholders* without taking into account the interests of people who we might regard as *stakeholders*?[413]

7   A STORY FOR POLITICAL SCIENCE

For scholars to respond to the Age of Populism is a complicated business, because every academic discipline has its own principles, procedures, and goals, in which case to take into account a large and important set of new conditions and characters requires considerable professional adjustment. However, the American Political Science Association, with over 12,000 members, embraces more than sixty fields and subfields about people, institutions, issues, and research methods, and we share a signature concern for the exercise and impact of power relationships. Therefore, we are equipped to deal with this challenge if some of us will want to do that.

In these circumstances, I have proposed that appropriate responses to the Age of Populism should relate to a variety of factors. These include insights we inherit from great thinkers, procedural and substantive democracy, good citizenship, the shape of multiversities, a metaphorical Temple of Science, mainstream economics, indices of gross domestic product, needs and wants, economic growth, entrepreneurship, neoliberalism, *homo economicus*, *homo politicus*, free trade, shareholders, stakeholders, scarcity, public goods, the decline of the middle class, beleaguered truth, humanism, opposition to tyranny, problem-centered research, power studies, real people, and real markets.

The trends among these factors are fueled in large part by creative destruction, which generates dislocations in various realms of life to the point where many citizens resent the modern economy and distrust leaders and institutions – from politicians to journalists, from professors to bankers – who have praised innovation but done little to mitigate its adverse consequences. Therefore, I have proposed that some political scientists will take a special interest in those consequences, contributing to the public conversation about neoliberalism by investigating and highlighting the costs of economic growth.

Lists and Stories

It remains for us to consider how political scientists might most effectively present their findings in the national debate over neoliberalism. To this end, several factors are worth adding to those I have described so far. One of these is what I have called elsewhere the "list syndrome," which we should avoid.[414]

The list syndrome is a matter of weak "framing."[415] It shows up when liberal politicians such as John Kerry, Barack Obama, Charles Schumer, and Hillary Clinton propose a jumble of new government policies to deal with what they regard as social and economic problems.[416] It also appears when liberal social critics write about what strikes them as social and economic difficulties, each critic treating a particular problem – say global warming, nuclear proliferation, racism, pesticides, automation, misogyny, gun control, illegal immigration, and more – but not clearly relating it to others.[417] In other words, the list syndrome shows up when politicians and critics "string together one policy proposal after another (there are the lists) rather than organize those proposals around short and powerful statements, repeated endlessly, about what such proposals represent together and why they should be adopted."[418]

In *Politics Without Stories* (2016), I wrote about how, for historical and philosophical reasons, including Weberian disenchantment and Deweyan pragmatism, the list syndrome reflects a liberal lack of powerful political stories.[419] This absence is a serious rhetorical handicap, because political stories, told again and again, can relate to various policy proposals and may enlist for them public support to the extent that stories seem to link those proposals in a vision of large ends worthy of collective action.[420]

On that score, approximately speaking, Bernie Sanders promoted a dramatic story of inequality culminating in the "One Percent," which gave shape to his campaign, and Donald Trump promoted a vivid story of the "swamp" in Washington, which invited resentful voters to support him as their champion against haughty elites. At the same time, Hillary Clinton, whose official campaign website offered solution after solution for a wide range of policy issues,[421] promoted a disjointed list of policy proposals and lost the election.[422]

Political scientists as such are not running for office. But avoiding the list syndrome is essential for the project I am proposing. Critics of the modern economy and its consequences – of capitalism and its bag of mixed blessings – have already written, and will continue to write, about what should be repaired or ameliorated in that economy. Their output fills libraries, bookstores, the internet, and social media. But, as Naomi Klein observed, saying "no [for example, saying no to oligarchic banking] is not enough ... What was too often missing [in recent protest movements] was a clear and captivating vision [story] of the world beyond that no."[423]

In other words, although Klein did not say this, we may take our inspiration from Judith Shklar. As a matter of principle, Shklar pointed us toward opposing tyranny. That is her goal, as a matter of principle. But if, as a matter of practice, in order to pursue tyranny we will employ the sort of problem-driven research that Ian Shapiro recommends, we should rhetorically clothe our indignant findings in effective terms.

To that end, neoliberalism's critics need stories to step up their case's appeal, and this is especially so because neoliberalism's supporters use stories to powerfully defend it. Some of the pro-capitalist stories are implicit in the kind of mainstream economic thought that we explored in earlier chapters, which is about individualism, utility seeking, scarcity, and more-is-better, and which legitimizes the national enthusiasm for long-term economic growth punctuated by creative destruction. And some of these stories infuse political speech on the American right – which I have treated elsewhere[424] – where flagship conservatives like William Buckley, Barry Goldwater, Ronald Reagan, George Will, Robert Bork, Charles Murray, Newt Gingrich, Rush Limbaugh, Grover Norquist, Paul Ryan, and Tucker Carlson, who helped to install neoliberalism in America before Donald Trump took center stage, already promoted a powerful rhetorical vision of personal freedom, free markets, small government, welfare queens, evil empires, reckless "elites," robust patriotism, and divine sanction for American exceptionalism.

A Tale for Political Scientists

In sum, political scientists have the research tools needed to deal with our populist age. And some of us should move in that direction. And we should frame our messages in a story, or interlocking stories, about the target of our disaffections and what to do about it.

However, as I have explained elsewhere, no one knows for sure how to create long-term, popular, and inspiring political stories.[425] Leave aside philosophical and historical debates on this matter. In plain terms, it is impossible to describe in words, amounting to clear guidelines, how to create gripping and unforgettable stories because what must somehow be generated are qualities as ethereal as a *beautiful* painting, a *melodious* sonata, a *spellbinding* potboiler, a *riveting* haiku, an *enthralling* anecdote, a *melancholy* requiem, an *entrancing* blouse, or a *harrowing* fairy tale. Furthermore, if a modern story-teller, such as Stephen King or J. K. Rowling, succeeds in generating any of those results, it may be that the intended effect will emerge for only some in the audience and not for others. Thus those of us who, say, fashion television commercials or political stump speeches, work hard at what we do but cannot guarantee success for our own creations.

So there is a difficulty on this score. Accordingly, without trying to create a durable, popular, inspiring, and explicit political story, I suggest that critics should place neoliberalism at the center of their messaging, where doing that repeatedly is

itself an implicit message.[426] They should constantly pound
home neoliberalism's name in association with descriptions
of wretched outcomes for "losers" across the land, for energetic and decent neighbors who do not deserve to be judged
solely by their economic "efficiency." They should write
about responsible citizens who are in fact victims of forces
over which they have no control, about people who might be
small towners, suburbanites, slum dwellers, farmers, minority
citizens, factory workers, college students, single parents,
high-tech geeks, soccer moms, office clerks, homeschoolers,
nurses, NRA members, feminists, mall-store "associates,"
devout congregants, gig economy temps, the *precariat*, click-
bait journalists, and more, who could do better in life if they
would see themselves all in the same boat and in politics act
accordingly.

Neoliberalism, in this implicit tale of continual wronging,
should be identified, and shamed, as a perpetuation of *contrived*
markets – remember, there are no *natural* markets – which arise
at least partly from unequal power relations,[427] which value
trinkets more than people, and which measure the dollar value
of everything instead of the ethical value of anyone.[428] We need
not deny that neoliberalism is often creative, and we should
agree that key parts of economic growth may contribute to
prosperity. But insisting that some of neoliberalism's results
are shameful, may over time generate an inclination to doubt
the wisdom of letting economic events run their course as if an
invisible hand will really produce most of the outcomes that
society needs.[429]

An Immoral Index

In public talk, political scientists should leave preaching to
others. We can count on some of those to warn against pursuing material wealth endlessly. For example, priests tell us
about Luke insisting that "You cannot serve both God and
money."[430] And ministers remind us about Jesus warning that
"it is easier for a camel to go through the eye of a needle, than

for a rich man to enter the Kingdom of God."[431] And rabbis and imams echo similar sentiments, citing the Torah or the Koran.

Still, as Judith Shklar might say, scholars can see, even without the benefit of clergy, scholars can see that some situations are extraordinarily disagreeable, and those we should move to condemn. Therefore, scholarly critics should insist, in impartial terms, that neoliberalism is guilty of measuring merit in modern times by immoral indices.

Thus, when pro-marketeers assume that everyone should behave like *homo economicus*, they are assigning some people to failure through no fault of their own. This is because in actual life, as opposed to what abstract economic theories describe, various amounts of economic talent, imagination, and energy are allocated in normal curves to real people. The result is that some people naturally receive more efficacy resources and others receive less, after which, in a job market where good jobs are constantly being automated out of existence or outsourced away, some workers will get the jobs that remain and others will trail in the economic race.[432]

The standard neoliberal response to this situation is to argue, with or without acting to budget the necessary funds, that America needs extensive job retraining programs. The assumption is that if there are not enough jobs to go around, unemployed workers can be retrained to do tasks that are not presently being performed or are being performed inadequately, after which entrepreneurs will find these workers and creatively hire them to upgrade existing projects or fashion new ones.

Well, yes. The country should welcome retraining programs. Certainly it is better to have some such programs than to have none. But retraining will not solve the problem of modern unemployment, because if idle workers will be upgraded by job training, good American jobs will still be automated away. Moreover, even if millions of new and lucrative jobs will be generated in America, there is no assurance that they will stay there, because countries like China and India have many millions of people at or near the top of their normal curves of competence who are, relatively speaking, inexpensively available in the international job market for so long as mobile capital and free trade are cornerstones of neoliberalism. And if Thomas Friedman and Michael Mandelbaum, on behalf of the modern economy, really believe that the country can retrain workers to the point where the normal curve for American workers will rise – where, like the cherished children of Garrison Keillor's Lake Webogan, they will all be "above average" in talents and skills – then neoliberals should consult with scholars in the Temple of Science's psychology column about the limits of normal curves.[433]

In principle, Friedman and Mandelbaum deserve credit for insisting that what victims of economic growth and creative destruction need is thoughtful and community-wide action to help people who cannot keep up on the economic treadmill. Unfortunately, it is exactly this sort of shared mitigation, probably requiring political decisions, which most neoliberals will not promote because, having adopted the mainstream economic notion of incomes based on rational behavior, they view society as a collection of individuals who should take care of themselves.[434]

For example, neoliberals usually reject comprehensive proposals for deliberately sheltering a wide range of familiar American industries and enterprises.[435] And they are unlikely to favor enacting statutes to forbid "venue shopping," whereby corporations – like Amazon – play American cities and states off against one another to receive tax concessions that deprive local governments of adequate funding for education, roads, sewers, libraries, and other public services.[436]

Another Immoral Index

On this score, the fact that neoliberals praise nation-wide or "average" gains from globalization, as if life for all of us is getting better all the time, amounts to using a second immoral index to justify existing practices. The Ricardian notion of comparative advantage, which neoliberals endorse, says that two countries engaging in free trade will both benefit.[437] And we will know this is happening when GDP, at home and abroad, goes up.

In this view, free trade is a win–win situation. Now, that may sometimes be true for *countries*. But this piece of conventional wisdom tells us nothing about the *people* who live in those countries.[438] For many of them, average is an irrelevant yardstick because, in truth, some of these people will prosper greatly and others will suffer from comparative inefficiency. For example, if workers in America need wages of fifteen dollars per hour to make even basic ends meet, some of them will surely not achieve that if globalization offers new jobs to poor, crowded, and corrupt countries where workers make no more than several dollars a day.

In social science terms, to regard average incomes as an index of well-being and prosperity is to ignore differences in the "distribution" of incomes. One way to do this is to speak of high incomes – such as the sometimes irritating billions collected by the One Percent – as if, for the most part, they flow justifiably from unusual efforts and initiative. To this end, the concept of entrepreneur is conveniently available, and famous examples – such as Sam Walton, Oprah Winfrey, Michael Bloomberg, and Mark Zuckerberg – come easily to mind.

Another way for neoliberals to avoid distribution issues, however, is to assume that lesser incomes depend on the routine marginal utility contributions of people who don't live in One Percent neighborhoods. That is, if mainstream marginal utility theory is valid, the market provides everyone who works with an income, however modest, which is exactly equivalent to that person's contribution to society's happiness.[439] In which case, there is no need for public discussion of income distribution because it is already being done automatically and fairly by the private realm.[440]

Well, not really. Technically speaking, social science research shows that in existing markets many high incomes depend (1) on exploiting various kinds of "rents," such as when patents prevent potential competitors from challenging a current producer,[441] or (2) on creating what economists call "network effects," as, for example, when so many people join a digital system that you feel you must join to be able to communicate with its members even if the system is technically second-rate.[442] Facebook is an obvious recent example of a network effect, because many people open accounts on Facebook in order not to be left out of its community. And that impulse enables Mark Zuckerberg and his co-investors to make inordinate profits from selling the personal information that Facebook collects on each of its users. Another network effect favors Bill Gates, whose engineers designed the word processing program called Microsoft Word. Many people choose to buy that program (thereby enhancing Gates' income) and write with it because it is compatible with what many other people are using (which is also Microsoft Word).[443]

Social scientists know, then, that the unequal distribution of income is often unfair, and this is a large strike against neoliberalism. But inequality also leads to a situation we noted earlier, which is that when incomes are unequal, some people will be able to turn their surplus income (wealth) into political power (lobbying, funding electoral campaigns, underwriting think tanks, sponsoring referenda, hiring consultants, owning media outlets, etc.). As a result, economic inequality in America today is an enormous political problem.[444]

Neoliberals are largely indifferent to this problem, especially after, in *Citizens United v. Federal Elections Commission* (2010) and *McCutcheon v. Federal Elections Commission* (2014), the Supreme Court decided that throwing heaps of money at politics, sometimes anonymously, is not an abuse of power but a legitimate exercise of free speech. This indifference to inequality invites a strong response among those who will investigate the Age of Populism's human ecology. Here they will find many matters of fact that should be presented front and center, again and again, in a message about the downsides of creative destruction.

Among those downsides, for example, we should pay attention to how creativity in the invention of new commercial instruments – such as junk bonds, securitized mortgages, credit swaps, and derivatives in companies led by entrepreneurs like Ivan Boesky, Sanford Weill, Michael Milkin, Jack Welch, Kenneth Lay, Angelo Mozilo, and Richard Fuld[445] – generated the growth of financial institutions that caused the Crash of 2008 but were "too big to fail" and now account for 20 percent of the country's GDP even though mostly they make profits rather than things.[446] In other words, contrary to the way neoliberals usually tell their story, it turns out that gainful creativity is not always a matter of inventing patently useful goods like transistors, Corningware, standardized shipping containers, and Ibuprofen.[447]

In sum, there are principles and practices in our special times that should be analyzed and criticized by some political scientists. In order to avoid activating the list syndrome, however, which might reduce the public impact of their findings, they should frame those findings in a relentless message, shared among scholars, about the downsides of neoliberalism as it is driven by creative destruction. As I noted, no one knows exactly how to create large-scale stories that will surely be popular, therefore such a story critical of dangerous current trends need not be specified explicitly, like in a religious catechism. But we are entitled to hope that it might grow over time out of repeatedly underlining undesirable, market-based, neoliberal outcomes in American life.

Hartz's Story

Even more hopefully, a shortcut may be available to this end, because there already exists a simple but powerful story of American exceptionalism that scholars could promote, at least in part, as applicable to the nation's situation today. That is the story about centrist, moderate, and democratic political values and institutions told by Louis Hartz in *The Liberal Tradition in America* (1955).

Very briefly, as Hartz put it, his book "contains … what might be called the storybook truth about American history: that

America was settled by men who fled from the feudal and clerical oppressions of the Old World."[448] We may leave aside the gender problem in that sentence and take it for what Hartz intended, which was that ordinary men and women came to America's Atlantic coast and made a forward-looking Revolution even while, by and large, the class structure and moral orthodoxies of Britain did not follow them. That is, the British did not export to the colonies a small but powerful aristocracy and a mass of credulous workers, peasants, and tenant farmers. As a result, Americans were able to espouse and promote political values belonging to European Liberals, who thrived as a sector of society between the wealthy above and the poor below.[449]

Most importantly for Hartz in this tale, the late-stage feudalism of the Old Order (*ancien regime*) of Europe, including large and powerful established churches, was not much present in the American colonies.[450] Consequently, there were few defenders of that Order who could try, during and after the Revolution, to violently overthrow what was basically a Liberal American society. Consequently, that society eventually (but not immediately) produced a polity marked by balances of power, separation of religion and state, widespread civil rights, and many middle-class citizens. In these circumstances, the absence of a European-style Reaction, led by philosophers like Joseph de Maistre and statesmen like Prince Klemens von Metternich, according to Hartz helped the American Liberal regime to survive and prosper, even while Europe for a century-and-a-half endured terrible conflicts fueled by ethnic and class distinctions that animated competing ideologies of monarchy, empire, nationalism, fascism, and communism.

In 1957, the APSA awarded Louis Hartz the Woodrow Wilson Prize for best book in political science, and in 1977, the APSA added to that prize its prestigious Lippincott Prize for a political theory book of enduring importance. Nevertheless, as years passed and social attitudes in America evolved, scholars fiercely debated whether Hartz had been right about America and even what he meant. For example, Ira Katznelson accepted

Hartz's thesis that Liberalism has long been the central current in American life. But he insisted that that current has been challenged repeatedly by complex alternatives, variations, and illiberal legacies in relations between groups such as workers and employers, whites and blacks, men and women, Jews and Gentiles.[451] Somewhat similarly, James Kloppenberg and Rogers Smith argued that Hartz's story was unrealistic because, perhaps in keeping with his time, he overestimated the nation's commitment to Liberalism by not sufficiently accounting for anti-democratic American expressions of racism and misogyny.[452] Additional scholars, like Corey Robins and Michael C. Desch, focused more on foreign affairs and rebuked Hartz for, in their opinion, mainly overlooking Liberalism's penchant for fueling American imperialism and brutality on the world stage.[453]

Alan Wolfe, however, decided in 2005 that "Hartz got the large picture astonishingly right."[454] And there is the evaluation on which we can build today.[455]

Where Hartz was Right

For our purposes, Hartz was right in two important respects. On the one hand, he argued that most Americans believe strongly in Liberal values. In Hartz's terms, and especially by comparison with the full mosaic of European political thinking, Liberal sentiments in America added up to a fairly homogeneous notion of American exceptionalism.[456] It was as if, generation after generation, Americans believed that the country, dedicated to democracy (as Lincoln defined it in his Gettysburg Address, "government of the people, by the people, and for the people"), was morally outstanding – that is, a "light unto the nations"[457] or "a city on a hill"[458] – in which case all Americans should pledge their allegiance to that inspiring vision.

Of course, many of the people who Hartz regarded as "Liberals" supported segregation, scorned immigrants, oppressed Native Americans, ignored feminism, and condemned unconventional genders. Nevertheless, whatever generosity may have been lacking at one time or another in Liberal politics, Hartz focused less on what was missing than on what was present. Therefore he described most Americans in 1955, deep into the Cold War, as confidently believing that, apart from some awkward deviations, they shared a democratic, constitutional, and pluralistic political tradition that they should defend against all detractors.

There was, however, a problem with this American solidarity that entails, in a way, orthodox thinking. As Hartz pointed out, when they feel threatened, some of America's like-minded may become hostile to unusual views or unconventional people. When that happened in the past, as in the Red Scare in 1919–1920 and during McCarthyism after World War II, some Liberals came together to call for, in effect, government committed to "America First" policies. Thus, at that point, those true-believers recommended a government devoted to excluding or marginalizing people in their country who they (the true believers) regarded as different, as not sufficiently American or even, perhaps, un-American. And that is where, obviously, Hartz's story of American exceptionalism may be at least somewhat relevant to populism and its manifestations, such as the election of President Donald Trump, a contemporary champion of America First,[459] of border walls, and of inviting progressive congresswomen to leave America, that is, to "go back" to the "places from which they came."[460]

Hartz was also right on a second point, which relates to how he described America as fortunate because, in the absence of late-stage feudalism in America, the country could acclaim its Liberal sentiments and, for generations, with little opposition, maintain Liberal institutions. Hartz may have praised early Liberalism too highly. On that score, we can be thankful, and he was, too,[461] that there is room in America for living up more fully than originally to the great principles that were enshrined in the Declaration of Independence even though some of the men who signed it enslaved black Africans, devastated Native Americans, and demeaned women.[462] Thus, the country has over time, and at considerable cost, significantly adjusted its practices in realms involving race, difference, and identity. More needs doing, but progress has been made.[463]

We should note, however, apart from the details, that Hartz's second point, about America's good fortune for lacking a reactionary opposition, is now directly relevant to politics in our time. In the seventeenth and eighteenth centuries, as Hartz observed, Americans did not bring into the country, from outside, feudal classes and institutions that, in Europe, opposed Liberal ideas and practices. But in the late twentieth and early twenty-first centuries, a troublesome new force appeared in America itself, a force that was not imported but arose at home, and that, like the remnants of feudalism once did in Europe, now challenges Liberal principles and projects.[464]

The new and anti-Liberal force is neoliberalism,[465] which critics named after Hartz wrote,[466] but which insists that Liberals should not try to work through government in a humanistic way to provide happiness and well-being for all Americans. In the neoliberal view, Liberals must, instead, permit markets to make large decisions about such matters, on the grounds that markets can do that efficiently whereas voters and elected officials will necessarily err.[467] And if the result in America today is large disparities of income, respect, and health, like in historically feudal societies, we are admonished to leave those alone because they flow, justifiably, from an invisible hand exercising a special sort of moral competence.

In other words, Hartz's thesis from 1955 implies, in a way, that the convictions and demands of neoliberalism after he wrote can be regarded as analogous to historical elements of the European Reaction.[468] Yet what that means is that political scientists can use Hartz's story to argue that neoliberalism, as a local amalgam of ideas, disciples, interest groups, donors, spokespeople, and policy proposals, should be criticized now because, in some respects, it holds back the positive side of the Liberal Tradition in America, which might otherwise be capable of mitigating or preventing damages caused by neoliberalism's central project of creative destruction.[469]

It is as if, to borrow from other stories, the country waited, for generations, for barbarians to arrive at the city's gate. Fortunately, the ones that Washington, Jefferson, Adams, Franklin, Madison, and their colleagues feared never came. Today, though, it is as if Americans must repel new, modern barbarians, soft-spoken and well-dressed, acclaimed by articulate surrogates and steered by efficient strategists, who are already inside the city and must be confronted there.[470]

Politics

I have said all along that some political scientists should deal directly with the Age of Populism. To the matrix of factors that I proposed taking into account to that end, let us add two final elements, which are (1) a willingness to seriously consider promoting *redistribution* of income and wealth, and (2) an understanding that to do this would probably require substantial *political action*.

Years ago, these sentiments frequently went hand in hand, as in President Franklin D. Roosevelt's Second Inaugural Address, during the Great Depression, when he declared that "The test of our progress is not whether we add more to the abundance of those who have much; it is whether we provide enough for those who have too little."[471] Some rearrangement of incomes, then, was clearly on the New Deal agenda. More recently, however, American politicians, pundits, scholars, and activists have focused mainly on issues of race, identity, and gender. The problem there, as Walter Benn Michaels explained, is that such cultural issues, important though they are, draw attention away from broad elements of material inequality, from diverse economic outcomes that can fuel some of the intense resentment that underlies our era.[472]

Redistribution
With regard to inequality, then, the case for political action comes after that for redistribution.[473] Neoliberals argue that

political action is biased and fallible whereas markets are just and effective, in which case government should be small and markets should encourage creative destruction. But in reality, markets create uneven distribution – what I have called winners and losers – which generates inequality, which breeds resentment, which fuels populism, which brings us squarely to the Age of Populism and its downsides.[474] And those downsides are, after all, what political scientists should investigate and whose parameters they should publicize to encourage voters and politicians to reduce some of the inequalities that, inevitably, flow from economic growth. Therefore, at least *some* redistribution is a necessary step for our times, although there will be intense arguments about how much of it should be fostered.

Political Action

Once the need for redistribution becomes clear, the need for *political action* must also be recognized, because to the extent that social science findings about creative dislocations and destructions will emerge, achieving more equitable conditions will flow mainly from taking political action to adjust the neoliberal system from without, from beyond the marketplace and its uneven allocations. In plain language, our living rooms are occupied by an 800-pound gorilla.[475] And this gorilla will not restrain itself.[476] Therefore, ordinary men and women must together curb him by exercising their sovereign power as democratic citizens.[477]

In which case, if scholars will draw public attention to the downsides of America's economy – to the massive use of fossil fuels, to the decline of Main Street, to the growth of temporary work, to the corrosion of character,[478] to losses of status and self-esteem, to disdain for traditional virtues, to the rise of digital dependence, to the inordinate power of financial institutions, and more – they must be prepared to accept, and even recommend, along with other citizens, that government will make some or many of the adjustments necessary for spreading happiness and well-being throughout society more evenly than they exist there today.

Just Say No?

Arguments about exactly how far government should intervene in markets, if at all, are endless and cannot be resolved here.[479] We should consider one approach to this issue, though, which suggests that a substantial amount of governmental activism could be helpful to Americans across the board, from various groups, from various regions, from various identity sectors, and from various political persuasions.

Here is what happened. As neoliberalism gathered strength, Nancy Reagan argued that America did not need to fashion legislative solutions to the destruction caused by narcotic drugs. In a classic illustration of the neoliberal tendency to regard society mainly as a collection of individuals, President Ronald Reagan's wife declared in 1986 that the national drug problem could be solved if only children would personally resist the temptations of heroin and crack cocaine dealers and "just say no" to drugs.[480] The First Lady campaigned earnestly and wholeheartedly, but the drug epidemic continued.

The moral of this story is, I think, that formal rules and collective strategies should not be rejected in principle, as Mrs. Reagan apparently did. Rather, in some cases, they may be necessary if a society wants to move closer to shared well-being.[481] And this is certainly so in modern America, where economic competition and constant change sometimes compel individuals to choose between manifest decency and economic success or even survival.

Thus, again and again, a lack of overall rules forces many Americans to deal personally with stark moral dilemmas. For example, within the framework of free trade, should I continue to operate my cookie factory in Chicago, or should I discharge my Chicago employees, move the factory to a poor country such as Mexico, and utilize cheap labor there?[482] Or, if it is my business to make 3D printers, should I stop producing them because I know that, somewhere down the road, those printers will throw millions of people out of work? Or if, along with companies like Monsanto and Dupont, I can develop genetically modified seeds and crops, should I do that even if my selling them profitably locks growers into a system of highly capitalized agribusiness that ruins traditional farming and farm families?[483]

Furthermore, if I earn or inherit a great deal of money, should I donate to an Ivy League university some of that money for new laboratories so that that school will admit my child rather than a more energetic and talented youngster from East St. Louis? Or, if I am managing part of the American aerospace industry, should I, on behalf of American workers in companies like Boeing, Lockheed-Martin, and Raytheon, favor selling precision-guided missiles and advanced fighter planes to Saudi Arabia, whose violent ruling family oppresses its citizens, exports religious fanaticism, and bombs its neighbors in Yemen?[484]

Such dilemmas demonstrate that if a society wants to enable its citizens to behave virtuously, so that they may live together effectively in the pursuit of happiness, it must sometimes create rules – that is, governmental guidelines and injunctions – which constrain everyone (although not in everything), to the point where all people can afford to follow their best instincts because they will know that others must refrain from following their worst. Among great thinkers, George Bernard Shaw made this point years ago, in *The Intelligent Woman's Guide to Socialism and Capitalism* (1928), and with his insight, we can conclude.

George Bernard Shaw

Choices to make are everywhere. For most of them, we need no guidelines from government. Will I open a business or work for someone else? Will I teach children or sell life insurance? Will I prefer country music by Dolly Parton or twelve-tone symphonies by Arnold Schoenberg? Will I spend my time on Twitter or reading great novels? Will I live in a big city or a small town? Will I marry? Will I, or my partner, decide to have children?

These are personal matters, which most people address by themselves and then hope for the best. However, some of our personal decisions add up to collective difficulties that now afflict an entire generation, which is reeling from *neoliberalism*, which demands *economic growth*, which is rooted in *creative destruction*, which perpetuates *change*, and which thereby breeds *resentment*, to a point which generates *populism*.[485]

In these circumstances, said Shaw, experience shows "that social problems cannot be solved by personal righteousness, and that under capitalism not only must men [and women] be made moral by an Act of Parliament [or Congress], but they cannot be made moral any other way, no matter how benevolent their dispositions may be."[486]

NOTES

Preface

1 John B. Judis, *The Populist Explosion: How the Great Recession Transformed American and European Politics* (New York: Columbia Global Reports, 2016).

2 Jan-Werner Muller, *What is Populism?* (Philadelphia, PA: University of Pennsylvania Press, 2016).

3 Benjamin I. Page and Martin Gilens, *Democracy in America: What Has Gone Wrong and What We Can Do About It* (Chicago: University of Chicago Press, 2017).

4 Edward Luce, *The Retreat of Western Liberalism* (New York: Atlantic Monthly Press, 2017).

5 Pankaj Mishra, *Age of Anger: A History of the Present* (New York: Farrar, Strauss, and Giroux, 2017).

6 Mark Lilla, *The Once and Future Liberal: After Identity Politics* (New York: HarperCollins, 2017).

7 David Runciman, *How Democracy Ends* (New York: Basic Books, 2018).

8 Steven Levitsky and Daniel Ziblatt, *How Democracies Die* (New York: Crown Books, 2018).

9 William Galston, *Anti-Pluralism: The Populist Threat to Liberal Democracy* (New Haven, CT: Yale University Press, 2018).

10 Francis Fukuyama, *Identity: The Demand for Dignity and the Politics of Resentment* (New York: Farrar, Strauss, and Giroux, 2018).

11 Robert Kuttner, *Can Democracy Survive Global Capitalism?* (New York: Norton, 2018).

12 Barry Eichengreen, *The Populist Temptation: Economic Grievances and Political Reaction in the Modern Era* (New York: Oxford University Press, 2018).

13 Yascha Mounk, *The People vs. Democracy: Why Our Freedom is in Danger & How to Save It* (Cambridge, MA: Harvard University Press, 2018).

14 John L. Campbell, *American Discontent: The Rise of Donald Trump and Decline of the Golden Age* (New York: Oxford University Press, 2018).

15 Paul Starr, *Entrenchment: Wealth, Power, and the Constitution of Democratic Societies* (New Haven, CT: Yale University Press, 2019).

16 Sophia Rosenfeld, *Democracy and Truth: A Short History* (Philadelphia, PA: University of Pennsylvania, 2019).

17 On economic resentment, see especially Campbell, *American Discontent*, pp. 17–18, 31–55, *et passim*.

18 Rogers Smith, *That is Not Who We Are! Populism and Peoplehood* (New Haven, CT: Yale University Press, forthcoming in 2020).

19 Literature about the populist debate multiplies rapidly. For example, against policy proposals made by Eichengreen and Mounk, see Chris Lehmann, "The Populist Morass: Why Liberal Savants Deplore Rule by the People," at https://thebaffler.com/salvos/the-populist-morass-lehmann.

20 For example, Edward Luttwak points out that half of all American households in 2016 could not afford to buy a new car, and he argues that this hard-times fact generated some of the anger that fueled the electoral success of Donald Trump and Bernie Sanders. See www.the-tls.co.uk/articles/public/trump-dynasty-luttwak/.

21 Thus John Sides, Michael Tesler, and Lynn Vavreck, *Identity Crisis: The 2016 Presidential Campaign and the Battle for the Meaning of America* (Princeton, NJ: Princeton University Press, 2018), pp. 12–32, *et passim*, maintain that Trump and Clinton voters in 2016 were motivated more by group identity than by economic anxiety.

22 Economic trends may exacerbate even structural issues, such as charges of institutional unfairness. Thus American farming requires fewer *Little-House-on-the-Prairie*-style

families than in the past. Consequently, rural populations decline, but each rural state keeps its two senators, whereupon the Senate becomes even more unrepresentative than it has been in the past, to the point where, by 2040, 30 percent of the population will elect 70 percent of American senators, while nation-wide majorities (according to opinion polls) of citizens already cannot shape their country's public policies. See www.nytimes.com/2016/11/21/upshot/as-american-as-apple-pie-the-rural-votes-disproportionate-slice-of-power.html and www.washingtonpost.com/news/politics/wp/2017/11/28/by-2040-two-thirds-of-americans-will-be-represented-by-30-percent-of-the-senate/?noredirect=on&utm_term=.d0eb113bdbe7.

23 See www.nytimes.com/2018/12/10/world/europe/macron-france-yellow-vests.html. In this speech Macron recognized, among demonstrators, the "anger and indignation that many Frenchmen share…"

24 Macron did not initially grasp the depth of resentment that fueled the yellow-vest demonstrations. See Didier Fassin and Anne-Claire Defosser, "An Improbable Movement?" *New Left Review* (January/February, 2019) at https://newleftreview.org/II115/didier-fassin-anne-claire-defossez-an-improbable-movement.

25 For example, see Salena Zito and Brad Todd, *The Great Revolt: Inside the Populist Coalition Reshaping American Politics* (New York: Crown Forum, 2018) and Fukuyama, *Identity: The Demand for Dignity and the Politics of Resentment.*

26 The importance of facts depend on which "facts" are at stake. Many liberals are concerned with what we might call *sociological facts*, which may be revealed by research and may change over time, whereas many conservatives are concerned with what they regard as *moral facts*, which may be discovered by theology or philosophy and never change. This dichotomy (and many of its implications) is described at length in Robert O. Self, *All in the Family: The Realignment of American Democracy Since the*

1960s (New York: Bloomsbury, 2012). Along these lines, the American conservative thinker Richard M. Weaver, in his *Ideas Have Consequences* (orig., 1948; Chicago: University of Chicago Press, 1984), pp. 1–17, but esp. 3–6, argued that, since William of Occam's doctrine of "nominalism" in the fourteenth century denied that "universals" really exist, liberals have attributed too much importance to mundane "facts" while they have abandoned faith in transcendental "truth." Weaver's ideas still inspire conservatives today. No one knows what he would have thought of a Republican president who invents facts and ignores the truth.

1 The Age of Populism

27 The phrase was first used by economist Joseph A. Schumpeter, *Capitalism, Socialism and Democracy*, 3rd edn (New York: Harper and Row, 1947), pp. 81–86.

28 Amy Goldstein, *Janesville: An American Story* (New York: Simon and Schuster, 2017). Working space at the GM plant in Janesville was larger than the 3.7 million square feet of office space in the Pentagon. See www. britannica.com/topic/Pentagon.

29 An exception to this generalization is Jane Mansbridge, "What is Political Science For?" *Perspectives on Politics* (March, 2014), pp. 8–17. Mansbridge was APSA president for 2013 and this article is a presidential address.

30 This is the general idea in F. H. Buckley, *The Republican Workers Party: How the Trump Victory Drove Everyone Crazy, and Why It Was Just What We Needed* (New York: Encounter Books, 2018). See also Tucker Carlson, *Ship of Fools: How a Selfish Ruling Class is Bringing America to the Brink of Revolution* (New York: Free Press, 2018), p. 3: "Trump's election wasn't about Trump. It was a throbbing middle finger in the face of America's ruling class." For a more academic justification of Trump's willingness to disregard conventional standards and practices, and especially to

reject rule by (p. 92) "America's expert class," see Salvatore Babones, *The New Authoritarianism: Trump, Populism, and the Tyranny of Experts* (Cambridge, MA: Polity, 2018), which (pp. 93–111) refers to Trump as "the populist purgative." Conservative intellectuals will tend to set aside Trump's personal qualities, as they did Senator Joseph McCarthy's, and argue that his cause, of attacking liberalism, was justified. For example, see William Voegeli, "Trump and His Enemies," *Claremont Review of Books* (Summer, 2016): "Sometimes, worthy causes have unworthy champions." At www.claremont.org/crb/article/trump-and-his-enemies/.

31 This is the general idea in Michael Wolff, *Fire and Fury: Inside the Trump White House* (New York: Henry Holt and Company, 2018). See also Michael Lewis, *The Fifth Risk* (New York: Norton, 2018), which is shocked by Trump's ignorance of the vital services that government agencies provide for America and by his willingness to appoint agency managers who are similarly ignorant.

32 Several eras of great upheaval and danger in American life are described in Jon Meacham, *The Soul of America: The Battle for Our Better Angels* (New York: Random House, 2018). As Meacham says (p. 7) of American history, "imperfection is the rule, not the exception."

33 In other words, today's anxious polarization is not new. For example, on the right in 1938, Congressional conservatives created the House Committee on Un-American Activities, which after World War II contributed substantially to what became known as McCarthyism. Almost simultaneously, liberal Americans in 1937 established the National Lawyers Guild, which, unlike the National Bar Association at that time, accepted African American lawyers to membership. The Guild was named in the Attorney General's List of Subversive Organizations starting in 1947.

34 A similar unemployment rate today would be terrible but less painful than before World War II, because fewer

women worked (for pay) in the 1930s than now, in which case 25-percent unemployment then meant that almost a quarter of the country's families had no breadwinner.

35 My 29-year-old uncle, Daniel Hutner, joined the Communist Party in New York City, enlisted among 2800 American volunteers in the Lincoln Brigade to fight on behalf of the Republican Government of Spain, sailed to Europe on the Queen Mary in April of 1937, and was killed in Belchite, Zaragoza, fighting against fascist forces in September five months later. During the McCarthy era, federal agents assumed that his Manhattan garment industry widow, my Aunt Florence Morgenstein, was a dangerous communist and therefore interrogated her. Some of her relatives, including my father, a federal government lawyer in Washington, DC, were also questioned.

36 For example, in the Declaration, "We hold these truths to be self-evident, that all men are created equal, and that they are endowed by their Creator with certain unalienable [natural] rights..."

37 The increasing fragility of democratic theory and faith between World War I and World War II is discussed in Edward A. Purcell, Jr., *The Crisis of Democratic Theory: Scientific Naturalism and the Problem of Value* (Lexington, KY: The University Press of Kentucky, 1973). See also David M. Ricci, *The Tragedy of Political Science: Politics, Scholarship, and Democracy* (New Haven, CT: Yale University Press, 1984), pp. 88–96.

38 This is the central message of Meacham, *The Soul of America*. Optimism informed by the need for sobriety and hard work on behalf of decency and progress appears also in Steven Pinker, *Enlightenment Now: The Case for Reason, Science, Humanism and Progress* (London: Allen Lane, 2018).

39 Changes in farming and food production are among the realms of modern economic creativity, plagued by social destruction, and causing resentment, which worry liberals *and* conservatives. See the sources in n. 478.

40 On the Trump White House as a reality show, see https://
thebaffler.com/the-poverty-of-theory/the-real-world-trump-
edition and www.vanityfair.com/hollywood/2018/06/
is-reality-tv-really-to-blame-for-president-donald-trump.
On the character of reality shows paid for by advertising
in America's largely for-private-profit economy, see
Jenifer L. Pozner, *Reality Bites Back: The Troubling Truth
About Guilty Pleasure TV* (Berkeley, CA: Seal Press, 2010).
Pozner describes TV reality shows – such as *Survivor*, *The
Bachelor*, *The Apprentice*, and *The Swan* – as shilling for
"consumerism," that is, as a format designed to persuade
viewers to adopt a lifestyle promoted by producer-
driven messages. In that sense, commercial TV is today a
reflection of "neoliberalism," which I will discuss in later
chapters.

41 See the books by scholars and journalists cited in
notes 1–16, 18. Many of those writers contend that
populism characteristically denies political complexity.
Surely that description can be applied to the referendum
held on Brexit, when the enormously complicated matter
of the United Kingdom's economic, political, social,
emotional, and historical relations with most of Europe
was put to a yes-or-no vote before roughly 33 million UK
voters. Why experienced politicians would propose and
permit such a simplistic vote is not clear.

42 Eichengreen, *The Populist Temptation*, p. 3. See also p. 13.

43 Mounk, *The People vs. Democracy*, pp. 7–8. What Mounk and
his colleagues describe as populism can be seen in Donald
Trump's speech to the Republican National Convention in
2016, when the candidate declared to "the American people"
that "I am your voice." See www.vox.com/2016/7/21/12253426/
donald-trump-acceptance-speech-transcript-republican-
nomination-transcript. See also Trump's "Inaugural Address,"
wherein the president announced that "… today… we are
transferring power from Washington, D.C. and giving it
back to you, the American People." See www.whitehouse.
gov/briefings-statements/the-inaugural-address/. On the

evolution – from Andrew Jackson to Donald Trump – of the populist notion of a leader who, while promoting "common sense," will stand up for "the people" against "experts" and "elites," see Rosenfeld, *Democracy and Truth*, pp. 92–136.

44 As of early March, 2019, President Trump had withdrawn or threatened to withdraw from "the Paris climate accord, the Trans-Pacific Partnership, UNESCO, the multilateral nuclear accord with Iran, NAFATA, the Universal Postal Agreement, the Intermediate-Range Nuclear Forces Treaty, the Korean-United States Free Trade Agreement, and the World Trade Organization." See www.nybooks.com/articles/2019/03/21/king-and-i-chris-christie-cliff-sims/.

45 For example, Newt Gingrich, *Understanding Trump* (New York: Center Street, 2017), p. 61: "For decades, members of America's elite – in government, academia and the media – have steered the country in a direction counter to the will of the American people."

46 For example, James Kalb, *The Tyranny of Liberalism: Understanding and Overcoming Administered Freedom, Inquisitorial Tolerance, and Equality by Command* (Wilmington, DE: Intercollegiate Studies Institute, 2008); Terrence P. Jeffrey, *Control Freaks: 7 Ways Liberals Plan to Ruin Your Life* (Washington, DC: Regnery, 2010); Ben Shapiro, *Bullies: How the Left's Culture of Fear and Intimidation Silences Americans* (New York: Simon and Schuster, 2013); Mark R. Levin, *Rediscovering Americanism and the Tyranny of Progressivism* (New York: Simon and Schuster, 2017); Buckley, *The Republican Workers Party*; Jerome R. Corsi, *Killing the Deep State: The Fight to Save President Trump* (West Palm Beach, FL: Humanix Books, 2018); Chris Buskirk, *Trump vs. The Leviathan* (New York: Encounter Books, 2018); and Jonah Goldberg, *Suicide of the West: How the Rebirth of Tribalism, Populism, Nationalism, and Identity Politics is Destroying American Democracy* (New York: Crown Forum, 2018).

47 In this view, "pluralism" promotes a commitment to side-by-side social components rather than a unified American

community, and moral relativism implies the legitimacy of alternative virtues rather than a shared commitment to Americanism as an overriding value.

48 E. J. Dionne, Jr., *Why Americans Hate Politics* (New York: Simon and Schuster, 1991), noticed this sentiment gathering strength long before the Age of Populism.

49 Lawrence M. Mead, "Scholasticism in Political Science," *Perspectives on Politics* (June, 2010), pp. 453–464, addresses this point.

50 Easton, "The New Revolution in Political Science," *American Political Science Review* (December, 1969), pp. 1051–1061, but esp. p. 1053.

51 Deutsch, "On Political Theory and Political Action," *American Political Science Review* (March, 1971), p. 11.

52 Snyder, *On Tyranny: Twenty Lessons From the Twentieth Century* (New York: Tim Duggan Books, 2017), pp. 118–120.

53 Fukuyama, "The End of History," *The National Interest* (Summer, 1989), pp. 3–18. Recently, Fukuyama has claimed that "identity politics" on the world stage, which political scientist Samuel Huntington predicted, may be stronger than Fukuyama earlier anticipated. See www.the-american-interest.com/2018/08/27/huntingtons-legacy/. See also Fukuyama, *Identity* (2018).

54 Benjamin Carter Hett, *The Death of Democracy: Hitler's Rise to Power and the Downfall of the Weimar Republic* (New York: Henry Holt, 2018).

55 *The People vs. Democracy*, p. 23.

56 Thus, in the Age of Populism, Orwell's *Animal Farm* (London: Penguin, 1945) and *1984* became best-sellers long after their original publication dates. See www.independent.co.uk/news/world/politics/2017-isn-t-1984-it-s-stranger-than-orwell-imagined-a7555341.html.

57 Milosz, *The Captive Mind* (New York: Knopf, 1953), pp. 25–53, but esp. p. 28: "The man of the East cannot take Americans seriously because they have never undergone the experiences that teach men how relative

their judgments and thinking habits are. Their resultant lack of imagination is appalling. Because they were born and raised in a given social order and in a given system of values, they believe that any other order must be unnatural, and that it cannot last because it is incompatible with human nature." Part of what Milosz had in mind was American ignorance of East European atrocities later described in Timothy Snyder, *Bloodlands: Europe Between Hitler and Stalin* (New York: Basic Books, 2010). Snyder describes American ignorance of, or indifference to, the deliberate murder of 14,000,000 civilians by Nazi and Soviet forces between 1933 and 1945 in what he calls the "bloodlands" of, chiefly, Poland, the Baltic states, Ukraine, western Russia, and Belarus. Even the Holocaust, which occurred mostly in that region, became a subject of scholarly attention and civic consciousness in America only after the 1961 publication of Raul Hilberg, *The Destruction of the European Jews*, 3rd edn (orig., 1961; New Haven, CT: Yale University Press, 2003).

58 That academic thinking can restrict our vision is the central message of Daniel T. Rodgers, *Age of Fracture* (Cambridge, MA: Harvard University Press, 2011). Rodgers analyzes a wide range of standard academic concepts, such as rational choice theory, efficient markets, gender, culture, and class, in disciplines such as philosophy, economics, history, political science, and sociology. Joseph J. Ellis recommends, instead, "an ongoing conversation between past and present from which we all have much to learn." See Ellis, *American Dialogue: The Founders and Us* (New York: Knopf, 2018), pp. 3–9, but esp. p. 4.

59 If some political scientists will go down that road, they will find their colleague Steven B. Smith already there. As Smith says, "The history of political thought is not an antiquarian appendage to the real business of research … I am not suggesting for a moment that the study of political philosophy can serve as a substitute for empirical studies of political problems. I am suggesting [though] that

without being anchored in the history of political theory
empirical studies are likely to be cast adrift without a map
and with no sense of destination." See Smith, "Political
Science and Political Philosophy: An Uneasy Relation,"
PS: Political Science and Politics (June, 2000), p. 190.

60 Yeats, "The Second Coming," (1919) at www.potw.org/
archive/potw351.html.

2 The Temple of Science

61 See Donald M. Freeman (ed.), *Foundations of Political
Science: Research, Methods, and Scope* (New York: Free
Press, 1978); Alan S. Isaak, *Scope and Methods of Political
Science: An Introduction to the Methodology of Political Inquiry*
(Homewood, IL: The Dorsey Press, 1985); Janet Buttolph
Johnson, H. T. Reynolds, and Jason D. Mycoff, *Political
Science Research Methods*, 8th edn (Washington, DC: C.Q.
Press, 2015); Paul M. Kellstedt and Guy D. Whitten, *The
Fundamentals of Political Science Research*, 3rd edn (Cambridge
University Press, 2018); and David Marsh and Gerry
Stoker (eds), *Theory and Methods in Political Science*, 4th edn
(New York: Palgrave MacMillan, 2018).

62 On political science and power, see Robert E. Goodin,
The Oxford Handbook of Political Science (Oxford: Oxford
University Press, 2011), pp. 4–7.

63 For the convention's program, see https://convention2.
allacademic.com/one/apsa/apsa18/index.php?cmd=Online
+Program+Load+Focus&program_focus=browse_by_sub_
unit_submissions&PHPSESSID=ct3iap5g5su5is94e2uejnq
8l4#unit_type_1739. The divisions, or organized sections,
are now represented by twenty separate, specialized
journals, which contribute to pluralism or, less admirably,
facilitate the fracturing of concepts and findings within
the discipline. See the ad for these journals in *American
Political Science Review* (May, 2019), p. 292.

64 Gary King, Kay Lehman Schlozman, and Norman
H. Nie (eds), *The Future of Political Science: 100 Perspectives*

(Cambridge, MA: Harvard University Press, 2009). The same pluralism shows up in "Significant Works in Political Science: Some Personal Views," *PS: Political Science and Politics* (Spring, 1983), pp. 196–204, where colleagues do not agree on which works to list as most significant.

65 "What Happened to the British Party Model?" *American Political Science Review* (March, 1980), p. 9.

66 *PS: Political Science and Politics* (Autumn, 1988), pp. 828–842. The essay "Separate Tables" is reprinted in Gabriel Almond, *A Discipline Divided: Schools and Sects in Political Science* (London: Sage Publications, 1990), pp. 13–31. See also the lack of agreement among symposium participants concerning the achievements of their discipline in Jennifer L. Hochschild, "APSA Presidents Reflect on Political Science: Who Knows What, When, and How?" *Perspectives on Politics* (June, 2005), pp. 309–334.

67 On getting involved "politically," see n. 357.

68 See Lucien Pye, "Political Science and the Crisis of Authoritarianism," *American Political Science Review* (March, 1990), pp. 3–19.

69 "Communities" usually contain many people, pursuing many ends. "Organizations" usually pursue one major goal, like armies fight wars, Boeing manufactures airplanes, the Internal Revenue Service collects income taxes, and the Catholic Church pursues salvation.

70 For example, innumerable articles on democracy and on citizenship appear in the discipline's in-house journal *PS: Politics and Political Science*, while the discipline's historical commitment to both is described in books such as Ricci, *The Tragedy of Political Science*.

71 Levi, "Why We Need a New Theory of Government," *Perspectives on Politics* (March, 2006), pp. 5–19.

72 Michael Sandel has challenged what he calls the "procedural republic" in his *Democracy's Discontent: America in Search of a Public Philosophy* (Cambridge, MA: Harvard University Press, 1996), pp. 274–315.

73 I have discussed substantive citizenship in Ricci, *Good Citizenship in America* (New York: Cambridge University

Press, 2004), esp. pp. 227–252, where the aim is not just to maintain legal citizenship but also to practice "good" citizenship, which consists of virtuous acts or, in a way, citizenship not just of rights but also responsibilities.

74 Benjamin I. Page and Martin Gilens, *Democracy in America? What Has Gone Wrong and What We Can Do About It* (Chicago: University of Chicago Press, 2017).

75 See also Frank R. Baumgartner, Jeffrey M. Berry, Marie Hojnacki, David R. Kimball, and Beth L. Leech, *Lobbying and Policy Change: Who Wins, Who Loses, and Why* (Chicago: University of Chicago Press, 2009).

76 Page and Gilens, *Democracy in America?*, esp. pp. 11–14.

77 The point is made in the 2018 APSA presidential address by Kathleen Thelen, "The American Precariate: U.S. Capitalism in Comparative Perspective," *Perspectives on Politics* (March, 2019), p. 20: "Surely the equality to which we aspire in a democracy is not just a matter of democratic procedures, as important as those are. It is animated as well by substantive ambitions and a sense of what a just society looks like."

78 I am making here a point about formal knowledge. I am not suggesting that people who don't study at universities are less important than those who do. Many people in modern societies have little "higher" education but do work that is absolutely vital to civilization and everything decent. Therefore, I totally agree with David Graeber, *Bullshit Jobs: A Theory* (New York: Simon and Schuster, 2018), that such people should be paid generously and respected more than they are today.

79 For example, see John Witherspoon, *Lectures on Moral Philosophy* (London: Forgotten Books, 2012). These lectures were delivered in the 1770s by John Witherspoon, president of the College of New Jersey (later called Princeton University). Witherspoon was the only clergyman to sign the Declaration of Independence, and he taught James Madison, Aaron Burr, and more than eighty students who became congressmen, senators, governors, cabinet members, and Supreme Court justices.

80 Ricci, *The Tragedy of Political Science*, pp. 29–45, but esp. p. 30.

81 Kerr, *The Uses of the University* (Cambridge, MA: Harvard University Press, 1963), pp. 1–45.

82 On the influence of money over colleges and universities, see Stanley Aronowitz, *The Knowledge Factory: Dismantling the Corporate University and Creating True Higher Education* (Boston: Beacon Press, 2000); Derek Bok, *Universities in the Marketplace: The Commercialization of Higher Education* (Princeton, NJ: Princeton University Press, 2003); James Engell and Anthony Dangerfield, *Saving Higher Education in the Age of Money* (Charlottesville, VA: University of Virginia Press, 2005); Christopher Newfield, *Unmaking the Public University: The Forty-Year Assault on the Middle Class* (Cambridge, MA: Harvard University Press, 2008); and Suzanne Mettler, *Degrees of Inequality: How the Politics of Higher Education Sabotaged the American Dream* (New York: Basic Books, 2014).

83 Kerr himself remarked that the job of chancellor came to be defined as "providing parking for the faculty, sex for the students, and athletics for the alumni." Kerr is quoted in www.berkeley.edu/news/media/releases/2003/12/02_kerr.shtml.

84 Robert Maynard Hutchins, *The Higher Learning in America* (New Haven, CT: Yale University Press, 1936); Robert Paul Wolff, *The Ideal of the University* (Boston: Beacon Press, 1969); Allen Bloom, *The Closing of the American Mind: How Higher Education Has Failed Democracy and Impoverished the Souls of Today's Students* (New York: Simon and Schuster, 1987); Ellen Screcker, *The Lost Soul of Higher Education: Corporatization, the Assault on Academic Freedom, and the End of the American University* (New York: The New Press, 2010); and William Deresiewicz, *Excellent Sheep: The Miseducation of the American Elite and the Way to a Meaningful Life* (New York: Free Press, 2014).

85 For the sake of simplicity, I will write about "departments" in the text above, even though all modern universities have "institutes" which may consist of

related departments, such as German Literature, French
Literature, and Italian Literature.

86 In praise of this flexibility, and against a one-size-fits-
all plan for modern universities, see David F. Labaree,
*A Perfect Mess: The Unlikely Ascendancy of American Higher
Education* (Chicago: University of Chicago Press, 2017).

87 To me, universities look like congeries of this and that; it
is probably my disciplinary background that leads me to
view them that way. But sociologists and anthropologists,
using research methods favored in their disciplines,
find that those congeries manifest patterns of behavior
that generate significant social consequences. That is,
such scholars look for, find, and highlight persistent
structures and functions in what Kerr described, more
or less, as an administrative contraption. For example,
see Jerome Karabel, *The Chosen: The Hidden History of
Admission and Exclusion at Harvard, Yale, and Princeton*
(New York: Houghton Mifflin, 2005); Richard Arum and
Josipa Roksa, *Academically Adrift: Limited Learning on College
Campuses* (Chicago: University of Chicago Press, 2011);
and Elizabeth A. Armstrong and Laura T. Hamilton, *Paying
for the Party: How College Maintains Inequality* (Cambridge,
MA: Harvard University Press, 2013).

88 In Carroll's book *Through the Looking Glass* (1871), from the
poem "The Walrus and the Carpenter," in chapter 4. See
the poem at www.poetryfoundation.org/poems/43914/
the-walrus-and-the-carpenter-56d222cbc80a9.

89 I first suggested the Temple of Science metaphor in Ricci,
The Tragedy of Political Science, pp. 54–56, 212–214.

90 That the Temple metaphor describes *academic* knowledge
does not mean that it is *merely* about academic knowledge.
In modern times, where most people of influence while
young have studied in institutions of higher education,
the shape of knowledge there bears heavily on how
worldly people outside universities think.

91 There are unwritten rules in the Temple, and one of
them is that most scholars in one column do not easily

introduce into their work information and techniques that exist in other columns. It seems to me obvious, for example, that real-world "politics" cannot be understood thoroughly without some understanding of "history." But in order to recommend that simple thought to his colleagues, Paul Pierson wrote about "path-dependence" in Pierson, "Increasing Returns, Path Dependence, and the Study of Politics," *American Political Science Review* (June, 2000), pp. 251–267.

92 If we extend this metaphor, the Temple has grown top-heavy in recent years because its superstructure is growing faster than the number or size of its columns. See the increasing number of administrators described in Benjamin Ginsberg, *The Fall of the Faculty: The Rise of the All-Administrative University and Why It Matters*, 2nd edn (New York: Oxford University Press, 2013).

93 During the twentieth century, and even today, this dichotomy has troubled people who do not want to belittle the "humanities" as opposed to the "sciences" but find themselves at a loss to explain why anyone would want to rely on knowledge that cannot be certain, definitive, or conclusive. Philosopher Ernest Gellner summed up their dilemma when he argued, in early Cold War days, that the main problem of modernity is that the *clerc* no longer has the same authority as the scientist. See Gellner, "The Crisis in the Humanities and the Mainstream of Philosophy," in J. H. Plumb (ed.), *Crisis in the Humanities* (London: Penguin, 1956), p. 72f.

94 For example, see the distinction drawn at Stanford University between "fuzzies" and "techies" in Jennifer Summit and Blake Vermeule, *Action versus Contemplation: Why an Ancient Debate Still Matters* (Chicago: Chicago University Press, 2018), esp. pp. 63–97.

95 In academic terms, the aspiration for teachings that will go beyond what a single column can provide has sometimes been expressed in support for the principle of "interdisciplinary research." Thus researchers are

encouraged to study more than one discipline, to combine the techniques and knowledge of both, and to present an amalgam to students and the public. The aspiration is admirable, but little interdisciplinary research gets done. Evidence of the quantitative difficulty is easy to find. For example, in the Oxford University Press series entitled "Very Short Introductions," each volume contains approximately 120 pages and covers an interesting and important subject from "accounting" and "adolescence" to "World War II" and "World Music." Since 1995, the series has published more than *640* volumes. And the list continues to grow. The current list is available at https://global.oup.com/academic/content/series/v/very-short-introductions-si/?type=listing&lang=en&cc=il. For a case study, Jamie Cohen-Cole, *The Open Mind: Cold War Politics and the Sciences of Human Nature* (Chicago: University of Chicago, 2014), pp. 164–189, explains how the Center for Cognitive Studies at Harvard University failed to maintain an interdisciplinary approach.

96 I say "scholars" in this sentence because we should not forget that religious leaders, who do not usually specialize in secular knowledge, offer general advice based on theology rather than science, and many people accept it from them.

97 Consider that one powerful tactical ploy among social and political philosophers is to argue, like John Stuart Mill, in favor of a "marketplace for ideas," or, like Michael Oakeshott, for a "great conversation." The assumption is that no one philosopher or book will provide all that we must know to prosper, in which case we should consult many sources and somehow decide from among them what we should do. Implicitly, there is an admission here that, in Temple of Science terms, individual scholars, in separate fields, are not able enough to (1) put together definitively everything we need to know in one place, and thereby (2) tell us exactly how to live accordingly. Arthur Koestler wrote his satirical novel, *The Call Girls*

(New York: Random House, 1973), about this conundrum, where leading social theorists meet in a Swiss chalet, discuss the dangerous state of world affairs, fail to agree on what should be done, and send the transcript of their conversation to the president so that *he*, from their learned observations, can figure out the way forward by himself.

98 Conservative Republican Newt Gingrich, in *Understanding Trump*, praised the president's penchant for fast food as an indication that he was the kind of candidate who could identify with working-class voters and be seen by them as representing their preferences and lifestyle. Trump's "personal taste leaned toward main street American fast food. Friends who saw him in Palm Beach at the fancy Sunday brunch at his golf course reported ... [that] Trump would wander through the line and get a cheeseburger and fries" (p. xx).

3 Mainstream Economics

99 See Andrew Gamble, *Can the Welfare State Survive?* (Malden, MA: Polity Press, 2016) for a discussion of competitive capitalism and democratic socialism as two alternative ideologies, mostly in Western societies. See also Jonas Pontusson, *Inequality and Prosperity: Social Europe vs. Liberal America* (Ithaca, NY: Cornell University Press, 2005).

100 Jeff Madrick, *Seven Bad Ideas: How Mainstream Economists Have Damaged America and the World* (New York: Knopf, 2014) and Juliet B. Schor, *True Wealth: How and Why Millions of Americans Are Creating a Time-Rich, Ecologically Light, Small-Scale, High-Satisfaction Economy* (New York: Penguin, 2011), p. 67. Roger E. Backhouse, *The Puzzle of Modern Economics: Science or Ideology?* (New York: Cambridge University Press, 2010), p. 154 describes "mainstream" economics. The same is true of David Orrell, *Economyths: 11 Ways Economics Gets It All Wrong* (London: Icon Books, 2017), pp. xvii–xviii.

101 Avner Offer and Gabriel Soderberg, *The Nobel Factor: The Prize in Economics, Social Democracy, and the Market Turn* (Princeton, NJ: Princeton University Press, 2016), pp. 18–19.

102 Earle, Moran, and Ward-Perkins, *The Econocracy: The Perils of Leaving Economics to the Experts* (Manchester: Manchester University Press, 2017), pp. 37–38.

103 Baker, *Rigged: How Globalization and the Rules of the Modern Economy Were Structured to Make the Rich Richer* (Washington, DC: Center for Economic and Policy Research, 2016), pp. 17–18.

104 Pontusson, *Inequality and Prosperity*, p. 4.

105 For example, Backhouse, *The Puzzle of Modern Economics*, p. 154: "… there is a set of approaches, albeit one with very fuzzy boundaries that change all the time, that can be found in the top journals and leading university departments, variously referred to as the 'orthodoxy' or, less critically, 'the mainstream,' as well as groups of economists, publishing in other outlets, who do not fit in."

106 Stiglitz, *Freefall: America, Free Markets, and the Sinking of the World Economy* (New York: Norton, 2010), p. 238.

107 Robert Heilbroner and William Milberg, *The Crisis of Vision in Modern Economic Thought* (New York: Cambridge University Press, 1995), pp. 109–117, claim that academic economics is all about capitalism although it (economics) purports to be about behavior present in all societies. That is, economists claim to view all human behavior objectively but actually express the values of a particular society dedicated to maintaining what we now call capitalist production, private ownership, and open markets. (What Heilbroner and Milberg say contradicts what Lawrence Summers claims about economics in n. 138, that "One set of [economic] laws works everywhere.") This is not just a point in theory but has enormous practical implications. For example, in America for generations, native people seemed to

men like Andrew Jackson to be "primitive" and remiss
for not placing land under private ownership like white
immigrants did. In which case, the newcomers were
morally entitled to take and "develop" tribal lands, such
as when much of Oklahoma was removed in 1889 from
tribal control and opened up to mostly white settlement.
For a recent, inadvertent example of capitalism as the
default setting in American economics, see economist
Dani Rodrik in http://bostonreview.net/class-inequality/
dani-rodrik-rescuing-economics-neoliberalism.
108 Edward N. Luttwak, *The Endangered American
Dream: How to Stop the United States From Becoming a
Third-World Country and How to Win the Geo-Economic
Struggle for Industrial Supremacy* (New York: Simon and
Schuster, 1993); Noah, *The Great Divergence: America's
Growing Inequality Crisis and What We Can Do About It*
(New York: Bloomsbury Press, 2012); Smith, *Who Stole
the American Dream* (New York: Random House, 2012);
Packer, *The Unwinding: An Inner History of the New America*
(New York: Farrar, Straus, and Giroux, 2013); Reich, *Saving
Capitalism: For the Many, Not the Few* (New York: Vintage
Books, 2016); Ehrenreich, *Third Wave Capitalism: How
Money, Power, and the Pursuit of Self-Interest Have Imperiled
the American Dream* (Ithaca, NY: Cornell University Press,
2016); and Chris Hedges, *America: The Farewell Tour*
(New York: Simon and Schuster, 2018). For references
to economic research on downsides in the modern
economy, see the blog www.economicprincipals.com/.
109 Richard H. Thaler, *Misbehaving: The Making of Behavioral
Economics* (New York: Norton, 2015), p. 5. Furthermore,
leading textbooks of economics, used widely in
introductory courses, present and generally agree on what
they consider to be basic principles of the subject – such
as methodological individualism, marginal utility, general
equilibrium, efficient markets, and the goal of growth.
110 For when the term "mainstream economics" came
into use among economists, and for how it evolved as

time passed, see www.ineteconomics.org/perspectives/
blog/how-the-term-mainstream-economics-became-
mainstream-a-speculation.

111 I will say that one source that struck me as particularly
useful was Offer and Soderberg, *The Nobel Factor*, pp. 16–41.

112 This means that there is little or no room in
economic theory for what psychologists, sociologists,
anthropologists, and historians might call "groupthink."
See the classic Irving Lester Janis, *Victims of Groupthink: A
Psychological Study of Foreign Policy Decisions and Fiascos*
(Boston: Houghton Mifflin, 1972). Furthermore, even
if it could deal with cases of groupthink, mainstream
economics cannot systematically analyze decisions made
by a chain-of-command structure, like when Toyota
Motors raises its car prices. The prices got raised. But who,
exactly, did that? And why? In fact, who *is* Toyota Motors?

113 Actually, many economists study or speculate about
hypothetical rather than *real* individuals, such as when
postulating – in thought experiments or vignettes –
situations (1) involving imagined rather than real
individuals, and (2) designed to tease out the likelihood
of rational or irrational behavior. Thus the joke about an
economist stranded on a desert island proposing to other
castaways to open a washed-up can of soup by assuming
the existence of a can opener. On the postulations of
economists versus real economic behavior, see Jonathan
Schlefer, *The Assumptions Economists Make* (Cambridge,
MA: Harvard University Press, 2017), *passim*.

114 For example, Thaler, *Misbehaving*, p. 25: "Normative
theories tell you the right way to think about some
problem. By 'right' I do not mean right in some moral
sense; instead, I mean logically consistent, as prescribed
by the optimizing model at the heart of economic
reasoning, sometimes called rational choice theory."

115 Thus the distinction between what economists call
rational and what philosophers call reasonable is a
central theme in John Rawls, *Political Liberalism*, Expanded

Edition (New York: Columbia University Press, 2005),
passim, but esp. pp. 48–54.

116 That mainstream economists regard utility as legitimately
subjective contradicts the traditional ethical warning in
Judges 17:6 – "In those days, there was no king in Israel,
but everyone did what was right in his own eyes."

117 Public choice theory emphasizes what can be learned from
analyzing "thought experiment" games such as Prisoners'
Choice, in which people assumed to be prisoners seek to
minimize their chances of punishment and maximize their
chances of being set free. It is a game predicated for the
most part upon self-interest. To be loyal to other prisoners
in the game is regarded as an unrealistic strategy.

118 Buchanan used public choice theory to explain democracy
in James Buchanan and Gordon Tullock, *The Calculus of
Consent: Logical Foundations of Constitutional Democracy* (Ann
Arbor, MI: University of Michigan, 1962). See also Anthony
Downs, *An Economic Theory of Democracy* (New York: Harper,
1957). On some anti-government implications of this use
of public choice theory, see Nancy MacLean, *Democracy in
Chains: The Deep History of the Radical Right's Stealth Plan for
America* (New York: Penguin, 2017).

119 The concept of extending equal prices to all buyers
underlies the Elkins Act of 1903, which forbade
railroads from paying rebates (kickbacks) and thereby, as
previously, extending special and unfair shipping prices
to companies like John D. Rockefeller's Standard Oil
Company (which shipped oil in tanker cars).

120 See Smith, *An Inquiry into the Nature and Causes of The
Wealth of Nations* (orig., 1776; New York: Modern Library,
1937), (970 pages). Economists regard Smith as the
founder of modern economic theory, but the term
"invisible hand" appeared in *The Wealth of Nations* only
once, in Bk. IV, ch. 2, p. 423.

121 Smith used the phrase "invisible hand" only several
times in all of his writings, and we cannot be sure
that he meant it to refer to God. The assumption is

reasonable, though, because as a moral philosopher Smith was undoubtedly uncomfortable recommending an economy where avarice becomes acceptable or even admirable because, when it fuels marketplace trading, it can be said to produce virtuous results. On economics and theology, see Duncan K. Foley, *Adam's Fallacy: A Guide to Economic Theology* (Cambridge, MA: Harvard University Press, 2006), esp. pp. 1–4.

122 John Maynard Keynes insisted that if an economic equilibrium exists at any time, it may not come even close to maximizing the utility that available resources can supply. He had in mind the Great Depression before World War II, when unemployed workers, idle factories, and starving families were in equilibrium side by side. See Keynes, *The General Theory of Employment, Interest, and Money* (New York: Harcourt, Brace & Co., 1935).

123 *The Nobel Factor*, p. 20.

124 www.theguardian.com/politics/2013/apr/08/margaret-thatcher-quotes. Mrs. Thatcher did not explain how some people might behave as benevolent members of families but continue to act as selfish individuals when participating in other groups or networks. For example, she ignored how the people of Great Britain, commonly known as a "society," stood up together against Nazi Germany during World War II.

125 We should note that GDP, because it is measured in dollars, is much easier to track than if we would try, from one year to the next, to count specific utility items in order to decide if people are enjoying themselves more or less from one year to another. To track specific utility items would require economists to accomplish the impossible task of figuring out how many tables, and chairs, and jeans, and gallons of ice cream, and smartphones, and cars, and whatever else, are sold from one year to the next.

126 As I said above, the mainstream is a complicated business and the vocabulary is problematical. So let readers

beware. Economists across the board know very well that
GDP is not an index of welfare. They understand that
it includes the dollar values of "bads" (say, cigarettes)
as well as "goods" (say, heart stents). On this point, see
Diane Coyle, *GDP: A Brief but Affectionate History* (Princeton,
NJ: Princeton University Press, 2014), pp. 40, 91, 105,
and see Joseph E. Stiglitz, Amartya Sen, and Jean-Paul
Fitoussi, *Mismeasuring Our Lives: Why GDP Doesn't Add Up*
(New York: The New Press, 2010). Nevertheless, most
economists and politicians insist that we should try
to raise GDP constantly, via what they call "economic
growth." In so insisting, they apparently believe
that somehow, overall, in the last analysis, all things
considered, elevating GDP is desirable. But that makes
sense only if they believe that, when GDP goes up, it
indicates that Americans are enjoying more welfare than
previously. So where practical politics meet everyday
beliefs, GDP *is* an index of welfare. Complaining that
this is so, see Clifford Cobb, Ted Halstead, and Jonathan
Rowe, "If the GDP is Up, Why is America Down?" *The
Atlantic Monthly* (October, 1995), pp. 59–78.

127 On the economic theory of markets creating value, see
Dani Rodrik, *Economic Rules: The Rights and Wrongs of the
Dismal Science* (New York: Norton, 2015), pp. 117–120.
There is a crucial philosophical point here, which is
explained in William Davies, *The Happiness Industry: How
the Government and Big Business Sold Us Well-Being*
(London: Verso, 2016), *passim*, but esp. pp. 41–69. If
"values" are (1) measured by moral, philosophical, and
theological precepts, there are a limited number of
values and society can (but not easily) dedicate itself to
maximizing them. But if valued items are (2) created by
marketplace exchanges, where individuals decide which
commodities are of value to them, there is no limit to
the number and quantity of values that can be produced.
In those circumstances, in effect, society is condemned
to run (after "values") on a treadmill, driven by an

endless process of creative destruction and consumption. Economists like Adam Smith, David Ricardo, Karl Marx, and John Stuart Mill until the late 1800s promoted thinking along the lines of (1). Then marginal utility theory was invented by economists like William Stanley Jevons, Leon Walrus, and Carl Menger. Adopting that theory, mainstream economists began to regard individual deal-makers as competent to decide what is valuable and what is not, which reflected thinking along the lines of (2). Thus they justified the current treadmill.

128 Political scientists should note that if "value" is created *only* by trade, there is little or no place in mainstream economic analysis for a concept of "value" created by political action, where legislators, encouraged by voters, enact a law (such as the National Labor Relations Act, 1935) that they presume will benefit (be of value to) the community. Different concepts of value constitute an enormous difference between what economists and political scientists study and teach.

129 Alan S. Blinder, *Hard Heads, Soft Hearts: Tough-Minded Economics for a Just Society* (New York: Addison-Wesley, 1987), pp. 16–17. Here is an example of a leading economics professor, at Princeton University and formerly a Vice Chairman of the Federal Reserve Bank, talking proudly about what some people call "mainstream economics."

130 William Greider, *The Soul of Capitalism: Opening Paths to a Moral Economy* (New York: Simon and Schuster, 2004), esp. pp. 1–22, postulates that promoting more rather than less is characteristic of capitalist economic thought and practices. In which case, economic growth is the national goal. He argues, however (p. 9), that twentieth-century Americans solved "the [age-old] economic problem," in the sense that the nation's economy, based on science and technology, can finally make enough food, shelter, and clothing to provide survival for all of its citizens. Nevertheless, American capitalism persists in producing

more tradeable commodities, in a market-driven process that, in effect, disdains "humanism" (see esp. pp. 300–324, where Greider calls for social and political creativity but does not refer explicitly to humanism) because it (capitalism) denies that people together, rather than markets, can decide deliberately what sort of society – stable, decent, moderate, responsible, considerate, neighborly, environmentally sound, and so forth – they wish to live in. We will return to humanism especially in Chapter 6.

131 Dirk Philipsen, *The Little Big Number: How GDP Came to Rule the World and What to Do About It* (Princeton, NJ: Princeton University Press, 2015), p. 49.

132 See the classic jeremiad on this subject by E. J. Mishan, *The Costs of Economic Growth* (Baltimore: Penguin Books, 1967).

133 How, when, and why driving up GDP became a governmental goal throughout most of the world is explained in Lorenzo Fioramonti, *Gross Domestic Problem: The Politics Behind the World's Most Powerful Number* (New York: Zed Books, 2015), *passim*.

134 *Ibid.*, p. 149.

135 For example, see Marion Fourcade, Etienne Ollion, and Yann Algan, "The Superiority of Economists" (2015), which analyzes "the dominant positon of economics within the social science network of the United States." At www.maxpo.eu/pub/maxpo_dp/maxpodp14-3.pdf.

136 Some valuable activities, such as child care at home, are not handled thoroughly or at all by mainstream economists because they (the activities) do not entail a financial expenditure.

137 E. Roy Weintraub, *How Economics Became a Mathematical Science* (Durham, NC: Duke University Press, 2002). For example, see Robert E. Lucas (Nobel Prize winner in economics, 1995), quoted in David Warsh, *Knowledge and the Wealth of Nations: A Story of Economic Discovery* (New York: Norton, 2007), p. 168: "Like so many others

in my cohort, I internalized its view that if I couldn't formulate a problem in economic theory mathematically, I didn't know what I was doing … Economic theory *is* mathematical analysis. Everything else is just pictures and talk."

138 Economist Lawrence Summers, Chief Economist of the World Bank, Secretary of the Treasury, President of Harvard University, Director of the National Economic Council: "Spread the truth – the laws of economics are like the laws of engineering. One set of laws works everywhere" (1991). Quoted in Naomi Klein, *Shock Doctrine: The Rise of Disaster Capitalism* (New York: Picador, 2007), p. 275.

139 This view is promoted by Maurice Allais (Nobel Prize winner in economics, 1988): "An Outline of my Main Contributions to Economic Science," p. 243: "Firstly, the prerequisite of any science is the existence of regularities which can be analyzed and forecast. This is for example the case in celestial mechanics. But it is also true of many economic phenomena. Indeed, their thorough analysis displays the existence of regularities which are just as striking as those found in the physical sciences. This is why Economics is a science…." https://assets.nobelprize. org/uploads/2018/06/allais-ecture.pdf?_ga=2.97089372.21 3120061.1536601189-1440850594.1536601189.

140 On the centrality of metaphors in economics, see Deirdre N. McClosky, *The Rhetoric of Economics* (Madison, WI: University of Wisconsin Press, 1985).

141 For example, see the 1992 Nobel Prize in economics lecture by Gary S. Becker, "The Economic Way of Looking at Life," https://old.nobelprize.org/nobel_prizes/economic-sciences/laureates/1992/becker-lecture.html. See also Becker, *The Economic Way of Looking at Behavior* (Stanford, CA: The Hoover Institution, 1996).

142 Friedman, *Capitalism and Freedom* (Chicago: University of Chicago Press, 1962), p. 13.

143 In their enthusiasm for "behavioral economics," some economically minded thinkers today recommend that

government itself should get into the nudge business. See
Nobel Prize winner (economics, 2017) Richard H. Thaler
and Cass R. Sunstein, *Nudge: Improving Decisions About
Health, Wealth, and Happiness* (New York: Penguin, 2009).

144 Thus, Paul A. Samuelson and William Nordhaus,
Economics, 14th edn (New York: McGraw-Hill, 1992),
a widely used textbook for courses in introductory
economics, is 727 pages long but does not discuss
advertising or marketing. Neither commercial practice
appears in the book's index or glossary.

145 See *ibid.*, p. 38, on consumer sovereignty, where
(a) consumers (all of us), and (b) technology (controlled
by producers) are described as jointly "in charge" of
markets. Therefore, "Just as a broker helps to match
buyers and sellers, so do markets act as the go-betweens
who reconcile the consumer's tastes with technology's
limitations" [D. R. – the limitations are embodied in
producers' production capacities]. In this formulation
of market activity, advertising does not appear.
Samuelson and Nordhaus observe that consumers express
"innate or acquired tastes," but they do not explain where
the acquired tastes come from or what that might signify.

146 Bringing Galbraith up to date, spending on ads in the US
for 2017 was estimated at more than $200 billion. See
www.emarketer.com/Report/US-Ad-Spending-eMarketers-
Updated-Estimates-Forecast-2017/2002134.

147 Galbraith, *The New Industrial State* (Boston: Houghton
Mifflin, 1967), pp. 198–218. In his *The Affluent Society*
(Boston: Houghton Mifflin, 1958), pp. 124–130, Galbraith
called much the same process "the dependence effect,"
where consumers were dependent on producers.

148 See Eli Cook, *The Pricing of Progress: Economic Indicators and
the Capitalization of American Life* (Cambridge, MA: Harvard
University Press, 2017), pp. 243–250.

149 Kahneman's major work for lay people is his *Thinking,
Fast and Slow* (New York: Penguin, 2011). See also Michelle

Bradley, *Behavioural Economics: A Very Short Introduction* (New York: Oxford University Press, 2017).

150 Hacker (ed.), *The Corporation Take-Over* (New York: Doubleday, 1964), p. 7.

151 See Stuart Ewen, *PR! A Social History of Spin* (New York: Basic Books, 1996).

152 See Eric Clark, *The Want Makers: Inside the World of Advertising* (New York: Penguin, 1988), and Tim Wu, *The Attention Merchants: The Epic Scramble to Get Inside Our Heads* (New York: Knopf, 2016).

153 On needs versus wants, see Juliet B. Schor, *The Overspent American: Why We Want What We Don't Need* (New York: Harper Perennial, 1998).

154 A good example of this claim, made in a leading economics journal, is Jack Hirshleifer, "The Expanding Domain of Economics," *American Economic Review* (December, 1985), p. 53: "There is only one social science … [because] our analytical categories – scarcity, cost, preferences, opportunity, etc. – are truly universal in application … Thus, economics does really constitute the universal grammar of social science." (After I drafted this chapter, I read Gary Saul Morson and Morton Schapiro, *Cents and Sensibility: What Economics Can Learn from the Humanities* (Princeton, NJ: Princeton University Press, 2017) and saw (p. 2, *et passim*) that they also write about economic "imperialism.")

155 There is a commercial expression of this academic imperialism. People who work in financial institutions – banks, brokerage houses, insurance companies, etc. – think in economic terms. As a result, they are likely to believe that many different sorts of social problems can be treated, and perhaps resolved, by an application of economic principles and strategies, say, by consulting firms such as McKinsey and Company. Anan Giridharadas, *Winners Take All: The Elite Charade of Changing the World* (New York: Knopf, 2018), *passim*, but esp. pp. 30–34, argues that the result is

an outlook that he calls MarketWorld, where people who are involved in creating the present social situation via capitalist markets believe that they are uniquely qualified and competent to repair the downsides – in all domains – of that situation. In Giridharadas' thesis, it is as if academic economic training has become a locus of cure-all advice in the commercial world.

156 (New York: McGraw-Hill, 1997).

157 (New York: Penguin, 2006).

158 (New York: Basic Books, 2007).

159 (New York: Harper Perennial, 2010).

160 (New York: Simon and Schuster, 2012).

161 (Boston: Little, Brown, 2008).

162 Thus, one blurb about Nobel Prize winner (economics, 1992) Gary S. Becker, *A Treatise on the Family* (Cambridge, MA: Harvard University Press, 1993), says that the book "cuts through the romantic mist that so often blinds social scientists to the hard choices faced by families and their members." Another blurb, about Avinash K. Dixit and Barry J. Nalebuff, *The Art of Strategy: A Game Theorist's Guide to Success in Business and Life* (New York: Norton, 2008), says that "Since reading it, I've been seeing everything in terms of game theory, and it feels like having put on a pair of x-ray goggles to view the world." Another blurb, about Tim Harford, *The Logic of Life: Uncovering the New Economics of Everything*, says that "Reading this book, you'll discover that the unlikeliest of individuals – racists, drug addicts, revolutionaries and rats – comply with economic logic, always taking account of future costs and benefits."

4 Creative Destruction

163 In 1959, Richard Nixon and Nikita Khrushchev met at an American exhibition in Moscow and the vice president extolled the virtues of American affluence by praising American home appliances on display in the exhibition.

See the transcript of their conversation at www.cia.gov/
library/readingroom/docs/1959-07-24.pdf.

164 On the virtues of growth, see Benjamin Friedman, *The Moral
Consequences of Economic Growth* (New York: Vintage, 2006).

165 Brink Lindsey and Steven M. Teles, *The Captured
Economy: How the Powerful Enrich Themselves, Slow Down
Growth, and Increase Inequality* (New York: Oxford
University Press, 2017), pp. 179–180.

166 Philipsen, *The Little Big Number*, p. 93.

167 That both Keynesians and monetarists favor
maintenance of demand is a central message of David
W. Noble, *Debating the End of History: The Marketplace,
Utopia, and the Fragmentation of Intellectual Life* (Minneapolis,
MN: University of Minnesota Press, 2012).

168 The efficacy of pumping up supply, even before it is
demanded, was championed especially by Arthur Laffer.
His "Laffer Curve" was described and praised by the *Wall
Street Journal*'s Jude Wanniski, *The Way the World Works*
(New York: Touchstone, 1978), pp. 97–107, *et passim*. See
a later explanation of that curve from the conservative
Heritage Foundation at www.heritage.org/taxes/report/
the-laffer-curve-past-present-and-future.

169 Breaking with his colleague President Ronald Reagan,
President George H. W. Bush called the supply-side view
"voodoo economics." See www.washingtonpost.com/
business/economy/before-trumps-tax-plan-there-was-
voodoo-economics-hyperbole/2016/12/21/c37c97ea-c3d2-
11e6-8422-eac61c0ef74d_story.html?noredirect=on&utm_
term=.7d57477c120c.

170 Galbraith, *The Culture of Contentment* (orig., 1992;
Princeton, NJ: Princeton University Press, 2017), p. 84.

171 See Robert Collins, *More: The Politics of Economic Growth in
Postwar America* (New York: Oxford University Press, 2000),
pp. 166–213, on how important the supply-side concept
was to Ronald Reagan and the Republican Party.

172 These presidents should be noted because supply-side tax
cuts for the well-to-do have reduced government revenues

and therefore limited the provision of social services that might ease the costs of living born by resentful citizens. That thesis is a central theme in Jacob S. Hacker and Paul Pierson, *Off Center: The Republican Revolution & the Erosion of American Democracy* (New Haven, CT: Yale University Press, 2006); Jacob S. Hacker, *The Great Risk Shift: The New Economic Insecurity and the Decline of the American Dream* (New York: Oxford University Press, 2006); and Jacob S. Hacker and Paul Pierson, *Winner-Take-All Politics: How Washington Made the Rich Richer – and Turned its Back on the Middle Class* (New York: Simon and Schuster, 2010).

173 The American Dream story appears today in, among other places, inspirational literature written by, or commissioned by, people who have been very successful economically. Recent examples include (Koch Industries) Charles G. Koch, *Good Profit: How Creating Value for Others Built One of the World's Most Successful Companies* (New York: Crown Business, 2015); (Amway) Rich DeVos, *Simply Rich: Life and Lessons from the Cofounder of Amway: A Memoir* (New York: Howard Books, 2016); (Dollar General) Cal Turner, *My Father's Business: The Small-Town Values That Built Dollar General into a Billion-Dollar Company* (Nashville, TN: Center Street, 2018); and (Home Depot) Ken Langone, *I Love Capitalism: An American Story* (New York: Portfolio, 2018).

174 The counter-argument, from outside of mainstream economics, is that success in life is only partly due to "individualism" but also to a political, social, and economic environment, friendly to commercial success, which is built and maintained by many people, including taxpayers, other than the entrepreneur. We will return to this alternative view, promoted by books such as Stephen J. McNamee and Robert K. Miller, Jr., *The Meritocracy Myth*, 3rd edn (New York: Roman and Littlefield, 2014), and Robert H. Frank, *Success and Luck: Good Fortune and the Myth of Meritocracy* (Princeton, NJ: Princeton University Press, 2016). See also n. 248.

175 These terms come from John Lanchester, *How to Speak to Money: What Money People Say – and What It Really Means* (New York: Norton, 2014), pp. 65–229.

176 On empathy, one can assume that people who work in finance are accustomed (when they work) to think of things in economic rather than human terms, in which case one can argue that the government officials who handled the Crash of 2008 may have understood that there were millions of "mortgages" at risk but not that there were millions of "mortgage-holders" – that is, "homeowners" and "households," desperate men and women – also at risk, that is, on the edge of bankruptcy, which if it occurred would impose on them terrible and perhaps irreparable personal costs. On this point, see Robert Skidelsky and Edward Skidelsky, *How Much is Enough? Money and the Good Life* (New York: Other Press, 2012), p. 41.

177 See Rana Foroohar, *Makers and Takers: How Wall Street Destroyed Main Street* (New York: Crown Business, 2017), pp. 165–188. See also Neil Barofsky, *Bailout: How Washington Abandoned Main Street While Rescuing Wall Street* (New York: Free Press, 2012). Those who left most small debtors in the lurch were less critical than Foroohar of what they did, emphasizing their goal of preventing a systemic meltdown and overall depression. On this score, see Timothy F. Geithner, *Stress Test: Reflections on Financial Crises* (New York: Broadway Books, 2015), written by the Secretary of the Treasury after the Crash of 2008, "Epilogue: Reflections on Financial Crises," pp. 492–528, but esp. 505: "[As to helping Wall Street more than Main Street, there was]… no other way to prevent a financial calamity from crushing the broader economy." See also Ben S. Bernanke, *The Courage to Act: A Memoir of a Crisis and its Aftermath* (New York: W. W. Norton, 2015), written by the economics professor who was Chairman of the Federal Reserve Bank during the crisis, which notes that there was little political support for helping homeowners, which

notes that the Fed had little jurisdiction over the subject of home ownership debt, which devotes 6 out of 579 pages to home mortgage foreclosures, and which provides no figures on how many foreclosures occurred on Bernanke's watch.

178 Many working Americans are too poor to participate creatively in the modern economy and therefore, except to protest about being treated badly by it (as some Trump voters did), center their lives mainly on family, tradition, and community. For example, see Barbara Ehrenreich, *Nickel and Dimed: On (Not) Getting by in America* (New York: Owl Books, 2001); David K. Shipler, *The Working Poor: Invisible in America* (New York: Vintage, 2005); Robert D. Putnam, *Our Kids: The American Dream in Crisis* (New York: Simon and Schuster, 2015); Arlie Russell Hochschild, *Strangers in Their Own Land: Anger and Mourning on the American Right* (New York: The New Press, 2016); J. D. Vance, *Hillbilly Elegy: A Memoir of a Family and Culture in Crisis* (New York: HarperCollins, 2016); Eliza Griswold, *Amity and Prosperity: One Family and the Fracturing of America* (New York: Farrar, Straus, and Giroux, 2018); and Sarah Smarsh, *Heartland: A Memoir of Working Hard and Being Broke in the Richest Country on Earth* (New York: Scribner, 2018). See also Guy Standing, *The Precariat: The New Dangerous Class* (New York: Bloomsbury, 2014).

179 John Patrick Leary, *Keywords: The New Language of Capitalism* (Chicago: Haymarket Books, 2018), argues that neoliberalism rules public conversation in America and the English-speaking world. Therefore he lists, defines, and analyzes the vocabulary of neoliberalism, that is, hundreds of everyday (p. 180) "terms that celebrate profit and the rule of the market..."

180 On this point, one can compare (professor of economics) Avinash K. Dixit and (professor of management) Barry J. Nalebuff, *The Art of Strategy: A Game Theorist's Guide to Success in Business and Life* (New York: Norton, 2008), to (professor of history) John Lewis Gaddis, *On Grand Strategy* (New York: Penguin, 2018). The first book sees economic

factors as underlying almost every human transaction, and the second describes cultural, political, *and* economic reasons in history for making some of the world's greatest strategic decisions concerning war and peace.

181 Schumpeter, *Capitalism, Socialism and Democracy*, pp. 81–86.

182 For example, Paul A. Samuelson and William D. Nordhaus, *Economics*, 19th edn (New York: McGraw-Hill, 2010), chapter 25: "Economic Growth," pp. 501–518. See also N. Gregory Mankiw, *Principles of Economics*, 6th edn (Mason, OH; Andover: South-Western, 2012), chapter 25: "Production and Growth," pp. 531–553. See also Moore McDowell, Rodney Thom, Ivan Pastine, Robert Frank, and Ben Bernanke, *Principles of Economics*, 3rd edn (New York: McGraw Hill, 2012), chapter 20: "Economic Growth, Productivity and Living Standards," pp. 499–524.

183 This point is discussed in Lanchester, *How to Speak Money*, p. 53, which notes that neoliberals insist that inequality is not just the outcome but also the necessary condition for economic growth and consequent prosperity. See also n. 237.

184 A good example of economic thinking that regards innovation (creativity) and entrepreneurship (creative people) as essential to economic progress is William J. Baumol, Robert E. Litan, and Carl J. Schramm, *Good Capitalism, Bad Capitalism, and the Economics of Growth and Prosperity* (New Haven, CT: Yale University Press, 2007), *passim*, but esp. pp. 1–14.

185 As a matter of "framing" after World War II, the phrases "creative destruction" and "free enterprise," which are both presumably driven by "entrepreneurs," served in the Cold War as American substitutes for "capitalism" and "capitalists." The aim was to avoid negative connotations that some people attached to the latter.

186 Reich, *Saving Capitalism*, pp. 206–207: "When Instagram … was sold to Facebook for about $1 billion in 2012, it had thirteen employees and thirty million customers. Contrast

this with Kodak, which had filed for bankruptcy a few months before. In its prime, Kodak had employed 145,000 people."

187 See www.aei.org/publication/the-netflix-effect-is-an-excellent-example-of-creative-destruction/.

188 The relentless process of economic change is plainly described by (non-mainstream) economist Robert L. Heilbroner, *The Nature and Logic of Capitalism* (New York: Norton, 1985), p. 36, *et passim*. The formula is $M\text{-}C\text{-}M^1$, where M, capital-as-money, is invested to produce C, capital-as-commodities, which are sold to produce M^1, capital-as-more-money (including profit). M^1 may then be used to finance innovation, otherwise the original capital of M will become obsolete and worthless when its traditional usage is undermined by the process of creative destruction.

189 In the service of creative destruction, Facebook officers offered euphemisms instead of war slogans with their early motto of "Move fast, break things." When critics began to regard that sort of Facebook behavior as reckless and irresponsible, Facebook eventually softened its motto to "Move fast with stable infrastructure."

190 See Clayton M. Christensen and Michael E. Raynor, *The Innovator's Solution: Creating and Sustaining Successful Growth* (Boston: Harvard Business Review Press, 2003), pp. 31–65, on the (recommended) "disruptive innovation model." Recommending the same process of ceaseless economic change, see also business administration professor Gary P. Pisano, *Creative Construction: The DNA of Sustained Innovation* (New York: Public Affairs, 2019). In fact, creative social media such as Facebook and Twitter may have already disrupted the American political process – elections, parties, campaigning, etc. – to the point where democracy as we knew it may no longer continue. For Jill Lepore's criticism of Christensen's praise for disruption, see www.newyorker.com/magazine/2014/06/23/the-disruption-machine.

191 Thus economic growth is often described mainly as an outpouring of welcome consumer products, and we are reminded by economist Diane Coyle, *GDP*, p. 63, that "Meyer Rothschild, the richest man in the world of his time, died in 1836 for want of an antibiotic to cure an infection." Alternatively, Louis Hyman, *Temp: How American Work, American Business, and the American Dream Became Temporary* (New York: Viking, 2018), explains a great downside of economic growth by showing how many American companies creatively increased their profits by turning full-time jobs, which included social benefits, into temporary jobs that paid little but increased personal and financial insecurity for many workers. In that critical vein, Barry C. Lynn, *End of the Line: The Rise and Coming Fall of the Global Corporation* (New York: Currency Books, 2005), describes how innovations in management and organization decentralized great corporations, which are now more profitable than previously but no longer provide long-term jobs in production, research, and development like, for example, General Motors, General Electric, Motorola, and Bell Telephone used to provide.

192 One sees this in some literary descriptions of competition. Thus the sixteenth-century proverb: "Everyman for himself, and the Devil take the hindmost." Or, from Oliver Goldsmith's "The Deserted Village," an eighteenth-century poem against land enclosures in England: "Ill fares the land, to hastening ills a prey. Where wealth accumulates, and men decay." In www.poetryfoundation.org/poems/44292/the-deserted-village. Or Alfred Lord Tennyson, *In Memoriam*, canto LVI, "Nature, red in tooth and claw." In https://babel.hathitrust.org/cgi/pt?id=uc2.ark:/13960/t2r49rk91;view=1up;seq=60. Proponents of economic growth might quote, in response, the mixed blessings described in Bernard Mandeville's poem, *The Grumbling Hive: or, KNAVES turn'd Honest* (1705): "The worst of all the

Multitude, did something for the common Good ... Such were the Blessings of that State; Their Crimes conspired to make 'em Great ... Thus every Part was full of Vice, Yet the whole Mass a Paradice." See https://andromeda. rutgers.edu/~jlynch/Texts/hive.html.

193 Accordingly, the business world is replete with tough-minded self-help books. For example, Antony Jay, *Management and Machiavelli: A Prescription for Success in Your Business* (Englewood Cliff, NJ: Prentice Hall, 1996). And, of course, Donald Trump and Bill Zanker, *Think Big and Kick Ass in Business and Life* (New York: HarperCollins, 2008).

194 Climate change, as a downside of affluence and GDP prosperity, is already killing coffee bushes and causing Central American coffee farmers to emigrate. See www.nytimes.com/2019/04/13/world/americas/coffee-climate-change-migration.html.

195 See David Landes, *The Wealth and Poverty of Nations: Why Some Are so Rich and Some so Poor* (New York: Norton, 1999), pp. 290–291.

196 Martin Ford, *The Rise of the Robots: Technology and the Threat of Mass Unemployment* (New York: Basic Books, 2015), pp. 169–186, speaks explicitly of the downside of creative destruction and discusses both 3D printing and driverless cars as examples of foreseeable destruction. See also Sam Schwartz, *No One at the Wheel: Driverless Cars and the Road of the Future* (Boston: Public Affairs, 2018).

197 Kirkpatrick Sale, *Rebels Against the Future: The Luddites and Their War on the Industrial Revolution* (New York: Basic Books, 1996).

198 A good example of optimism on this score is Thomas Friedman, *The Lexus and the Olive Tree: Understanding Globalization* (New York: Anchor Books, 2000), pp. 101–111, where Friedman, exercising his talent for rhetorical creativity, explains that in the maelstrom of globalization, countries are, to their own benefit, constrained by a "golden straightjacket." That is, they should change their ways (in effect, abjure Ludditism) to fit into a worldwide process that is beyond their control, whereby doing so

will assure them prosperity. For examples of damage
from creative destruction, together with firm support
for it because although sometimes painful it also fuels
commendable progress, see also W. Cox and Richard Alm
at www.econlib.org/library/Enc/CreativeDestruction.html.

199 See "The Great Horse Manure Crisis of 1894" in www.
historic-uk.com/HistoryUK/HistoryofBritain/Great-Horse-
Manure-Crisis-of-1894/.

200 The reasoning might be as follows. Neoliberals believe
that people are responsible for finding a job and working
hard to make their way in the world. In other words,
we are not ethically obliged to help them. Many social
scientists regard life as more complicated than that. For
example, they know that various talents and abilities are
naturally distributed according to normal curves, which
means that some people are destined, through no fault
of their own, to maneuver in life less successfully than
others. Apart from individual talents and achievements,
though, there is a question of why some communities
more than others create new jobs and prosperity for their
members. This question is discussed by Timothy P. Carney,
Alienated America: Why Some Places Thrive While Others Collapse
(New York: Harper, 2019). Carney argues that communities
that remain faithful to traditional religions, which
promote marriages and tight families rather than divorces
and anchorless children, which disdain Big Government
and Big Business, and which foster the little platoons of
civil society, are most likely to "thrive" and reject populist
politics. In other words, Carney, writing as a visiting
fellow at the American Enterprise Institute, argues that
America's main problem is cultural rather than economic.
See esp. pp. 29–46, chapter 3: " 'They've Chosen Not to
Keep Up,' Is it Economics or Culture?"

201 I should qualify what I said here. Some economists *are*
writing about destruction. My argument is not that
there are *no* such writings but that there are *too few*. For
an excellent example of focusing on the downside, see
Nobel Prize (economics, 2001) winner Joseph E. Stiglitz,

Rewriting the Rules of the American Economy: An Agenda for Growth and Shared Prosperity (New York: Norton, 2016), p. 169: "The American economy no longer works for most people in the United States." Notice, though, that even in his title, Stiglitz wants to promote growth, if only a somewhat more benign growth.

202 Reich, *Saving Capitalism*, p. xiv.

203 Law students will recognize here the reasoning that led Justice Oliver Wendell Holmes to issue his dissent in the case of *Lochner v. New York* 198 U.S. 45 (1905), when he famously (but to no avail) criticized the Court majority for, in effect, accepting as legitimate arguments made by the economic theory of laissez-faire in favor of unregulated markets (the Court struck down a New York State law which limited bakery employee work to ten hours per day and sixty hours per week).

204 In truth, many trades involve bystanders who may be hurt when a trade is consummated. Economists refer to what those people gain or lose as "externalities," or "external costs." But if those externalities are undesirable (although the Coase Theorem, in mainstream economics, is not outraged by externalities), economists leave it to other people to repair the damage by, say, enacting laws that will permit government to forbid business deals that impose external costs on third parties. And if government does not make such laws, it is politicians rather than economists who are culpable for the damage. This is the sort of argument made by people who blame a lack of government regulation rather than greedy bankers and brokers for the Crash of 2008. On the Coase Theorem, which says that a person who causes external costs (say, downstream pollution) should be enabled to negotiate permission to do so by agreeing to compensate the aggrieved party (the theorem is taught via a "thought experiment" where there is one offender and one victim), see Moore McDowell, Rodney Thom, Ivan Pastine, Robert Frank, and Ben Bernanke, *Principles of Economics*,

3rd edn (New York: McGraw Hill, 2012), pp. 313–315. The Coase Theorem exemplifies economic rather than moral reasoning, that is, the pursuit of what economists call efficiency rather than what a political philosopher like Michael J. Sandel might call decency. Largely for his authorship of this theorem, Coase received the Nobel Prize in economics in 1991. For Sandel's view of this sort of notion, see Sandel, *What Money Can't Buy: The Moral Limits of Markets* (New York: Farrar, Straus, and Giroux, 2012).

205 Thus Thomas Sowell, *Markets and Minorities* (New York: Basic Books, 1981), p. 4: "[In this book,] by 'market' transactions are meant such transactions as are voluntarily made on terms chosen or negotiated by the transacting parties themselves."

206 Philosophers might say that Walmart's offer is "rational" but not "reasonable." See John Rawls in n. 115. See also the hypothetical, unjust land rental case described in Jason Stanley, *How Propaganda Works* (Princeton, NJ: Princeton University Press, 2015), p. 105.

207 Smith, *The Wealth of Nations*, Bk. I, ch. 8, pp. 66–67.

208 On the dog that did not bark in the night, see https://sherlock-holm.es/stories/pdf/a4/1-sided/silv.pdf.

209 For example, when Marx and Engels, in *The Communist Manifesto* (1848), called on workers "to unite" and throw off their chains, few if any workers throughout the world, either in home countries or in colonies, had a right to complain against capitalism via the ballot box. Nevertheless, many later Marxists, including Lenin and Stalin, interpreted Marx and Engels to mean that armed rebellion against even elected, later-day governments is legitimate.

210 Within America's somewhat monolithic Liberal tradition (which we will explore in Chapter 7), not just many economists but most American social scientists have never used or promoted Marxian concepts. Nevertheless, within political science, some Marxian works appear in the journal *New Political Science*. That journal grew

out of the Caucus for a New Political Science, which was founded in 1967. And Charles E. Lindblom, APSA president in 1981, in his presidential address entitled "Another State of Mind," *American Political Science Review* (March, 1982), pp. 9–21, very gingerly suggested (p. 20) that his conventional colleagues would do well to "call more heavily on radical thought," which in Lindblom's lexicon included Marxism. The fact that many poor white citizens approve of Donald Trump has encouraged some writing and talk about the significance of what Marxists regard as "class" in America. For example, on working-class characteristics and consequences, see Smarsh, *Heartland: A Memoir of Working Hard and Being Broke in the Richest Country on Earth* (2018).

211 American conservatives criticize American liberals for promoting modern social practices that sometimes push aside traditional principles and practices. But some of the damage is done by capitalism, which many conservatives admire even though it constantly innovates. See Daniel Bell, *The Cultural Contradictions of Capitalism* (orig., 1976; New York: Basic Books, 1996), which points out, among other instances of displacement, how credit cards mock the traditional (Protestant) virtues of prudence and frugality.

212 On the damage in Port Clinton, Ohio, see Putnam, *Our Kids*.

213 A 2018 report, from Brown University's Watson Institute for International and Public Affairs, estimates the cost of American Middle East wars at $5.9 trillion in current dollars (spent and obligated) after 9/11. The report appears at https://watson.brown.edu/costsofwar/files/ cow/imce/papers/2018/Crawford_Costs%20of%20War%20 Estimates%20Through%20FY2019.pdf.

214 For an example of how American economists, basing themselves on mainstream orthodoxies, describe life in America as a non-Marxian story, see George A. Akerlof and Robert J. Shiller, *Animal Spirits: How Human Psychology Drives the Economy and Why It Matters for Global Capitalism*

(Princeton, NJ: Princeton University Press, 2009). This book was written by two Nobel Prize winners (economics, 2001, 2013); it was published by one of the leading academic publishers of our generation; it appeared just after the calamitous Crash of 2008, when huge banks and brokerage houses had bought and sold securities they knew were over-priced; it attributes the terrible failure of capitalism in that moment of crisis to personal frailty (human nature) rather than to greedy institutions (group behavior); in short, it is based on methodological individualism rather than sociological and anthropological realities. When I read *Animal Spirits*, I felt like I was looking at America through the wrong end of a telescope.

215 That mainstream American economics slights democratic-socialist principles and practices – say as they are epitomized in the public life of Norway and Sweden – is described in Offer and Soderberg, *The Nobel Factor*.

5 Targeting Neoliberalism

216 Polanyi, *The Great Transformation: The Political and Economic Origins of Our Time* (orig., 1944; Boston: Beacon, 1957), p. 33. Polanyi extended this passage by saying that "Such household truths of traditional statesmanship, often … reflecting the teachings of a social philosophy inherited from the ancients, were in the nineteenth century erased from the thoughts of the educated by the corrosive of a crude utilitarianism combined with an uncritical reliance on the alleged self-healing virtues of unconscious growth."

217 Between the American Civil War and World War I, "Social Darwinists" assumed that "survival of the fittest" was a law of natural behavior, enjoining implacable competition, in which case that behavior should be encouraged by society so that the nation would progress. Critics – later called "Reform Darwinists" – responded with exactly Polanyi's argument, insisting that although we have some aggressive instincts, it is entirely possible

to progress by creating a civilization that mutes those
instincts. See the two points of view described in
Richard Hofstadter, *Social Darwinism in American Thought*
(orig., 1944; New York: Beacon, 1955). See a discussion
of neoliberalism as a "rebirth" of Social Darwinism
in Robert Reich, *Beyond Outrage: What Has Gone Wrong
with Our Economy and Our Democracy, and How to Fix It*
(New York: Vintage, 2012), pp. 67–76.
218 Keeping Polanyi in mind helps us to understand the
arguments of, for example, Martin Wolf, *Why Globalization
Works* (New Haven, CT: Yale University Press, 2004),
pp. 24–25. Wolf says that the "fundamental value"
of a "free society" (he means a "market economy") is
"individual freedom" (which is not "the welfare of the
community" to which Polanyi refers). Then he goes on to
maintain that "Liberalism means perpetual and unsettling
change. Most of its enemies have, at bottom, hated it for
that reason." Wolf shows little sympathy for critics (in his
category of "enemies") who do not "hate" liberal markets
but only want them to do a better job (less destructive)
for everyone (in the "community"). We should note
that Wolf's book was published by the prestigious Yale
University Press, which indicates that his views will
receive special weight within the academic community.
219 It seems to me (I cannot prove this) that, in America's
public conversation, creative destruction doesn't
draw as much criticism as it should because it fuels
economic growth, and that growth is assumed to
be a project that improves social life year after year.
There is a sense, though, in which economic growth
is not *part of the solution* but actually *part of the problem*.
After all, constant growth means constant change,
and constant change undermines the conditions that
maintain society itself. These are the circumstances that
Avner Offer describes as "the conventions, habits, and
institutions of commitment." In his formulation, these
circumstances crumble because "affluence [resting on

economic growth] is driven by novelty [creativity], and that novelty unsettles [destroys]." See Offer, *The Challenge of Affluence: Self-Control and Well-Being in the United States and Britain since 1950* (New York: Oxford University Press, 2006), pp. vii and 358.

220 Robert D. Putnam, "The Public Role of Political Science," *Perspectives on Politics* (June, 2003), pp. 249–250. This was Putnam's 2002 presidential address to the APSA.

221 For example, (anthropology) David Harvey, *A Brief History of Neoliberalism* (New York: Oxford University Press, 2005); (global studies) Manfred B. Steger and Ravi K. Roy, *Neoliberalism: A Very Short Introduction* (New York: Oxford University Press, 2010); (economics) Philip Mirowski, *Never Let a Serious Crisis Go to Waste: How Neoliberalism Survived the Financial Meltdown* (New York: Verso, 2014); (political science) Wendy Brown, *Undoing the Demos: Neoliberalism's Stealth Revolution* (New York: Zone Books, 2015); (psychology) Ehrenreich, *Third Wave Capitalism*; and (history) Quinn Slobodian, *Globalists: The End of Empire and the Birth of Neoliberalism* (Cambridge, MA: Harvard University Press, 2018).

222 See John Kenneth Galbraith, *The Great Crash 1929* (Boston: Houghton Mifflin, 1961).

223 The Glass-Steagall Act of 1933 banned any bank from engaging in all these activities; the Gramm-Leach-Bliley Act of 1999 repealed the Glass-Steagall prohibition.

224 On the rise of conservative organizations, see Thomas B. Edsall, *Building Red America: The New Conservative Coalition and the Drive for Permanent Power* (New York: Basic Books, 2006), and Sidney Blumenthal, *The Rise of the Counter-Establishment: The Conservative Ascent to Political Power* (New York: Union Square Press, 2008). The *Citizens United v. Federal Elections Commission* (2010) case, in which the Supreme Court overruled government limitations on campaign contributions from organizations, was brought to court by the conservative Citizens United organization, founded in 1988. Republican federal judgeship candidates,

such as John Roberts, Neil Gorsuch, and Brett Kavanaugh, are now vetted by the conservative Federalist Society organization, founded in 1982.

225 This is a central theme in Brown, *Undoing the Demos*, esp. pp. 79–111.

226 Smith, *The Wealth of Nations*, Bk. I, ch. II, p. 13.

227 On the nineteenth-century origins of the term *homo economicus*, see Kate Raworth, *Doughnut Economics: Seven Ways to Think Like a 21st-Century Economist* (New York: Random House Business Books, 2018), pp. 95–99.

228 For Kant, it is a "categorical imperative" that people should not use other people as means to someone else's ends but should relate to them as ends in themselves. See Immanuel Kant, *The Philosophy of Kant: Immanuel Kant's Moral and Political Writings*, ed. Carl Friedrich (New York: Modern Library, 1949), "Metaphysical Foundations of Morals (1785)," pp. 176–178.

229 For example, Reid Hoffman and Ben Casnocha, *The Start-Up of You: Adapt to the Future, Invest in Yourself, And Transform Your Career* (New York: Random House, 2013).

230 Thomas Hobbes, *Leviathan, or the Matter, Forme and Power of a Commonwealth Ecclesiasticall and Civil* (orig., 1651; Oxford: Oxford University Press, 1960), Part 1, chapter 13, p. 82.

231 Some scholars refer to this neoliberal approach to economic success as "the portfolio society." See Gerald F. Davis, *Managed by the Markets: How Finance Re-Shaped America* (New York: Oxford University Press, 2009), esp. "Chapter 6: From Employee and Citizen to Investor: How Talent, Friends, and Homes Became 'Capital'," pp. 191–234.

232 Aronowitz, *The Knowledge Factory*, pp. 125–156. Megan Erickson, *Class War: The Privatization of Childhood* (New York: Verso, 2015), pp. 70–80, *et passim*, describes how American public schools have been shaped, in recent decades, according to neoliberal notions of educating children to compete for work in a market-driven society, starting with the Reagan-era report, sponsored by Secretary of Education Terrel Bell,

entitled *A Nation at Risk: The Imperative of Educational Reform* (Washington, DC: United States Government Printing Office, 1983). For example, see Governor Rick Scott, Florida: "If I'm going to take money from a citizen to put into education then I'm going to take that money to create jobs … Is it a vital interest of the state to have more anthropologists? I don't think so." And see President Barack Obama: "I promise you, folks can make a lot more, potentially, with skilled manufacturing or the trades than they might with an art history degree." Scott and Obama are quoted in www.insidehighered.com/news/2014/01/31/obama-becomes-latest-politician-criticize-liberal-arts-discipline. See also David Skorton, president of Cornell University, delivering the university's commencement address in 2014: "Each of you starts the next portion of your life's journey with the tremendous benefit of a Cornell education. I hope that you'll carry with you … a continuing commitment to build human capital so that more will have opportunities to pursue their dreams." At http://news.cornell.edu/stories/2014/05/build-human-capital-skorton-tells-2014-graduates.

233 The phrase is from Thoreau's *Walden* in Brooks Atkinson (ed.), *WALDEN, And Other Writings of Henry David Thoreau* (New York: Modern Library, 1937, 1950), p. 7. On life in the modern economy, see Richard Sennett, *The Corrosion of Character: The Personal Consequences of Work in the New Capitalism* (New York: Norton, 1998), and Richard Sennett, *The Culture of the New Capitalism* (New Haven, CT: Yale University Press, 2006). See also Jules Henry, *Culture Against Man* (New York: Vintage Books, 1963), as a forerunner to Sennett's ideas on the inhumanity of much modern economic activity.

234 See Moshe Adler, *Economics for the Rest of Us: Debunking the Science That Makes Life Dismal* (New York: The New Press, 2011), pp. 113–150. Adler discusses what economists call the theory of wages. Classical economists such as

176 NOTES TO PAGE 70

Smith and Ricardo said that wages are determined by the bargaining powers of employers (capital) versus the bargaining powers of employees (labor). Neoclassical economists, starting with John Bates Clark, rejected Smith and Ricardo on this point and said that wages are determined by the marginal utility contribution of each person to the final product. Adler insists, however, that it is impossible to calculate any person's VMP (value of marginal product) because it is impossible to isolate one person's contribution to a collective project. For example, remove the taxi driver, and the taxicab will stand still, generating no fares. Remove the taxicab, and the driver will stand still, generating no fares. So who contributed what, or did each contribute 100-percent utility to the rides and fares? (On the difficulties of measuring VMP, see also Schlefer, *The Assumptions Economists Make*, pp. 99–120.) Let's put that another way. From the total sum of fares, how much should the employee driver be paid and how much should the taxicab owner take home? For social purposes, the bottom line here is that, if bargaining power is really the key factor to setting wages, then modern society, which does not limit how many investors can get together to form powerful corporations, should also not limit how many workers can unite to form powerful labor unions. But neoliberals usually regard labor unions unfavorably, to the point where they prefer that workers bargain separately with their employers. And neoliberals who praise banks and "entrepreneurs" for their contributions to economic growth make no objection to CEOs awarding themselves, while in control of their boards of directors, salaries and benefits which are hundreds of times more generous than what they are willing to pay average rank-and-file workers in the same corporations. On CEO pay in 2017 at S&P 500 Index firms, see the research reported in *Forbes Magazine* at www.forbes.com/sites/dianahembree/2018/05/22/ceo-pay-skyrockets-to-361-times-that-of-the-average-worker/#67c2b203776d.

235 The common-sense answer to how much people earn is that it mostly depends on their bargaining power. Having less power, one earns less. Having more power, one earns more. Which is why Walmart designates its salespeople "associates" instead of "workers," because the latter have a legal right, according to the National Labor Relations Act of 1935, to organize and join labor unions, whereas the former (as part of the company's "management") can legally be fired by Walmart for doing either. In short, "workers" can acquire bargaining power by uniting with other workers, so Walmart tries to prevent them from doing that by calling them "associates."

236 Bartels, *Unequal Democracy: The Political Economy of the New Gilded Age* (Princeton, NJ: Princeton University Press, 2008), p. 29.

237 This is the main argument in Friedman, *Capitalism and Freedom*. It is also sometimes implied, as in Lindsey and Teles, *The Captured Economy*, where the title assumes that the economy is simply there (not created by society) to be captured or otherwise distorted.

238 Market-based decisions produce inequality of incomes. But neoliberals assume that this uneven distribution of economic rewards is necessary, because they believe that only large rewards can motivate the entrepreneurs who produce the economic growth that counts for neoliberals as progress. For a discussion of this point – as if "no pain [for the weak], no gain [for society]" – see Raworth, *Doughnut Economics*, pp. 163–170. Religion inspired an earlier pro-market approach to inequality, as in *Mark* 14:7: "… the poor you always have with you." Thus Edmund Burke didn't need secular theories to conclude that it is not "within the competence of Government, taken as Government, or even of the rich, as rich, to

supply to the poor, those necessities which it has pleased
the Divine Providence for a while to with-hold from
them." See Burke, "Thoughts and Details on *Scarcity*"
(1795), p. 32, at https://quod.lib.umich.edu/e/ecco/
004903053.0001.000?rgn=main;view=fulltext.

239 John Gray, *False Dawn: The Delusions of Global Capitalism*
(New York: New Press, 2000), pp. 17–18, 23–24, 26–34. See
also Dean Baker, *Taking Economics Seriously* (Cambridge,
MA: MIT Press, 2010), pp. 1–17.

240 Graeber, *Debt: The First 5,000 Years* (New York: Melville
House, 2012), pp. 21–41.

241 The central thesis of neoliberalism, as expressed by
Friedrich Hayek and like-minded colleagues, is that
government should protect natural markets so that
democratic forces will not prevent them from functioning
efficiently. This point, on the "encasement" of "states, laws,
and other institutions to protect markets," is explained
throughout Slobodian, *Globalists*, but see esp. pp. 2–6. For
a scholarly claim that neoliberalism's central thesis, of
keeping capitalism safe from democracy, underlies the
libertarian theories of economist James Buchanan and the
anti-government political philanthropy of businessmen
Charles and David Koch, see MacLean, *Democracy in
Chains*, esp. pp. 74–87. On leading neoliberal economists,
see Daniel Stedman Jones, *Masters of the Universe: Hayek,
Friedman, and the Birth of Neoliberal Politics* (Princeton,
NJ: Princeton University Press, 2012). For a recent example
of this neoliberal approach, see Raghuram G. Rejan, *Fault
Lines: How Hidden Fractures Still Threaten the World Economy*
(Princeton, NJ: Princeton University Press, 2011), p. 228: "It
is when democratic government ... tries to use modern
financial markets to fulfill political goals, when it becomes
a participant in markets rather than a regulator [of natural
markets], that we get the kind of disasters [the Crash
of 2008] that we have just experienced."

242 On the importance of entrepreneurs, see Nobel Prize
winner (economics, 2013) Robert J. Shiller, *Finance and
the Good Society* (Princeton, NJ: Princeton University

Press, 2012), p. 13: "Financial innovation is an underappreciated phenomenon." Moreover, according to Shiller, the people who practice it and earn great wealth, should (p. 235) extend "enlightened stewardship" to those who are less successful financially. The notion of rich people as enlightened administrators of great wealth was famously promoted by Andrew Carnegie, in his "The Gospel of Wealth" (1889), reprinted in Andrew Carnegie, *The Gospel of Wealth*, ed. Edward C. Kirkland (Cambridge, MA: Harvard University Press, 1962), pp. 14–49.

243 Daron Acemoglu and James A. Robinson, *Why Nations Fail: The Origins of Power, Prosperity, and Poverty* (New York: Crown Business, 2012), pp. 32, 430.

244 Supply-side economics is described in n. 168. This theory rejects the Keynesian notion that (a) *government* (politicians) can enact policies to avoid recessions and generate prosperity. Instead, it favors a notion, rejected by demand-side economists, that if government will just get out of the way, (b) *private industry and commerce* (entrepreneurs) will make such extensive investments (and consumers will buy whatever additional goods are produced) as to avoid recessions and generate prosperity.

245 On the golden straightjacket, see n. 198. An earlier wordsmith portrayed less favorably the strictures of economic growth and globalization. Thus, in *Hard Times*, Charles Dickens described Thomas Gradgrind, Victorian and Utilitarian schoolmaster: "He sat writing in the room with the deadly statistical clock, proving something no doubt – probably, in the main, that the Good Samaritan was a Bad Economist." See Dickens, *Hard Times* (orig., 1854; London: Penguin Classics, 1994), p. 192.

246 Ngaire Woods, *The Globalizers: The IMF, the World Bank, and Their Borrowers* (Ithaca, NY: Cornell University Press, 2006) offers analysis and constructive criticism. Richard Peet, *Unholy Trinity: The IMF, World Bank and WTO* (New York: Zed Books, 2003), provides a hostile overview of the globalizers.

247 Thus Max Weber's essay, "Science as a Vocation" (1917),
    in David Owen and Tracy B. Strong (eds.), *Max Weber: The
    Vocation Lectures* (Indianapolis, IN: Hackett, 2004), pp. 1–31.

248 See Baumol, Litan, and Schramm, *Good Capitalism, Bad
    Capitalism, and the Economics of Growth and Prosperity*,
    pp. 263–268.

249 Some philosophers use the term "interdependence" or
    related terms to indicate that any one person's success
    depends on what he or she receives from others. For
    example, see John Dewey, *Individualism Old and New* (orig.,
    1933; New York: Prometheus, 1999) and Liam Murphy
    and Thomas Nagel, *The Myth of Ownership: Taxes and Justice*
    (New York: Oxford, 2001). See also the case of Walmart,
    which makes great profits at least partly by paying its
    workers so little that many of them live in poverty and
    must use government food stamps. On Walmart and its
    more than $6 billion of annual government assistance,
    see www.forbes.com/sites/clareoconnor/2014/04/15/
    report-walmart-workers-cost-taxpayers-6-2-billion-in-
    public-assistance/#4dd18666720b. On government's
    contributions to private, high-tech productivity and
    profitability, see Linda Weiss, *America Inc? Innovation and
    Enterprise in the National Security State* (Ithaca, NY: Cornell
    University Press, 2014), and Mariana Mazzucato, *The
    Entrepreneurial State: Debunking Public vs. Private Sector Myths*
    (New York: Public Affairs, 2015).

250 Many Americans deplore the course of Native American
    history. But they all automatically, and mostly
    unthinkingly, enjoy the outcome of their predecessors'
    forcibly occupying approximately 3.8 million square
    miles of land (including Alaska and Hawaii) that were
    once home only to indigenous people. Thus Irving Berlin,
    who was a white, Jewish, Russian, Yiddish-speaking
    immigrant who arrived at Ellis Island in 1893 (the
    Apache chief Geronimo was last captured by US cavalry
    soldiers in 1886), wrote and sang, while leaving out the
    natives, "God bless America … From the mountains to

the prairies, to the oceans white with foam, God bless America, my home sweet home." And Richard Rogers and Oscar Hammerstein, for their quintessential 1943 Broadway musical show "Oklahoma," composed an inspiring story about the former Indian Territory (which is still home to scores of tribes), without placing Native American characters on the stage.

251 After the battle of Omdurman in 1898, where British soldiers fielded Maxim guns (recoil-operated machine guns), British dead were listed as 47–48, while Mahdist (Muslim) dead were estimated at 12,000. See www.britishbattles.com/war-in-egypt-and-sudan/battle-of-omdurman/. See also Hilaire Belloc on the Maxim gun in https://archive.org/stream/moderntraveller00belluoft/moderntraveller00belluoft_djvu.txt.

252 See Gaddis, *On Grand Strategy*, p. 288: "[FDR's country emerged from the war] with half the world's manufacturing capability, two-thirds of its gold reserves, three-fourths of its invested capital, its largest navy and air force, and its first atomic bombs."

253 The "story" cited in this quotation was told by David Ricardo in David Ricardo, *The Principles of Political Economy and Taxation* (orig., 1817; London: Dent & Sons, 1962), pp. 81–83 ff. The quotation itself comes from Krugman, *The Accidental Theorist: And Other Dispatches from the Dismal Science* (New York: Norton, 1998), pp. 113–114. See also Ian Fletcher, *Free Trade Doesn't Work: What Should Replace It and Why* (Sheffield, MA: Coalition for a Prosperous America, 2011), p. 3: "Ninety-three percent of American economists [professors?] surveyed [in 2003] support free trade."

254 See Krauthammer at www.washingtonpost.com/opinions/save-obama-on-trade/2015/05/14/aabaf342-fa65-11e4-9ef4-1bb7ce3b3fb7_story.html?utm_term=.298f9067086b.

255 See this optimism underlying Wolf, *Why Globalization Works*, p. 157: "… it makes more sense to focus on what has happened to poverty than to inequality." This is a financial argument, where rising GDP does not account

for what economists call "externalities." For example, Indonesian workers may now make more money than previously (that is, they may be further than previously from poverty because they receive money from their country's growing GDP). But the environment in which they live – rainforests, coral reefs, freshwater resources, etc. – is deteriorating because it is being exploited to push up GDP. On the environmental costs of Third World economic success, see Elizabeth L. Cline, *Over-Dressed: The Shockingly High Cost of Cheap Fashion* (New York: Portfolio/ Penguin, 2013), pp. 123–125.

256 Republican lawmakers in the Senate and House together voted *for* NAFTA 166–114, while Democrats in the Senate and the House voted *against* NAFTA 182–129.

257 Clinton should be classified as neoliberal on this point because labor unions protested strongly against NAFTA but Clinton signed it into law anyway. On the economic and global implications of NAFTA, see Greg Grandin, *The End of the Myth: From the Frontier to the Border Wall in the Mind of America* (New York: Metropolitan Books, 2019), pp. 233–248. As Grandin says (p. 233), "Clinton was Reagan's greatest achievement."

258 Dickens noted the ambiguity of average gains in *Hard Times*, pp. 50–51, where in Coketown the Utilitarian schoolmaster, Mr. M'Choakumchild, observes to "Sissy" Jupe, his student, that "in this nation, there are fifty millions of money. Girl number twenty, isn't this a prosperous nation? and a'n't you in a thriving state? 'What did you say?' asked Louisa. 'Miss Louisa [said Sissy], I said I didn't know. I thought I couldn't know whether it was a prosperous nation or not, and whether I was in a thriving state or not, unless I knew who got the money, and whether any of it was mine.'"

259 See Gabriel Zucman, *Global Wealth Inequality* (Cambridge, MA: National Bureau of Economic Research, January, 2019), Figure 1, p. 36, at https://papers.nber.org/tmp/ 38195-w25462.pdf. See also Chuck Collins and Josh

Hoxie, *Billionaire Bonanza: The Forbes and the Rest of Us* (Washington, DC: Institute for Policy Studies, 2017) at https://inequality.org/wp-content/uploads/2017/11/ BILLIONAIRE-BONANZA-2017-Embargoed.pdf. Collins and Hoxie claim that the three richest Americans – Bill Gates, Jeff Bezos, and Warren Buffett – "now own more wealth than the entire bottom half of the American population combined, a total of 160 million people or 63 million households."

260 www.cnbc.com/2018/07/19/income-inequality-continues-to-grow-in-the-united-states.html.

261 See his "The Social Responsibility of Business is to Increase its Profits" (1970) in http://umich.edu/~thecore/ doc/Friedman.pdf: "[T]here is one and only one social responsibility of business – to use its resources and engage in activities designed to increase its profits so long as it stays within the rules of the game, which is to say, engages in open and free competition without deception or fraud." For early scholarly support of this notion, see Michael C. Jensen and William H. Meckling, "Theory of the Firm: Managerial Behavior, Agency Costs and Ownership Structure," *Journal of Financial Economics* (October, 1976), pp. 305–360.

262 2012 Republican presidential candidate Mitt Romney was a successful venture capitalist with the firm of Bain Capital. For a positive view of venture capitalism's role in American life, see Edward Conard, *Unintended Consequences: Why Everything You've Been Told About the Economy is Wrong* (New York: Portfolio/Penguin, 2012). Conard is a former managing director of Bain Capital. For critical views of venture capitalism, see Louis Hyman, *Temp: How American Work, American Business, and the American Dream Became Temporary* (New York: Viking, 2018) and Eileen Appelbaum and Rosemary Batt, *Private Equity at Work: When Wall Street Manages Main Street* (New York: Russell Sage Foundation, 2014). Appelbaum and Batt offer a briefer version of

their book's argument in http://prospect.org/article/
private-equity-pillage-grocery-stores-and-workers-risk.

263 Sloan is cited in David Farber, *Sloan Rules: Alfred
P. Sloan and the Triumph of General Motors*, 2nd edn
(Chicago: University of Chicago, 2005), p. 59. Sloan was
a harbinger. The massive historical shift of business
organizations after 1970 in Sloan's direction (via
outsourcing, hiring temporary workers, pressuring
suppliers, exploiting consumers, and more) to fulfill the
theory that companies exist in order to make money
rather than things (or even progress) is described in
Hyman, *Temp, passim*. See also Hyman, *Temp*, pp. 180,
184: "The patriotic pride that GE's Ralph Cordiner could
feel in the 1950s at being the head of an 'American
manufacturing company ... devoted to serving the
United States' had been replaced [in late-twentieth-
century America] by the pride in a rising stock price ...
Only suckers made commodities."

264 In American constitutional law, see *Charles River
Bridge v. Warren Bridge* 36 US (11 Pet) 420 (1837). On
the declining power of the idea that corporations are
chartered to serve the public, see Shoshana Zuboff, *The
Age of Surveillance Capitalism: The Fight for a Human Future at
the New Frontier of Power* (New York: Public Affairs, 2019),
pp. 40–41.

265 Appelbaum and Batt, *Private Equity at Work*,
p. 15: "Shareholder-value maximization represents
a fundamental shift in the concept of the American
corporation – from a view of it as a productive enterprise
and stable institution serving the needs of a broad
spectrum of stakeholders to a view of it as a bundle
of assets to be bought and sold with an exclusive goal
of maximizing shareholder value." The older, larger
view of corporation responsibilities to the community
is at odds with the modern notion, going back to the
late nineteenth century, that corporations should be
regarded as real (not artificial) individuals possessing

constitutional rights and therefore in some respects not to be restrained by government regulation. One of the Supreme Court's recent decisions to that effect, in *Citizens United v. Federal Election Commission*, is disputed by Jeffrey D. Clements, *Corporations Are Not People: Why They Have More Rights Than You Do and What You Can Do About It* (San Francisco, CA: Barrett-Koehler, 2012).

266 See this in Julia C. Ott, *When Wall Street Met Main Street: The Quest for an Investors' Democracy* (Cambridge, MA: Harvard University Press, 2011), pp. 4–5, *et passim*.

267 For the New Deal outlook, see Adolf A. Berle and Gardiner C. Means, *The Modern Corporation and Private Property*, 2nd edn (orig., 1932; New York: Routledge, 1991). For the pro-market view, see Amity Shlaes, *The Forgotten Man: A New History of the Great Depression* (New York: Harper Perennial, 2008) and Kim Phillips-Fein, *Invisible Hands: The Businessmen's Crusade Against the New Deal* (New York: Norton, 2009). For the day-to-day endorsement of a shareholder-values set of validations and justifications by financial workers in Manhattan, see the anthropological study by Karen Ho, *Liquidated, An Ethnography of Wall Street* (Durham, NC: Duke University Press, 2009), pp. 122–212.

268 Mankiw, *Principles of Economics*, p. 4.

269 Blinder, *Hard Heads, Soft Hearts,* pp. 16–17.

270 Famine (scarcity of food), for example, does not occur because society lacks the capacity to produce enough food but because we do not distribute enough of it to people who are hungry. See Nobel Prize winner (economics, 1998) Amartya Sen, *Poverty and Famines: An Essay on Entitlement and Deprivation* (New York: Oxford University Press, 1981).

271 For a neoliberal argument along these lines, see James R. Rogers, "The Inescapable Tragedy of Postliberalism" at www.lawliberty.org/2019/07/24/the-inescapable-tragedy-of-postliberalism/?utm_source=LAL+Updates&utm_campaign=0c39d6e790-LAL_Daily_Updates&utm_medium=email&utm_term=0_53ee3e1605-0c39d6e790-72492621. There, Rogers cites "tragically scarce

resources" to claim – without distinguishing between needs and wants – that only the pursuit of endless economic growth can comfortably "sustain a world of 7.9 billion souls."

272 When technology in the twentieth century led to factories and farms that could produce more things than people needed, desires had to be evoked, via advertising, to buy up the surpluses. That is the story told in William Leach, *Land of Desire: Merchants, Power and the Rise of a New American Culture* (New York: Vintage, 1993). See also Susan Strasser, *Satisfaction Guaranteed: The Making of the American Mass Market* (Washington, DC: Smithsonian Institution Press, 1989).

273 See Fred Hirsch, *The Social Limits to Growth* (Cambridge, MA: Harvard University Press, 1978), *passim*, on "positional goods," which, when achieved, become unavailable to others.

274 Schor, *True Wealth*, pp. 27–48, calls this situation the "materiality paradox," in that we are addicted to material items not because they are functional (necessary) but because they are culturally attractive (desirable).

275 In the context of the concept of consumer sovereignty, one may envision corporations as if they were like Gulliver, a giant (say, Google) flat on its back tied down with many small strings by tiny Lilliputians (consumers).

276 Personal costs would include bad health due to fracking. See Griswold, *Amity and Prosperity*.

277 See Kate Ervine, *Carbon* (New York: Polity, 2018).

278 In David M. Ricci, *Why Conservatives Tell Stories and Liberals Don't: Rhetoric, Faith, and Vision on the American Right* (Boulder, CO: Paradigm Publishers, 2011), pp. 37–38, I call this thesis "the dollar fix."

279 Gernot Wagner and Martin L. Weitzman, *Climate Shock: The Economic Consequences of a Hotter Planet* (Princeton, NJ: Princeton University Press, 2015), p. 46.

280 I say "in strictly economic terms" because a carbon tax, like the existing federal gasoline tax, could be collected and enforced by relatively few government workers and would do its work automatically rather than require the creation and administration of numerous government regulations. In other words, a carbon tax is more of an economic than a political instrument, favored by people who regard most governmental activities as fallible and potentially tyrannical.

281 Wagner and Weitzman, *Climate Shock: The Economic Consequences of a Hotter Planet*, pp. 6, 23–28, 46, 75–79. By using the word "economic," this book's title unintentionally reveals that its authors are addressing secondary consequences of climate change.

282 Klein, *No is Not Enough: Resisting Trump's Shock Politics and Winning the World We Need* (Chicago: Haymarket Books, 2017), p. 81.

283 Paradoxically, James Kwak, *Economism: Bad Economics and the Rise of Inequality* (New York: Pantheon, 2010), p. 10, points out that neoliberalism (whose economic beliefs he calls "economism") is "influential" in America precisely because it is *not* a formal ideology but a diffuse (and therefore hard to formally disprove) set of values, assumptions, inclinations, preferences, and interpretations. Mirowski, *Never Let a Serious Crisis Go To Waste*, *passim*, also finds no catechism for neoliberalism and therefore analyzes a set of values, assumptions, expectations, etc., which he calls the Neoliberal Thought Collective. See also Philip Mirowski and Dieter Plehwe (eds), *The Road From Mont Pelerin: The Making of the Neoliberal Thought Collective* (Cambridge, MA: Harvard University Press, 2015), esp. pp. 433–440, which lists eleven neoliberal tenets.

284 That different groups or classes have distinctive and user-friendly ways of seeing the world is canonically discussed in Karl Mannheim, *Ideology and Utopia: An Introduction to*

the *Sociology of Knowledge* (New York: Harvest Books, 1936), *passim*, but esp. pp. 55–59.

285 On the ideology of the modern American middle class, see Noble, *Debating the End of History*, *passim*, but esp. p. 1.

286 Conard, *Unintended Consequences*, pp. 40–43.

287 Bain Capital was co-founded in 1984 by Mitt Romney, who was governor of Massachusetts from 2003 to 2007, was the Republican presidential nominee in 2012, and was elected to the Senate from Utah in 2018.

288 Nassau Senior, *An Outline of the Science of Political Economy* (orig., 1836; London: G. Allen & Unwin, 1951), p. 58.

289 What is called "economics" today was originally called "political economy" (as in David Ricardo, *The Principles of Political Economy and Taxation*, 1817, and John Stuart Mill, *Principles of Political Economy*, 1848), because it was widely understood that governments regulate economic activity in order to promote political ends. National budgets, for example, are used by political leaders to set nation-wide priorities, with some economic activities fostered and others discouraged. That economic thinkers managed to drop the "political" from "political economy" gradually, in the decades before World War I, made it seem like there were two separate realms, one of "economics" and the other of "politics." In which case modern "economists" sound like they are being scientific about what is, in reality, a matter of subjective priorities that are still heavily influenced by political considerations.

290 I am using the term "public good" as economists use it, to describe a good, like a public park or no-fee bridge or clean water or the American Air Force, which comes into existence and thereafter is available to be used by, or provide a benefit to, everyone. That is, *public goods* are not like *private goods*, because the latter, for example my car, cannot be used by anyone else unless the owner gives that person permission.

291 Neoliberals would disagree with my assertion that they are weak on public goods. They would say that they

favor using government taxes to provide law and order
(domestic tranquility) and armed forces (national defense)
in order to enable the competitive market to facilitate
prosperity (in the pursuit of happiness). Then they would
say that, for so long as that market is maintained, every
individual will receive what he or she deserves (justice),
and private property earned in the market will make
citizens financially strong enough to resist government's
tendency to become tyrannical (ergo, liberty will reign).

292 See Mancur Olson, *The Logic of Collective Action: Public
Goods and the Theory of Groups* (Cambridge, MA: Harvard
University Press, 1965), esp. pp. 5–52.

293 Conard, *Unintended Consequences*, p. 266. In favor of charging
user fees for many services now provided by government
agencies, see Lawrence W. Reed (ed.), *Private Cures for Public
Ills: The Promise of Privatization* (Irving-on-Hudson, NY: The
Foundation for Economic Education, 1996).

294 The philosophical issue around public goods is
discussed in Gamble, *Can the Welfare State Survive?*, p. 3,
et passim, and Offer and Soderberg, *The Nobel Factor*,
pp. 4–7, *et passim*. Both of these books explain that
most American economic thought differs in principle
from social democratic thought in Europe, epitomized
in Nordic countries. In America, most economic
thinkers regard individuals as morally obliged to work
hard to achieve their own economic security (there is
the rational, utility-seeking individual of mainstream
economics), whereas in Nordic countries, most
economic thinkers expect that economic risks threaten
everyone, if only in old age, should be handled by
pooling some resources and thereby providing security
for the entire community. In that case, goods like
welfare and child support in Norway and Sweden are
allocated to all citizens as benefits that they deserve
as members of society, whereas in America welfare
and child support are described as services provided
only to the poor, in which case many prosperous

people have no self-interest in them (the services) and don't support them politically. For example, William Voegeli, *Never Enough: America's Limitless Welfare State* (New York: Encounter Books, 2012), who is a senior editor at the conservative *Claremont Review of Books*, promotes the view that regards "welfare" programs as intended not for society at large, as in Nordic countries, but for the poor and less successful in America.

295 For example, see William Kristol, "The 1993 Kristol Memo on Defeating Health Care Reform," addressed to "Republican Leaders" on the subject of "President Clinton's health care reform proposal" and warning that Clinton's plan, if enacted, would persuade many voters that the Democratic Party is "the generous protector of middle class interests." At www.scribd.com/document/12926608/William-Kristol-s-1993-Memo-Defeating-President-Clinton-s-Health-Care-Proposal.

296 See Robert H. Frank and Phillip J. Cook, *The Winner-Take-All Society: Why the Few at the Top Get so Much More Than the Rest of Us* (New York: Penguin, 1996). The same economy is sometimes called "the casino economy," which is particularly apt vis-à-vis Sheldon Adelson, a major Republican donor, much of whose $40-billion fortune comes from casinos in Las Vegas, Macau, and Singapore.

297 See www.washingtonpost.com/news/wonk/wp/2017/12/06/the-richest-1-percent-now-owns-more-of-the-countrys-wealth-than-at-any-time-in-the-past-50-years/?noredirect=on&utm_term=.60b09dca4a83.

298 For Sanders' view, see a long version in Sanders, *The Speech: A Historic Filibuster on Corporate Greed and the Decline of Our Middle Class*, 2nd edn (New York: Nation Books, 2015) and see a short version in his 2015 Georgetown University speech at http://inthesetimes.com/article/18623/bernie_sanders_democratic_socialism_georgetown_speech.

299 See Ehrenreich, *Nickle and Dimed*, *passim*, trying to pay for basic needs by working as a waitress, hotel maid, house cleaner, nursing home aide, and Walmart salesperson. See also Shipler, *The Working Poor*.

300 The transformation of wealth into political power is summed up in Nobel Prize winner (economics, 2001) Joseph Stiglitz, "Of the 1%, By the 1%, and For the 1%," *Vanity Fair* (May, 2011) at www.vanityfair.com/news/ 2011/05/top-one-percent-201105. Stiglitz writes more about the One Percent and its powers in his *The Price of Inequality: How Today's Divided Society Endangers Our Future* (New York: Norton, 2012).

301 Many books describe the impact of money on politics. For example, see Frank R. Baumgartner, Jeffrey M. Berry, Marie Hojnacki, David R. Kimball, and Beth L. Leech, *Lobbying and Policy Change: Who Wins, Who Loses, and Why* (Chicago: University of Chicago Press, 2009); Lawrence Lessig, *Republic Lost: How Money Corrupts Congress – and a Plan to Stop It* (New York: Twelve, 2011); Zephyr Teachout, *Corruption in America: From Benjamin Franklin's Snuff Box to Citizens United* (Cambridge, MA: Harvard University Press, 2014); Martin Gilens, *Affluence and Influence: Economic Inequality and Political Power in America* (Princeton, NJ: Princeton University Press, 2014); Wendell Potter and Nick Penniman, *Nation on the Take: How Big Money Corrupts Our Democracy* (New York: Bloomsbury, 2016); and Benjamin I. Page, Jason Seawright, and Matthew J. Lacombe, *Billionaires and Stealth Politics* (Chicago: University of Chicago Press, 2019).

302 For political science, that money talks is summed up in Thomas Ferguson, *Golden Rule: The Investment Theory of Party Competition and the Logic of Money-Driven Political Systems* (Chicago: University of Chicago Press, 1995).

· Roughly speaking, "the golden rule" says that whoever has the gold, rules. In popular culture, see the ABBA song, "Money, Money, Money" – "All the things I could do, if I had a little money, it's a rich man's world."

303 On what major "donors" get in return for their
    political money, see Richard Hasen, *Plutocrats
    United: Campaign Money, the Supreme Court, and the
    Distortion of American Elections* (New Haven, CT: Yale
    University Press, 2016), pp. 37–59. On the endless
    hours that candidates spend raising money rather than
    serving the voters, see Potter and Penniman, *Nation on
    the Take*, pp. 8–9, 48–50.
304 Kenneth P. Vogel, *Big Money: 2.5 Billion Dollars, One
    Suspicious Vehicle, and a Pimp – On the Trail of the Ultra-Rich
    Hijacking American Politics* (New York: Public Affairs, 2014),
    and Jane Mayer, *The Hidden History of the Billionaires Behind
    the Rise of the Radical Right* (New York: Anchor Books, 2016).
    See also Alma Cohen, Moshe Hazan, Roberto Tallarita,
    and David Weiss, *The Politics of CEOs* – a study of 3500
    CEOs of S&P 1500 companies from 2000–2017, showing
    CEOs are between 2.6 and 3.2 times more likely to
    contribute to Republicans than to Democrats. At https://
    corpgov.law.harvard.edu/2019/04/02/the-politics-of-ceos/.
305 Orwell, *Animal Farm: A Fairy Story* (London: Penguin, 1945),
    p. 114.
306 On this score, consider the anecdote about Henry Ford II
    and Walter Reuther. While touring a Ford assembly
    plant in the 1950s and seeing there many early robots,
    the CEO of Ford asked (triumphantly) UAW President
    Reuther, "Walter, how are you going to organize [into
    the United Automobile Workers union] those machines?"
    Whereupon Reuther replied, "Henry, how are you going
    to get them to buy your Ford automobiles?"
307 Early warnings about the decline of the middle class
    appeared in Katherine S. Newman, *Falling from Grace: The
    Experience of Downward Mobility in the American Middle Class*
    (New York: Vintage, 1989) and Katherine S. Newman,
    Declining Fortunes: The Withering of the American Dream
    (New York: Basic Books, 1993).
308 Reich, *Saving Capitalism*, p. xi.

309 See www.washingtonpost.com/news/monkey-cage/wp/
2016/03/29/how-wall-street-became-a-big-chunk-of-the-
u-s-economy-and-when-the-democrats-signed-on/?utm_
term=.9c4c12e71b2a.

310 On the rise of temporary work and its effects, see Louis
Hyman, *Temp.*

311 A decline in living standards was postponed by many
families taking on debt to pay for even ordinary
commodities. Many of them were therefore bankrupted
by the Crash of 2008. On the growth of debt in America
since the 1970s, see Louis Hyman, *Debtor Nation: The
History of America in Red Ink* (Princeton, NJ: Princeton
University Press, 2011), pp. 173–287, and Louis Hyman,
Borrow: The American Way of Debt (New York: Vintage,
2012), pp. 180–247. See also Graeber, *Debt.*

312 Quart, *Squeezed: Why Our Families Can't Afford America*
(New York: Ecco, 2018), *passim.* Quart was preceded by
Elizabeth Warren and Amelia Warrent Tyagi, *The Two-
Income Trap: Why Middle-Class Mothers and Fathers Are Going
Broke* (New York: Basic Books, 2003).

313 Ganesh Sitaraman, *The Crisis of the Middle-Class Constitution:
Why Economic Inequality Threatens Our Republic* (New York:
Knopf, 2017), *passim*, but esp. pp. 111–160, 223–232.

314 *Ibid.*, pp. 274–302. Sitaraman is a law professor. Among
political scientists, but without projecting the same
historical analysis, much of Sitaraman's concern and
many of his findings are matched by Bartels, *Unequal
Democracy* and by Kay Lehman Schlozman, Sidney Verba,
and Henry E. Brady, *The Unheavenly Chorus: Unequal Political
Voice and the Broken Promise of American Democracy* (Princeton,
NJ: Princeton University Press, 2012). See also Jeffrey
A. Winters and Benjamin I. Page, "Oligarchy in the United
States?" *Perspectives on Politics* (December, 2009), pp. 731–
751. From philology and literature, see Emily Katz Anhalt,
Enraged: Why Violent Times Need Ancient Greek Myths (New
Haven, CT: Yale University Press, 2017). Anhalt contends

that Greek epics such as the *Iliad*, and Greek tragedies such *Ajax* and *Hecuba*, help us to understand that humans should control rage, should practice critical reflection, should improve political institutions, should realize that tolerance, rather than war, is good for both sides in a confrontation, and should accept responsibility for earthly events because the gods accept none.

315 Joseph E. Stiglitz, with Nell Abernathy, Adam Hersh, Susan Holmberg, and Mike Konezal, *Rewriting the Rules of the American Economy: An Agenda for Growth and Shared Prosperity* (New York: Norton, 2016), p. 169. Note that, while Stiglitz makes this claim, he leaves open the possibility that the American economy may be working well for some people *outside* the United States, which is what angers some Americans whose jobs were outsourced to other countries.

316 See Gray, *False Dawn*, pp. 194–208.

317 Reich, *Beyond Outrage*, Part I, "The Rigged Game," pp. 2–63, offers a liberal explanation of their plight. Baker, *Rigged*, *passim*, does the same. Carlson, *Ship of Fools*, *passim*, offers a conservative explanation.

318 This is, I believe, a simple but roughly accurate explanation for Hillary Clinton's defeat in 2016. For scholarship on this point, see Suzanne Mettler, *The Government-Citizen Disconnect* (New York: Russell Sage Foundation, 2018), which is based on survey research, and which explains why many pro-Trump voters, even while they received substantial income and services from the federal government, disliked that government and would therefore hold candidates like Hillary Clinton responsible for what they regarded as Washington's shortcomings. For journalism on this point, see Thomas Frank, *What's the Matter with Kansas? How Conservatives Won the Heart of America* (New York: Metropolitan Books, 2004), which argues that, spurred by conservative thinkers and candidates, many Kansas voters fear cultural deterioration more than they seek economic improvement.

319 I am arguing that "creative destruction" and
"neoliberalism," among other trends, especially underlie
the Age of Populism. Using different terms, something
very similar appears in Zito and Todd, *The Great Revolt*.
Zito and Todd interviewed self-declared Trump voters
particularly in the Great Lakes and Rust Belt states of
Michigan, Ohio, Pennsylvania, Wisconsin, and Iowa,
because those states swung to Trump in 2016 and assured
his victory in the Electoral College. Their book reports
(*passim*, but esp. p. 237) on widespread resentment
expressed by people who felt that they worked hard,
paid their taxes, volunteered at church, attended PTA
meetings, and still were called racists and ridiculed
by elites from large metropolitan areas. Summing up
their findings (p. 5), the authors claim that polling
experts and opinion pundits wrongly predicted the 2016
presidential election outcome because they ignored "the
… changes wreaking havoc in every other [non-elite, non-
metropolitan] part of American society."
320 Michiko Kakutani, *The Death of Truth: Notes on Falsehood in
the Age of Trump* (New York: Tim Duggan Books, 2018).
321 This process of stimulating demand appeared, for
example, when Apple's CEO Steve Jobs said that
customers "don't know what they want until we've
shown them." See www.forbes.com/sites/chunkamui/
2011/10/17/five-dangerous-lessons-to-learn-from-
steve-jobs/#3c44fd5f3a95. On the general problem
of advertisements corrupting language and making
coherent thinking difficult if not impossible, see Jean
Kilbourne, *Can't Buy My Love: How Advertising Changes the
Way We Think and Feel* (New York: Torchbooks, 2000),
passim, but esp. pp. 74–75.
322 See Neil Postman, *Amusing Ourselves to Death: Public
Discourse in the Age of Show Business* (New York: Penguin,
1986), p. 128: "A McDonald's commercial, for example,
is not a series of testable, logically ordered assertions.
It is a drama – a mythology, if you will – of handsome

people selling, buying, and eating hamburgers, and being driven to near ecstasy by their good fortune. No claims are made, except those the viewer projects onto or infers from the drama. One can like or dislike a television commercial, of course. But one cannot refute it."

323 Colbert is cited in Farhad Manjoo, *True Enough: Learning to Live in a Post-Fact Society* (Hoboken, NJ: John Wiley & Sons, 2008), pp. 188–189.

324 The mainstream economic view of life uses this rule of thumb. But in real life, it is clear (and I think most economists would agree) that just because people want something does not mean that their preference cannot and should not be challenged ethically and socially. For example, if alcoholics drink a great deal, we do not regard that as good for them because they are willing to pay. See Clive Hamilton, *Growth Fetish* (London: Pluto Press, 2003), p. 12.

325 See the philosophical point described in the text above n. 116. One wonders what Bentham would have thought of plastic bags and bottles.

326 See Ewen, *PR! A Social History of Spin*. Spin is so prevalent today as to encourage many people to believe that they are surrounded by dissembling, that no institutions are trustworthy, and that everyone is trying to manipulate everyone else. A ubiquitous example of such dissembling is how internet websites use "cookies" to invisibly vacuum up information about our habits and preferences and then sell that information to commercial interests who use it, profitably, to influence our thinking. This is a ruthless process of exploitation (which Facebook uses on more than 2 billion participants), which is usually covered up by deceptive explanations – mostly misleading and often false – such as: "Like many other sites, *The Globalist* uses cookies *to enable us to track your use of our site and make it more useful to you ...*" [emphasis supplied]. At www.theglobalist.com/. Is the tracking really "useful to you" or is it instantly valuable to *The Globalist*? Or, from

Politico, "To give you the best possible experience [of what?], this site uses cookies. If you continue browsing, you accept our use of cookies. You can review our privacy policy to find out more about the cookies we use." At www.politico.com/. Actually, you can "review" Politico's "privacy policy" but you won't understand it or its legal implications. Such announcements are grammatically correct but do not describe the situation they reference plainly, fully, and accurately. For example, what exactly does this sentence, from *The Walrus*, mean? "*This website or its third-party tools use cookies to improve functionality.*" [emphasis supplied] At https://thewalrus.ca/in-defence-of-hate/. Do ordinary browsers know what "third-party tools" or "functionality" are?

327 One classic anecdote on this point is that German Chancellor Otto von Bismarck is reported to have said (not disapprovingly) that politics (making laws) is like making sausages (salami, hot dogs, etc.). That is, you don't want to look too closely into exactly how it is done and what ingredients are used.

328 Unlike in President Donald Trump's tweets, truth as a public good (although without using that term) is recommended in the opening sentences of President Franklin D. Roosevelt's First Inaugural Address (1933). As Roosevelt put it, "I am certain that my fellow Americans expect that on my induction into the Presidency I will address them with a candor and a decision which the present situation of our Nation impels. This is preeminently the time to speak the truth, the whole truth, frankly and boldly. Nor need we shrink from honestly facing conditions in our country today." See the speech at http://avalon.law.yale.edu/20th_century/froos1.asp.

329 Snyder, *On Tyranny*, p. 71: "To abandon facts is to abandon freedom. If nothing is true, then no one can criticize power, because there is no basis on which to do so. If nothing is true, then all is spectacle. The biggest wallet pays for the most blinding lights."

330 Reality shows and advertisements are both "pseudo-
events" according to Daniel Boorstin, *The Image: A Guide to
Pseudo-Events in America* (New York: Harper Colophon, 1964).
Pseudo-events purport to reflect reality as it is embodied
in real events. But the former fashion invent what only
appear to be "facts" and then use those to displace the
truth (real facts). In Donald Trump's world, campaign
rallies, speeches, press conferences, and Twitter tweets
are powerful pseudo-events, where almost nothing real
actually happens even though the main character, who is
enormously talented at this sort of thing, draws attention
by performing on stage. Boorstin on pseudo-events and
the displacement of truth are discussed in Chris Hedges,
*Empire of Illusion: The End of Literacy and the Triumph of
Spectacle* (New York: Nation Books, 2009), pp. 47–53.

331 www.nbcnews.com/storyline/meet-the-press-70-years/
wh-spokesman-gave-alternative-facts-inauguration-crowd-
n710466. See Carlos Lozada, "Can Truth Survive This
President?" at www.washingtonpost.com/news/book-party/
wp/2018/07/13/feature/can-truth-survive-this-president-an-
honest-investigation/?tid=a_inl_manual&tidloc =5&utm_
term=.a8f58da33b09). Lozada argues that "[President George
W.] Bush [by attacking Iraq] wanted to remake the world.
President Trump, by contrast, just wants to make it up as he
goes along." Lozada's intimation of a false narrative matches
Michael Gerson's description of Trump as a man who
lives in "the eternal now – no history, no consequences."
www.nytimes.com/2018/10/18/us/politics/donald-trump-
foreign-leaders.html. See also Peter Pomerantsev, *This is Not
Propaganda: Adventures in the War Against Reality* (New York:
Public Affairs, 2019), p. 119: "There is nothing new about
politicians lying, but what seems novel [today] is their acting
as if they don't care whether what they say is true or false."

332 Because some truths emerge from the study of history,
Jo Guldi and David Armitage, *The History Manifesto*
(Cambridge: Cambridge University Press, 2014), insist
in their opening sentence that historians should speak

truth to power. Aaron Wildavsky made the same point
for political scientists. See his *Speaking Truth to Power: The
Art and Craft of Policy Analysis* (Boston: Little Brown, 1979).
On the indispensability of truth in democratic societies,
see Rosenfeld, *Democracy and Truth*, *passim*.

333 Hannah Arendt, *The Origins of Totalitarianism* (New York:
Harcourt, Brace and Company, 1951), *passim*. Arendt's
basic thesis (pp. 340–364) was that the erasure of
truth was the primary aim of "propaganda" promoted
by totalitarian regimes. See also Arendt, "Lying
in Politics: Reflections on The Pentagon Papers,"
New York Review of Books (November 18, 1971), on how
when "National Security Managers" in the Johnson
Administration separated their *thinking* (public relations,
in fact, to drum up electoral support for the war) about
Vietnam from *reality* (what was really happening in the
war), they wound up (mistakenly) "using excessive means
to achieve minor aims in a region of marginal interest."

334 Orwell, *1984* (New York: Harcourt, Brace, 1949), p. 69.
Perhaps with Winston Smith's formulation in mind,
former CIA Director Michael Hayden in 2018 updated
Orwell's warning by noting President Trump's scorn
for intelligence briefings and by suggesting that, in
his opinion, Donald Trump is unable to differentiate
between truth and fiction. See Hayden at
www.nytimes.com/2018/04/28/opinion/sunday/the-end-
of-intelligence.html. Or, as the president's lawyer Ruddy
Giuliani declared, cryptically but confidently, while
hinting that the president should avoid talking to special
counsel Robert Mueller, "Truth isn't truth." At www.
nytimes.com/2018/08/19/us/giuliani-meet-the-press-truth-
is-not-truth.html.

335 Mill, *Principles of Political Economy, With Some of Their
Applications to Social Philosophy* (orig., 1848; New York:
Augustus M. Kelly, Bookseller, 1961), p. 748.

336 *Ibid.*, p. 748. For modern discussions of what Mill
called the "stationary state," see Herman Daley,

Steady-State Economics (Washington, DC: Island Press, 1991); Serge Latouche, *Farewell to Growth* (Malden, MA: Polity Press, 2009); Richard Heinberg, *The End of Growth: Adapting to Our New Economic Reality* (Gabriola Island, BC: New Society Publishers, 2011); Tim Jackson, *Prosperity Without Growth: Foundations for the Economy of Tomorrow*, 2nd edn (London: Routledge, 2017); and Paul Craig Roberts, *The Failure of Laissez Faire Capitalism* (Atlanta, GA: Clarity Press, 2013). For opposition to the stationary-state notion, that is, opposition to the thesis that innovation and change should be restrained or mitigated, see Matt Ridley, *The Rational Optimist: How Prosperity Evolves* (New York: Harper Perennial, 2011), esp. pp. 349–359. In Ridley's estimation, pessimists say that if current trends will continue, disaster will strike. But current trends will not continue, says Ridley, because human creativity and innovation (and economic growth) will solve all problems as they arise. Therefore, p. 281, "The real danger comes from slowing down change."

337 The relation between change and progress is an enormously fraught philosophical subject, for which we have no space here. But see Jill Lepore, *These Truths: A History of the United States* (New York: Norton, 2018), pp. 735–738, for a discussion of (1) how belief in "progress" in the nineteenth century assumed that "change," flowing from science and technology, contributes to social improvements that are morally justifiable, whereupon (2) economists like Schumpeter, in the mid-twentieth century, moved to favoring change (creative destruction) because it boosts economic growth whose index of social improvement is an ever-rising GDP. In such a view, economist Alan Blinder does not need to ponder complex moral characteristics of "progress" but can simply stipulate, with GDP in mind, that "more is better." Along these lines (see n. 190), business professors Clayton Christensen and Michael Raynor sculpted

Schumpeter's concept of "creative destruction" into their concept of "disruptive innovation."

6 Humanism

338 Hacker and Pierson, *Off Center*, argues that American public policies, enacted and maintained by elected officials, have shifted to the right even though the national voting majority has not. At least part of that shift is caused by uneven political contributions.

339 The book you are holding is a product of qualitative research, although its source materials were quantitatively extensive. My guide on this score is historian William McNeill, who described his "method" as follows: "I get curious about a problem and start reading up on it. What I read causes me to redefine the problem. Redefining the problem causes me to shift the direction of what I'm reading. That in turn further reshapes the problem, which further redirects the reading. I go back and forth like this until it feels right, then I write it up and ship it off to the publisher." McNeill is quoted in John Lewis Gaddis, *The Landscape of History: How Historians Map the Past* (New York: Oxford University Press, 2002), p. 48.

340 I have discussed this dilemma in Ricci, *The Tragedy of Political Science*, esp. pp. 291–300.

341 Much that is bleak appears or is implicit in, for example, Kenneth J. Arrow, *Social Choice and Individual Values*, 2nd edn (New Haven, CT: Yale University Press, 1963); Matthew A. Crenson and Benjamin Ginsberg, *Downsizing Democracy: How America Sidelined its Citizens and Privatized its Public* (Baltimore, MD: Johns Hopkins University Press, 2002); Bryan Caplan, *The Myth of the Rational Voter: Why Democracies Choose Bad Policies* (Princeton, NJ: Princeton University Press, 2007); Kahneman, *Thinking, Fast and Slow* (2011); Nadia Urbinati, *Democracy Disfigured: Opinion, Truth, and the People* (Cambridge, MA: Harvard University

Press, 2014); Christopher H. Achen and Larry M.
Bartels, *Democracy for Realists: Why Elections Do Not Produce
Responsive Government* (Princeton, NJ: Princeton University
Press, 2016); and Ilya Somin, *Democracy and Political
Ignorance: Why Smaller Government is Smarter* (Stanford,
CA: Stanford University Press, 2016).

342 Marc J. Hetherington and Thomas J. Rudolph, *Why
Washington Won't Work: Polarization, Political Trust, and the
Governing Crisis* (Chicago: University of Chicago Press,
2015), p. 1.

343 Karen Orren and Stephen Skowronek, *The Policy State: An
American Predicament* (Cambridge, MA: Harvard University
Press, 2017), *passim*, but esp. pp. 192–198.

344 For theory, see Mancur Olson, *The Rise and Decline of
Nations: Economic Growth, Stagflation, and Social Rigidities*,
2nd edn (New Haven, CT: Yale University Press, 1984). For
details, see James A. Thurber and Antoine Yoshinaka (eds),
*American Gridlock: The Sources, Character, and Impact of Political
Polarization* (New York: Cambridge University Press, 2015).

345 Jason Brennan, *Against Democracy* (Princeton,
NJ: Princeton University Press, 2016), esp. pp. 172–230.
During World War II, when Germany and the Soviet
Union were governed by dictators who insisted that they
should rule because *they alone knew* the right path, Karl
Popper rejected the notion of rule by those who claim to
know. He wanted leaders who were not absolutely sure
but open-minded enough to learn new truths when those
might be discovered. For a summary of Popper's view, see
Ricci, *The Tragedy of Political Science*, pp. 114–125.

346 This side of the Enlightenment is explored by Jonathan
Israel, *A Revolution of the Mind: Radical Enlightenment and
the Intellectual Origins of Modern Democracy* (Princeton,
NJ: Princeton University Press, 2010); Anthony Pagden, *The
Enlightenment and Why It Still Matters* (New York: Random
House, 2013); and Pinker, *Enlightenment Now*.

347 Paine, "Common Sense" (1776), in Howard Fast (ed.),
The Selected Work of Tom Paine and Citizen Tom Paine
(New York: Modern Library, 1945), p. 18: "In the following

pages, I offer nothing more than simple facts, plain arguments, and common sense…"

348 Alexander Hamilton, John Jay, and James Madison, *The Federalist* (New York: Modern Library, 1937), No. 1, p. 3: "It has frequently been remarked that it seems to have been reserved to the people of this country, by their conduct and example, to decide the important question, whether societies of men are really capable or not of establishing good government from reflection and choice."

349 See FDR's fireside chat on April 28, 1935: "We have survived all of the arduous burdens and the threatening dangers of a great economic calamity. We have in the darkest moments of our national trials retained our faith in our own ability to master our destiny. Fear is vanishing and confidence is growing on every side, faith is being renewed in the vast possibilities of human beings to improve their material and spiritual status through the instrumentality of the democratic form of government." www.presidency.ucsb.edu/ws/index.php?pid=15046. That is, improvement may come *not* because of the invisible hand of the market but through deliberate (humanistic) politics.

350 Rorty, *Achieving Our Country: Leftist Thought in Twentieth Century America* (Cambridge, MA: Harvard University Press, 1998), p. 101. A similar notion inspires Bob Herbert, *Losing Our Way: An Intimate Portrait of a Troubled America* (New York: Anchor Books, 2012), p. 245: "America needs to be reimagined." Optimism inspired Abraham Lincoln, the greatest republican, and Republican, of them all. As he put it in 1854, "They said that some men are too ignorant, and vicious, to share in government. Possibly so, said we; and by your system, you would always keep them ignorant, and vicious. We proposed to give all a chance; and we expected the weak to grow stronger, the ignorant, wiser; and all better, and happier together. We made the experiment; and the fruit is before us." Lincoln is quoted in Lepore, *These Truths*, p. 151. An opposing view is proposed by Jay W. Richards, *Money, Greed, and God: Why Capitalism is the Solution and Not*

the *Problem* (New York: HarperCollins, 2010), *passim*, but esp. p. 6, which says that we should *not* judge the present by utopian standards and then lists them.

351 For an example of not factoring in optimism, Downs, *An Economic Theory of Democracy*, argues that parties try to ascertain where voters stand ideologically and then position themselves close to those points in order to win votes. A great deal of political science research has followed Downs over the years. What his theory misses is that occasionally, new leaders and new movements can inspire significant numbers of voters to *change* their ideological positions, in which case officials can serve *new* interests and even initiate social improvement. On Downs' narrow definition of leadership, see pp. 87–88.

352 Lowi, "The State in Political Science: How We Become What We Study," *American Political Science Review* (March, 1992), pp. 1–7, but esp. p. 5. Lowi's appeal for his colleagues to "join a more inclusive level of discourse" is similar to my recommendation for some political scientists to participate in the public conversation about neoliberalism.

353 Judith N. Shklar, "Redeeming American Political Theory," *American Political Science Review* (March, 1991), p. 7. This article is an APSA presidential address.

354 On this point, see the update on Burke's conservatism (by name) in Roger Kimball, "Mill, Stephen, and the Nature of Freedom," in Hilton Kramer and Roger Kimball (eds), *The Betrayal of Liberalism: How the Disciples of Freedom and Equality Helped Foster the Illiberal Politics of Coercion and Control* (Chicago: Ivan R. Dee, 1999), pp. 43–69. Kimball, editor of *The Spectator* and publisher of Encounter Books, criticized Mill's *On Liberty* (1859) for praising change in principle but not warning, like Burke did, that some changes can undermine social order and morality. For an additional Burkean sentiment, see Fox News anchor Tucker Carlson who, in his *Ship of Fools*, pp. 9–12, complains that "elites" (he probably means mainly

liberals), by encouraging too much immigration, caused massive "demographic change" and destruction in America.

355 Burke's skepticism about undisciplined change, echoed by Polanyi, appears also in writings by economist Thomas Piketty, who is not on the right, and who warns against an increasing modern "divergence" of incomes and wealth in his *Capital in the Twenty-First Century* (Cambridge, MA: Harvard University Press, 2015), *passim*, but esp. pp. 1, 33–36. See also Harvard Business School professor Shoshana Zuboff, who condemns Silicon Valley for embracing the concept of "inevitability," that is, for arguing that constant digital change is an irresistible force that should not be challenged by "retrograde" consideration for social values (Ludditism) even though big-tech companies like Google, Facebook, and Microsoft, searching constantly for profits, are increasingly manipulating our lives to serve their interests rather than ours. See Zuboff, *The Age of Surveillance Capitalism*, esp. pp. 221–227.

356 Mozorov, *To Save Everything, Click Here: The Folly of Technological Solutionism* (New York: Public Affairs, 2013), p. 1.

357 Quoted in Sherry Turkle, *Reclaiming Conversation: The Power of Talk in a Digital Age* (New York: Penguin, 2015), p. 317.

358 Quoted in Eric A. Davidson, *You Can't Eat GNP: Economics as if Ecology Mattered* (Cambridge, MA: Perseus, 2000), p. 142.

359 Huntington, "One Soul at a Time," *American Political Science Review* (March, 1988), pp. 3–4.

360 I don't mean that, for ethical reasons, political scientists should become more political in the sense of more partisan. I do mean that they should look in many places for the downsides of creative destruction and therefore interact with both Democrats and Republicans who are disadvantaged by the modern economy.

361 This search earned for Aristotle's sort of political thought the title of "master science" for many centuries. On this

all-embracing concept of politics, see Paul H. Rahe, "The Primacy of Politics in Classical Greece," *American Historical Review* (April, 1984), pp. 265–293.

362 Lasswell, *Politics: Who Gets What, When, How* (orig., 1935; Whitefish, MT: Literary Licensing, LLC, 2011).

363 The issue of distribution is one of the dividing lines between political scientists and mainstream economists. See James Kwak, *Economism*, p. 86: "For centuries, who should get what has been a central political question. Economism [Kwak's term for mainstream economics as expressed in Econ 101] removes the question from the political sphere to the abstract realm of theory, in which the competitive labor market provides the perfect, indisputable solution." That is, citizens (and mainstream economists) don't have to worry about who gets what because the market will correctly decide that for them. The issue is summed up by Binyamin Applebaum, *The Economists' Hour: False Prophets, Free Markets, and the Fracture of Science* (New York: Little, Brown, 2019), which observes that, when promoting economic growth, most economists "focus on the size of the pie rather than the size of the pieces."

364 Peter Bachrach and Morton S. Baratz, "Decisions and Nondecisions: An Analytical Framework," *American Political Science Review* (September, 1963), pp. 632–642.

365 Bartels, *Unequal Democracy*.

366 Hacker and Pierson, *Winner-Take-All Politics*.

367 Of course, this point can be disputed. The Founders agreed to make a representative and anti-tyrannical government (for whites) but did not agree to abolish slavery. If they had tried to do that, Southern-state delegates would have withdrawn from the Constitutional Convention and no national government would have emerged. From this point of view, the new government was a great but imperfect achievement of the European Enlightenment. It did some things *very* badly and others *very* well. But beyond the details, some of them

unspeakably *awful* and others still *inspiring*, it has provided, by historical and international standards, a *considerable measure* of equality, progress, prosperity, law, order, and loyalty for over 200 years. That is, I think, something worth building on in our troubled times.

368 " 'The Divine Science': Political Engineering in American Culture," *American Political Science Review* (March, 1976), p. 140. Ranney is a good example of engaging with great thinkers, because he cites John Adams, James Madison, John Witherspoon, and Alexander Hamilton.

369 This strategy can be promoted without mentioning the term "creative destruction." For example, see Greg Lukianoff and Jonathan Haidt, *The Coddling of the American Mind: How Good Intentions and Bad Ideas Are Setting Up a Generation for Failure* (New York: Penguin, 2018), *passim*, but esp. pp. 5–14. Their thesis is that some "good social changes" may lead to "bad consequences," but that in those circumstances, children should not be "coddled." That is, they should be taught to deal with what Lukianoff and Haidt call "problems of progress." In "folk wisdom," the authors say, this strategy is summed up (on an un-numbered page before the Introduction) as "Prepare the child for the road, not the road for the child."

370 See Nicole Aschoff, *The New Prophets of Capital* (London: Verso, 2015), pp. 76–106, on Oprah Winfrey, and about how Winfrey hides economic, political, and social "structures." Aschoff claims that Winfrey's programs, focused on therapy and self-healing, encourage their audiences to adjust to the system rather than the other way round.

371 See the 2018 book review essay on Shklar's political thought in *Foreign Policy*. At https://foreignpolicy.com/2018/07/16/whos-afraid-of-judith-shklar-liberalism/.

372 Judith N. Shklar, "The Liberalism of Fear," in Nancy Rosenblum (ed.), *Liberalism and the Moral Life* (Cambridge, MA: Harvard University Press, 1989), pp. 21–38. Shklar

208 NOTES TO PAGES 100-101

was a child refugee who fled to Canada with her family
from Riga to escape Nazism.

373 Isaiah Berlin, *Two Concepts of Liberty: An Inaugural Lecture
delivered before the University of Oxford on 31 October 1958*
(Oxford: The Clarendon Press, 1958).

374 By praising liberalism for continually opposing tyranny,
Shklar sidestepped the modern criticism of liberals that
complains that they embrace corrosive principles from
the Age of Reason but provide no replacement for the late-
stage feudal order, which entailed clear social standings
and meaningful spiritual stories. That is, the critics say that
liberals provide no shared sense of what post-eighteenth-
century society should look like, whereas Shklar said
that that is simply not their job. Along these lines, recent
critics of liberalism include Charles Taylor, *A Secular
Age* (Cambridge, MA: Harvard University Press, 2007);
Michael Allen Gillespie, *The Theological Origins of Modernity*
(Chicago: University of Chicago Press, 2008); Steven
D. Smith, *The Disenchantment of Secular Discourse* (Cambridge,
MA: Harvard University Press, 2010); Brad S. Gregory, *The
Unintended Reformation: How a Religious Revolution Secularized
Society* (Cambridge, MA: Harvard University Press, 2012);
and Patrick J. Deneen, *Why Liberalism Failed* (New Haven,
CT: Yale University Press, 2018).

375 Shklar, "The Liberalism of Fear," p. 29. For a more
popular version of the thesis that liberalism is mainly
about combatting cruelty, see Adam Gopnik, *A
Thousand Small Sanities: The Moral Adventure of Liberalism*
(New York: Basic Books, 2019), *passim*, but esp. pp. 30–33,
80–82, 134–135.

376 See also Alan Dershowitz, *Rights From Wrongs: A Secular Theory
of the Origins of Rights* (New York: Basic Books, 2005), which
concludes that even if we do not manage to agree on what
are rights, we should at least agree on what are wrongs.

377 See the sources in n. 178. Thus there is justification for
observing that some American activists from East and
West Coast cities "fly over" the center of the country
and therefore never meet the Americans, sometimes

economically stressed, who live in states from Appalachia to the Rocky Mountains. A visit to Detroit would widen their horizons. Similarly, I tell some of my academic friends that they should at least once browse in a Christian bookstore.

378 See Katherine J. Cramer, *The Politics of Resentment: Rural Consciousness and the Rise of Scott Walker* (Chicago: University of Chicago Press, 2016), and Francis Fukuyama, *Identity: The Demand for Dignity and the Politics of Resentment* (New York: Farrar, Straus, and Giroux, 2018).

379 We live in a populist age epitomized by Donald Trump, during which belief often overrides truth in politics, finance, journalism, social media, advertising, and other realms of communication. Therefore, I am assuming that if political scientists will investigate the downsides of creative destruction, they will report true findings to their audiences. Proper scholarship should always promote the truth, of course. (See n. 332.) In addition, we should regard *truth* as vital to Judith Shklar's insistence on opposing *tyranny*. Thus "truth" is a powerful weapon against "tyranny," says Bernard Williams, *Truth and Truthfulness* (Princeton, NJ: Princeton University Press, 2002), pp. 206–209, because tyrannical forces (Williams speaks of "governments") "are disposed to commit illegitimate actions which they will wish to conceal, as they also want to conceal incompetent actions." Then he adds that it is in liberal societies that citizens can most easily speak the truth. Here, Williams cites Shklar, but we can also link this point about anti-tyrannical truth to what Louis Hartz says, as we will see in Chapter 7, about America being, thankfully, a traditionally Liberal, and therefore democratic, society.

380 Shapiro, *The Flight from Reality in the Human Sciences* (Princeton, NJ: Princeton University Press, 2005), p. 40. I am simplifying here, because Shapiro (esp. pp. 37–41) in some respects endorses "scientific realism," which is one point of view in an enormously complicated philosophical debate familiar to political theorists. See

the essays in Matt Sleat (ed.), *Politics Recovered: Realist Thought in Theory and Practice* (New York: Columbia University Press, 2018).

381 *Ibid.*, pp. 86–96. On how public "problems" get defined, leading to public or private demands for new programs to solve those problems, see Frank R. Baumgartner and Bryan D. Jones, *The Politics of Information: Problem Definition and the Course of Public Policy in America* (Chicago: University of Chicago Press, 2015).

382 Hacker (Oxford: Oxford University Press, 2006).

383 Mettler (Chicago: University of Chicago Press, 2011).

384 For example, Hoffman and Casnocha, *The Start-Up of You.*

385 Friedman, "The Methodology of Positive Economics," in Milton Friedman, *Essays in Positive Economics* (Chicago: University of Chicago Press, 1953), pp. 1–27. Mankiw, *Principles of Economics*, posits utility-maximizing, rational individuals, who buy and sell according to indifference curves, and then asks, p. 461: "Do people really think this way?" No, Mankiw answers, they don't. "The theory of consumer choice [he says] does not try to present a literal account of how people [the utility maximizers] make decisions. It is a model ... The best way to view the theory of consumer choice is as a metaphor for how consumers make decisions." But, p. 462, "Just as the proof of the pudding is in the eating, the test of a theory is in its applications." In other words, like Friedman says, does the theory work? Is it useful? In sum, mainstream economics does not focus on real people.

386 See Standing, *The Precariat.*

387 Assuming that epistemology is the philosophical study of what justifies solid knowing rather than questionable opinion, "epistemic rot" is an appropriate description of the effect of constant lying and prevarications imposed on America by President Donald Trump and his spokespeople in and around the White House. The truth is, however, that that "rot" has long plagued digital communications, where to attract attention to themselves, many people say

awful things. On anger, bitterness, isolation, and vulgarity promoted by our digital instruments, see Jaron Lanier, *Ten Arguments for Deleting Your Social Media Accounts Right Now* (New York: Henry Holt and Company, 2018). See also Siva Vaidhyanathan, *Anti-Social Media: How Facebook Disconnects Us and Undermines Democracy* (New York: Oxford University Press, 2018).

388 Friedman said that if his "positive economics" model predicts usefully, the nature of real people is irrelevant to economic research. One reason why he said that was defensive, because it was, and still is, easy to demonstrate that in many cases real people are not the rational calculators assumed by the model. (For showing that most people are irrational, the psychologist Daniel Kahneman received in 2002 the Nobel Prize in economics.) A quirky demonstration of this point appears in Raymond Fisman and Edward Miguel, *Economic Gangsters: Corruption, Violence, and the Poverty of Nations* (Princeton, NJ: Princeton University Press, 2010), pp. 85–94. Fisman and Miguel report on the parking habits of foreign diplomats in Manhattan, where their diplomatic immunity permits them to ignore tickets assigned to them for parking violations. In terms of mainstream economic theory, to park one's car conveniently, in violation of parking laws, when no penalty will be enforced, is "rational" as an alternative to paying expensive fees for parking in private lots. However, this "rational" behavior is not exhibited by all of the diplomats surveyed, as if scofflawing were a law of human nature. Instead, diplomats who come from countries that are known to be corrupt are frequent violators, whereas diplomats who come from countries where citizens are more law-abiding incur fewer violations. Thus on an annual basis, according to the research, Kuwaitis, Albanians, and Pakistanis often parked illegally, while Norwegians, Swedes, and Danes received no tickets at all. In which case, human *nurture* (socialization) clearly influences human *nature* (inherited), and the rational-expectations model is obviously

unrealistic (which Milton Friedman says doesn't matter anyway).

389 William Graham Sumner, *What Do Social Classes Owe Each Other?* (orig., 1883; Caldwell, ID: Caxton Printers, 1961), who was a leading Social Darwinist, famously declared that every social class is morally obliged to take care of itself. Later, Tea Party activists criticized defaulting homeowners who, the Tea Partiers said, recklessly took out large mortgages and then wanted Washington (that is, the taxpayers) to cover their losses. (The original call for a modern "tea party," made in 2009 by CNBC business reporter Rick Santelli, complained about mortgage defaults by irresponsible homeowners. See www.cnbc.com/id/29299591.) More recently, Graeber, in *Bullshit Jobs*, raises questions about how much we owe workers who behave responsibly, but whose work earns for them so little that they suffer in the affluent society. We might even ask how much we owe some cities. That productive communities like Detroit helped America win World War II but later, when pressured by globalization, received from Washington little help in return, is one of those large puzzles we might think about. On what metropolitan Detroit and its workers did for the nation – producing between 1941 and 1945 an endless stream of tanks, guns, trucks, jeeps, bombers, artillery, ammunition, and more – see www.history.com/how-detroit-won-world-war-ii and www.smithsonianmag.com/smart-news/when-detroit-was-arsenal-democracy-180962620/.

390 See Paul L. Wachtel, *The Poverty of Affluence: A Psychological Portrait of the American Way of Life* (Philadelphia, PA: New Society Publishers, 1989) and Sennett, *The Culture of the New Capitalism*.

391 Sennett, *The Corrosion of Character*, esp. pp. 98–117, discusses the decline of vocational commitment and craftsmanship.

392 Barry Schwartz, *The Paradox of Choice: Why More is Less* (New York: Harper Perennial, 2004), esp. pp. 9–44.

393 On the plight of such people – artists, musicians, actors, journalists, editors, architects, poets, book reviewers, and more – under the reign of neoliberalism, see Scott Timberg, *Culture Crash: The Killing of the Creative Class* (New Haven, CT: Yale University Press, 2015), p. 7: "The price we ultimately pay [as a society] is in the decline of art itself, diminishing understanding of ourselves, one another, and the eternal human spirit."

394 That people behave irrationally is a central message of behavioral economics. On behavioral economics, see n. 149. Richard Thaler received the 2017 Nobel Prize in economics for his work on behavioral economics.

395 On personal "rationales" that go beyond "rationality" defined by economists, see David Graeber, *The Utopia of Rules: On Technology, Stupidity, and the Secret Joys of Bureaucracy* (New York: Melville House, 2016), pp. 38–39. One obvious case, not noted by Graeber, is when poor people bet on lotteries. The rational economist (or the behavioral economist) might call that betting irrational because the odds on winning the lottery do not justify buying a ticket. However, a particular individual may buy the ticket anyway, on the outside chance of transforming his or her own life to an extent that seems impossible in the gig economy.

396 Reich, *Saving Capitalism*, pp. 4, 8.

397 The classic case of over-optimism on this score in recent years is the so-called "efficient market" hypothesis, promoted by leading economists like Alan Greenspan, long-time Chairman of the Federal Reserve Board, and Nobel Prize winner (economics, 2014) professor Eugene Fama, of the Chicago School of economic thought. According to this hypothesis, the American stock market was not a bubble but an accurate indicator of economic values – until it collapsed in the Crash of 2008. If one takes into account the colossal destruction caused by this failure of mainstream economic theory, it is hard to speak of it politely. On the losses resulting from the Crash of 2008,

estimated as high as $22 *trillion* (not *billion*), see www.
gao.gov/assets/660/651322.pdf. On the efficient market
hypothesis, see Justin Fox, *The Myth of the Rational
Market: A History of Risk, Reward, and Delusion on Wall Street*
(New York: Harper, 2009), *passim*.

398 Joseph E. Stiglitz, George A. Akerlof, and A. Michael
Spence were jointly awarded the Nobel Prize in
economics (2001) for their theories of asymmetric
information in real markets.

399 Stock buybacks are made by companies with money that
might otherwise be invested to make more products and
sell them more cheaply than today. Buybacks are popular
with managers because buying up their company's
paper assets drives up the price of those assets in the
stock market, whereupon the managers (and other
shareholders) can sell off the shares they own and profit
handsomely even though the buyback contributed
nothing to production and prosperity. See
www.cnbc.com/2019/03/25/share-buybacks-soar-to-
a-record-topping-800-billion-bigger-than-a-facebook-
or-exxon-mobil.html. Stock buybacks were mostly
illegal until the Reagan-era Securities and Exchange
Commission decided to permit them in 1982. See
https://mavenroundtable.io/theintellectualist/news/
stock-buybacks-were-once-illegal-why-are-they-legal-now-
sHh6HZjtyk2styG-qLgnQg/.

400 The Bank raises interest rates to head off inflation, because
inflation reduces the worth of loans made by creditors
such as banks, insurance companies, appliance stores, car
dealers, credit card companies, and more. But raising interest
rates reins in various kinds of business activity that require
loans, and that causes some hard-working employees to be
discharged for no fault of their own. See the process noted
offhandedly, without complaint, by Paul Krugman, who
observes that selling billions of dollars' worth of arms to
Saudi Arabia will maintain a few tens of thousands of jobs
in America's aerospace industries. But, says Krugman, "the
Federal Reserve believes that we're at full employment, and

any further strengthening of the economy will [only] induce the Fed to raise interest rates [to check inflation]. As a result, jobs added in one place by things like arms sales will be offset by jobs lost elsewhere as higher rates deter investment or make the U.S. less competitive by strengthening the dollar." See this remark at www.nytimes.com/2018/10/22/opinion/khashoggi-saudi-trump-arms-sales.html.

401 On how some people, via politics, successfully perpetuate their advantages, see Paul Starr, *Entrenchment*. On employment advantages enjoyed by those who are already ahead, see Lauren A. Rivera, *Pedigree: How Elite Students Get Elite Jobs* (Princeton, NJ: Princeton University Press, 2015).

402 See Reich, n. 308.

403 Reich, *Saving Capitalism*, p. 8.

404 The phrase "autonomous vehicles" is a distortion of grammatical truth fashioned by public relations experts because they assume that the term "driverless cars" (and trucks and trains and buses) would sound to many people ominous.

405 There may be some, but not much, demand for such vehicles. For example, some companies are probably hoping to buy and deploy driverless trucks, which, unlike truck drivers now employed by the same companies, would not demand vacations or pensions or overtime pay.

406 For an example of this argument, see https://medium.com/waymo/lets-talk-self-driving-cars-72743d39cad8.

407 On corporations being more interested in profit than conscience, see Joel Bakan, *The Corporation: The Pathological Pursuit of Profit and Power* (New York: Free Press, 2004). Against this critical view of how large commercial organizations behave, pro-market thinkers are likely to emphasize the vocational sentiments of entrepreneurs rather than the get-along-together skills of bureaucratic managers. This is the approach in Michael Novak, *Business as a Calling: Work and the Examined Life* (New York: Free Press, 1996).

408 I am writing about cars and trucks. But of course this class of entities includes also buses, trolleys, locomotives,

motorcycles, fork-lift carts, and more. I am also writing about America. Worldwide potential profits are far larger than those forecast for America, because there are now more than a *billion* people-driven cars, trucks, and buses in the world. See www.carsguide.com.au/car-advice/how-many-cars-are-there-in-the-world-70629.

409 See Ford, *The Rise of the Robots*, pp. 175–186. The American Trucking Associations estimate that there were 3.5 million truck drivers employed in the United States as of 2016. See www.trucking.org/News_and_Information_Reports_Industry_Data.aspx.

410 The benefits and costs, personal and social, of moving to horseless carriages are discussed in Ann Norton Green, *Horses at Work: Harnessing Power in Industrial America* (Cambridge, MA: Harvard University Press, 2008), esp. pp. 244–274.

411 There is a terminological nuance here. One can speak of "substitution" as when workers move from an old to a new job and the main consideration is whether they maintain or lose income. But one can also observe that, when old jobs are eliminated and new ones created, the new jobs will have characters different from the old, requiring different skills and attitudes and providing different satisfactions. In that case, even if the old rate of pay is maintained in a new job, the transition may generate substantial emotional costs. On this point, see Nicholas Carr, *The Glass Cage: How Our Computers Are Changing Us* (New York: Norton, 2014), p. 33. Ridley, *The Rational Optimist*, p. 114, assumes that when creative destruction destroys jobs, it creates new ones. However, he does not discuss whether or not the new ones will be similar or equal to the old ones, and in what respects.

412 Annie Lowrey, *Give People Money: How a Basic Income Would End Poverty, Revolutionize Work, and Remake the World* (New York: Crowne, 2018), p. 8. The logic here is that a guaranteed income cannot be generous because a large payment might tempt able-bodied people away from

working at all. See also Phillippe van Parijs and Yannick Vanderborght, *Basic Income: A Radical Proposal for a Free Society and a Sane Economy* (Cambridge, MA: Harvard University Press, 2017).

413 When we see a disaster approaching, I believe it is reasonable for scholars to study the situation, to teach about it, and to publish suggestions, radical if necessary, about how up-coming damage might be avoided or mitigated. Often, however, only mild generalizations are offered, as in Ford, *The Rise of the Robots*, p. 285: "If … we can fully leverage advancing technology as a solution – while recognizing and adapting to its implications for employment and the distribution of income – then the outcome is likely to be … optimistic. Negotiating a path through these entangled forces and crafting a future that offers broad-based security and prosperity may prove to be the greatest challenge for our time." A more dramatic and ominous discussion of the personal and social dislocations that automation has brought, and will still bring, appears in Andrew Yang, *The War on Normal People: The Truth About America's Disappearing Jobs and Why Universal Basic Income is Our Future* (New York: Hachette Books, 2018). As Yang says, p. 68, "The challenge we must overcome is that humans need work more than work needs us." In classic political science terms, which Yang does not use, what his book describes is the need for a new "social contract," to help what he calls the many "normal people" who the modern economy is on course to discard.

7 A Story for Political Science

414 On the list syndrome, see David M. Ricci, *Politics Without Stories: The Liberal Predicament* (New York: Cambridge University Press, 2016), esp. pp. 40–41, 132–133.

415 Framing is necessary for "agenda setting." According to this social choice theory, problems and their solutions

will not move onto the agenda of political issues up
for treatment by leaders and activists if they (the
problems and solutions) will not be presented clearly
and persuasively. And one way of presenting them
successfully is to enclose them in stories of where the
nation has been, where it is now, and where it should
go in the future. On agenda setting, see John W. Kingdon,
Agendas, Alternatives, and Public Policies,
2nd edn (New York: HarperCollins, 1995), *passim*.

416 *Politics Without Stories*, pp. 37-39, 139-143.
417 I offer examples of such writings in *ibid.*, pp. 114-131.
418 *Ibid.*, p. 40.
419 *Ibid.*, pp. 63-95.
420 Rogers Smith, *Stories of Peoplehood, The Politics and Morals
     of Political Membership* (New York: Cambridge University
     Press, 2003), *passim*, and Frederick W. Mayer, *Narrative
     Politics: Stories and Collective Action* (New York: Oxford
     University Press, 2014), esp. pp. 27-29, 101-124, on
     how stories create the solidarity needed for collective
     action. Most lately, see Smith, *That Is Not Who We Are!*
     (forthcoming).
421 See www.hillaryclinton.com/issues/.
422 Ricci, *Politics Without Stories*, p. 211. After the election,
     some pundits argued that Clinton's policy proposals
     were aimed at groups animated by narrow "identity
     politics." That is, those groups did not regard themselves
     as integral to the national community but sought to
     improve their minority standings within the nation.
     Consequently, Clinton responded with separate proposals
     tailored to fit parts of America rather than the nation as
     a whole. See Mark Lilla, *The Once and Future Liberal: After
     Identity Politics* (New York: HarperCollins, 2017).
423 Klein, *No is Not Enough: Resisting Trump's Shock Politics and
     Winning the World We Need* (Chicago: Haymarket Books,
     2017), p. 220.
424 Ricci, *Why Conservatives Tell Stories and Liberals Don't*.
425 Ricci, *Politics Without Stories*, esp. pp. 189-201.

426 Along these lines, but using a different vocabulary, William Greider wrote in 2003 about what he called "the soul" of capitalism, which he described as a powerful narrative justifying faith in markets and the belief that efficiency is more important than community. See Greider, *The Soul of Capitalism*, esp. pp. 23–48. (For examples of the tension between efficiency and community while New York City has fostered gentrification in the last half-century, see www. currentaffairs.org/2018/02/everything-you-love-will-be-eaten-alive.) Greider did not describe the soul of capitalism in terms of "neoliberalism." Nevertheless, what America lacks, he argued, pp. 299–324, is an alternative narrative about what people should do with themselves and their society after capitalism has produced enough things to fulfill our needs. He asked, in other words, according to what stories and standards will we decide, after capitalism has satisfied our *needs*, what we (rather than markets) actually *want* beyond that?

427 See Hedrick Smith, *Who Stole the American Dream?* (New York: Random House, 2012), on how American laws and institutions were politically realigned between roughly 1970 and 2010 to favor employers and banks and thereby shift a great deal of wealth to a small fraction of the population. Some of Smith's milestone events are summarized in Ricci, *Politics Without Stories*, pp. 181–182.

428 John Kenneth Galbraith, *The New Industrial State* (Boston: Houghton Mifflin, 1967), p. 408: "This is the modern morality. St. Peter is assumed to ask applicants only what they have done to increase the GNP." Or, as Wolfgang Streeck, *Buying Time: The Delayed Crisis of Democratic Capitalism*, 2nd edn (New York: Verso, 2017), p. 58, says, there are two "competing principles of distribution" in democratic capitalism today, which are "market justice" and "social justice." Similarly, on dollar values versus ethical values, see Robert Kuttner, *Everything for Sale: The Virtues and Limits of Markets* (New York: Knopf, 1998); Raj

Patel, *The Value of Nothing: Why Everything Costs so Much More Than We Think* (New York: Harper Perennial, 2009); Debra Satz, *Why Some Things Should Not be for Sale: The Moral Limits of Markets* (New York: Oxford University Press, 2010); and Sandel, *What Money Can't Buy.*

429 President Donald Trump has perfectly expressed the neoliberal position on market-based morality. See his statement assuring the American people that he will maintain good relations with the government of Saudi Arabia after a CIA report concluded that that government was implicated in the murder and dismemberment, on October 2, 2018, of Saudi journalist Jamal Khashoggi in Istanbul. The main reason for continuing to maintain relations as usual, according to the president, is that Saudi Arabia is an excellent trading partner, whose business he should not risk losing to other countries. In other words, economic gain is the rule and ethics has nothing to do with the matter. See Trump's statement at www.whitehouse.gov/briefings-statements/statement-president-donald-j-trump-standing-saudi-arabia/.

430 *Luke* 16:13. Some writers find no intrinsic conflict between the pursuit of wealth and the service of God. See Richards, *Money, Greed, and God.*

431 *Matthew* 19:24.

432 See Martin Ford, *The Rise of the Robots*, pp. 250–251, on how many skilled jobs are disappearing, to the point where retraining people, in many cases, will simply qualify them for jobs that are anyway being eliminated by robots and algorithms.

433 Thomas L. Friedman and Michael Mandelbaum, *This Used to be Us: What Went Wrong with America – and How It Can Come Back* (Boston: Little Brown, 2011), chapter 7, "Average is Over," pp. 133–152.

434 For example, in his 2012 presidential campaign, Republican candidate Mitt Romney said that "the president [Barack Obama] starts out with 48, 49 percent [of voters] … These are people who paid no income tax

[but enjoy government services] … So my job is not to worry about those people [who will automatically vote for Obama]. I'll never convince them that they should take personal responsibility and care for their lives." At www.politifact.com/truth-o-meter/statements/2012/sep/18/mitt-romney/romney-says-47-percent-americans-pay-no-income-tax/.

435 President Donald Trump has raised and lowered some tariff rates. But he did that on an *ad hoc* basis, aiming to please constituents rather than to execute an overall plan. *Against* most protection, see Daniel Griswold, *Mad About Trade: Why Main Street America Should Embrace Globalization* (Washington, DC: Cato Institute, 2009). *For* at least some protection, according to a theory of recreating an "industrial commons" in America, see Gary P. Pisano and Willy C. Shih, *Producing Prosperity: Why America Needs a Manufacturing Renaissance* (Boston: Harvard Business Review Press, 2012).

436 On Amazon playing off states against one another to receive tax concessions, see www.nytimes.com/2018/01/18/technology/amazon-finalists-headquarters.html and see www.huffingtonpost.com/entry/amazon-headquarters-hq2-process_us_5beb6f28e4b0caeec2bf0ead. On the general practice of states competing for business, note that in 2010 the population of Delaware stood at 971,180. See http://worldpopulationreview.com/states/delaware-population/. Yet the Delaware State Division of Corporations reported in 2011 that there were 1.1 million business entities registered in the state, that is, there were more business entities than residents. At that time, 55 percent of all publicly traded American companies and 65 percent of the Fortune 500 were headquartered in Delaware formally (but not actually domiciled there) to take advantage of various business-friendly Delaware public policies. See https://icis.corp.delaware.gov/eCorp/.

437 This sort of optimism pervades Jagdish Bhagwati, *In Defense of Globalization* (New York: Oxford University

Press, 2007). See also Ridley, *The Rational Optimist*, and John Plender, *Capitalism: Money, Morals, and Politics* (London: Biteback, 2016).

438 This point is made in William Davies, *Nervous States: Democracy and the Decline of Reason* (New York: Norton, 2018), pp. 75–79. Similarly, Roger Eatwell and Matthew Goodwin, *National Populism: The Revolt Against Liberal Democracy* (New York: Pelican, 2018), pp. 179–222, but esp. pp. 212–222, describe "relative deprivation" as when, even in times of national prosperity, some members of the nation feel that they belong to groups that are losing ground, that are becoming less prosperous or respected than others. In those circumstances, resentment grows regardless of "average" gains.

439 Zygmunt Bauman, *Does the Richness of the Few Benefit Us All?* (Malden, MA: Polity, 2013) and Danny Dorling, *Do We Need Economic Inequality?* (Medford, MA: Polity, 2018); both discuss (and reject) the pro-market idea that enormous gaps in income and wealth in market-based economies are necessary in order to encourage a few efficient people to innovate and drive GDP up for the many. In other words, they discuss the trickle-down idea, which claims that gaps in income and wealth (the One Percent situation) are not intolerable but necessary characteristics of economies committed to generating economic growth.

440 These are technical considerations. There is also the fact that, as a discipline, economists do not usually ask whether the existing distribution of resources, income, and wealth has been skewed by historical events and actors and, if so, what should be done about it. On this point, see Earle, Moran, and Ward-Perkins, *The Econocracy*, p. 76–80. See also Geoffrey M. Hodgson, *How Economics Forgot History: The Problem of Historical Specificity in Social Science* (London: Routledge, 2001). Hodgson argues, pp. 14–16, that micro-economics, which claims to explain how individuals and firms act on the basis of rational

calculations, cannot accurately explain macro-economic behavior, which can only assume that the sum-total of small actors performs in ways that can be predicted in theory. In truth, says Hodgson, no theory can make such accurate predictions because collections of real economic individuals behave as groups, which means that they behave as (not entirely rational) historical, sociological, and anthropological entities.

441 On "rent-seeking," see Stiglitz, *The Price of Inequality*, *passim*, but esp. pp. 28–52. On rents, see also Lindsey and Teles, *The Captured Economy*, pp. 15–34.

442 For technical definitions of network effects, see www. nfx.com/post/network-effects-manual. For a discussion of leading examples of network effects, in Google, Facebook, Amazon, Microsoft, Uber, and Airbnb, see Nick Srnicek, *Platform Capitalism* (Cambridge: Polity Press, 2017).

443 In social science terms, one oddity here is that once an adequate Word program was fashioned, producing additional copies of it requires only that someone in Microsoft will push a copy button on his or her computer. In other words, once original expenses are recovered, the marginal cost of the latest copy of such a program, which may be priced at 100 or more dollars, is actually close to zero. Some of the implications of this situation, which does not fit well into conventional economic theory, are discussed in Jeremy Rifkind, *The Zero Marginal Cost Society: The Internet of Things, The Collaborative Commons, and the Eclipse of Capitalism* (New York: St. Martin's, 2015).

444 Thus Sitaraman, *The Crisis of the Middle-Class Constitution*, harked back to the advice of great thinkers like Polybius, Cicero, Machiavelli, Harrington, Jefferson, and Madison, and pointed out that the shrinking of America's middle class creates power imbalances that those thinkers feared and that now threaten the nation's constitutional form of government.

445 Such players are targeted by name and their careers are discussed in chapter after chapter of Jeff Madrick, *The Age*

of Greed: The Triumph of Finance and the Decline of America, 1970 to the Present (New York: Vintage, 2012).

446 See Christopher Witko, "The Politics of Financialization in the United States, 1949–2005," *The British Journal of Political Science* (April, 2016), pp. 349–370. For the reverse thesis, that the Crash was caused by government policy errors rather than by "blind faith in laissez-faire capitalism," see Richard Vedder, "A Financial Fairy Tale," in the *Claremont Review of Books*, at www.claremont.org/crb/article/a-financial-fairy-tale/.

447 Someone should write about how economic growth enthusiasts usually make their case by citing examples of useful creativity while ignoring profitable inventions that turn out to be harmful. Thus computers are praised but asbestos fireproofing goes unmentioned.

448 Hartz, *The Liberal Tradition in America: An Interpretation of American Political Thought Since the Revolution* (New York: Harcourt, Brace, and World, 1955), p. 3.

449 I will capitalize Liberals in the text above because Hartz used that word to denote a sector of post-Enlightenment society rather than to describe liberals in a twentieth-century world of liberals versus conservatives, or modern liberals as opposed to modern progressives. Similarly, Yascha Mounk, *The People vs. Democracy: Why Our Freedom is in Danger & How to Save It* (Cambridge, MA: Harvard University Press, 2018), pp. 25–26, observes that George W. Bush and Barack Obama, Ronald Reagan and Bill Clinton are all European-style liberals by virtue of their support for freedom of speech, separation of powers, and the protection of individual rights.

450 I am writing about "late-stage feudalism" in the text above because even Hartz admitted (in *The Liberal Tradition in America*, asterisk on p. 1) that "There is no precise term for feudal institutions and feudal ideas as they persisted into the modern period amid the national states and economic movements which progressively undermined them."

451 On Katznelson and Hartz, see Richard M. Valelly, "Ira
Katznelson: Toward a Useful Historical Political Science
of Liberalism," *PS: Political Science and Politics* (October,
2005), pp. 797–800.

452 James L. Kloppenberg, "In Retrospect: Louis Hartz and
The Liberal Tradition in America," *Reviews in American History*
(September, 2001), pp. 460–478, and Rogers M. Smith,
"Beyond Tocqueville, Myrdal and Hartz: The Multiple
Traditions in America," *American Political Science Review*
(September, 1993), pp. 549–566.

453 See Corey Robin, "Louis Hartz at 50: On the Varieties
of Counterrevolutionary Experience in America," at
https://digitalcommons.law.umaryland.edu/schmooze_
papers/19. See also Michael C. Desch, "America's Liberal
Illiberalism: The Ideological Origins of Overreaction in U.S.
Foreign Policy," *International Security* (Winter, 2007), pp. 7–43.

454 See Alan Wolfe in www.nytimes.com/2005/07/03/books/
review/nobody-here-but-us-liberals.html. See also Philip
Abbott, "Still Louis Hartz After All These Years: A Defense
of the Liberal Society Thesis," *Perspectives on Politics*
(March, 2005), pp. 93–109. While arguing in favor of
some of Hartz's ideas, Abbott provides a wide-ranging
survey of what many other scholars have said, mostly
critical, about Hartz's work.

455 I agree with Wolfe that Hartz was *mainly* right. I also
agree with the scholars who say that Hartz did not get
everything right. But neither does any book that focuses
on "One Great Idea," which in Hartz's case was that
America's dedication to Liberalism made the country
exceptional among most societies based in Europe. For
later-day, mixed assessments of *The Liberal Tradition*,
see Mark Hulliung (ed.), *The American Liberal Tradition
Reconsidered: The Contested Legacy of Louis Hartz* (Lawrence,
KS: University of Kansas Press, 2010). On "One Great Idea"
books, see Alan Wolfe at https://newrepublic.com/article/
152668/francis-fukuyama-identity-review-collapse-theory-
liberal-democracy.

456 On the point of homogeneity, Americans have not always
    agreed on how to interpret the sentiments and principles
    that Hartz called a Liberal tradition in America. Therefore,
    his thesis deserves qualification, especially from historians
    whose forte it is to remind us, from time to time, of
    uninspiring details in American life. (See Lepore in n. 462.)
    Nevertheless, Hartz's intent was to argue that, compared
    to a wide range of European political ideas and principles,
    Americans had imported mostly a particular part of an Old-
    World spectrum, in which case the Americans were – but
    not always generously or consistently – inspired by that
    part, with certain logical consequences. In that sense, Hartz
    was coming at American politics somewhat as an American
    historian but even more as a comparative politics scholar.

457 *Isaiah* 49:6.

458 *Matthew* 5:14.

459 On the history of "America First" and Trump's support
    for it, see Sarah Churchwell, *Behold America: The Entangled
    History of "America First" and "The American Dream"*
    (New York: Basic Books, 2018), *passim*, but esp. pp. 272–282.

460 At www.nytimes.com/2019/07/14/us/politics/trump-
    twitter-squad-congress.html. Among various groups
    and individuals condemned by Donald Trump in his
    promotion of America First, the president in August
    of 2019 accused American Jews of disloyalty. Opinions
    on Trump's remarks to that effect are so polarized that
    I leave readers to locate their own sources on Trump's
    charges. Just search for: Trump on disloyal Jews.

461 Hartz cannot testify on his own behalf now. But he was my
    doctoral dissertation advisor and I know that when, after
    World War II, he was comparing America favorably with
    Europe, the sins of American Liberalism pained him deeply.

462 Generalizations on this point do not always suffice;
    details are sometimes required. Therefore we need
    historians to remind us of accounts that may still need
    adjusting. For example, some Americans know that, in
    the portrait which appears on the nation's one-dollar
    bill, George Washington isn't smiling because he suffered

from terrible tooth decay and wore ill-fitting artificial dentures. But it takes a historian like Jill Lepore, *These Truths*, p. 120, to remind us that those dentures included nine real teeth "pulled from the mouths of his slaves."

463 Some conservatives may feel that on issues of identity, difference, and gender, not too little but too much has been done in recent decades. See Self, *All in the Family.* Self's thesis, approximately, is that most liberals seek to expand personal rights (for example, the right to an abortion and the right to denounce American wars) whereas most conservatives seek to preserve existing rights (for example, the right to belong to a man-is-the-breadwinner family and to live in a patriotic society). In which case, conservatives believe that liberals are innovating *too much* and liberals believe that conservatives are innovating *not enough*. On the right side of this equation, Fox News anchor Tucker Carlson, *Ship of Fools*, p. 10, complains that liberals have promoted so much immigration into America that the country now has "no ethnic majority, immense religious pluralism, and no universally shared culture or language."

464 Here is the argument. Adam Smith promoted capitalist economics to discredit the late-stage feudalism that constrained many eighteenth-century commoners in the United Kingdom. But today, new constraints are operating. They are sometimes called neoliberalism, and they are, together, holding back the very Liberalism that Smith promoted. Ironically, just as Hartz found it difficult to describe Smith's late-stage feudalism precisely, it is difficult today to get scholars to agree on exactly what neoliberalism is. On that difficulty, see Brown, *Undoing the Demos*, pp. 48–50. For scholars who have begun to refer to neoliberalism as "neofeudalism," see Milan Zafirovski, " 'Neo-Feudalism' in America? Conservatism in Relation to European Feudalism," *International Review of Sociology* (October, 2007), pp. 393–427, and Alain Supiot, "The Public-Private Relation in the Context of Today's Refeudalization," *International Journal of Constitutional Law* (January, 2013), pp. 129–145.

465 Our political vocabulary is inadequate here. Hartz's
    Liberal Tradition in America (a) commends Liberalism
    for its freedom and individual rights, and (b) criticizes
    Liberalism for its insularity (anti-socialism) and
    oppressions (such as slavery). Which means that there
    are two strands of political thought in Liberalism, one
    more generous and the other less so. Which means that a
    critic of what I have just written in the text above might
    argue that the "new force" is not anti-Liberal but an
    extension of Liberalism, in the sense of growing out of
    undesirable (pro-market) Liberal qualities.

466 In the early 1970s, mental illness struck Louis Hartz.
    He retired from Harvard University in 1974 and died in
    Istanbul in 1986.

467 Ronald Reagan expressed this sentiment famously in his
    first Inaugural Address. As he said then, "In this present
    crisis, government is not the solution to our problem;
    government is the problem." See www.presidency.ucsb.
    edu/documents/inaugural-address-11.

468 This analogy between the Reaction and neoliberalism
    can be inferred from what Corey Robin, using a different
    vocabulary, describes in *The Reactionary Mind: Conservatism
    from Edmund Burke to Sarah Palin* (New York: Oxford
    University Press, 2011).

469 The point here is that neoliberals (like Edmund Burke
    earlier) doubt that citizens can solve great social
    problems, whereas Hartzian Liberals (like Thomas
    Paine) are actually humanists. This clash, between the
    skepticism of neoliberalism and the humanism of the
    Founders, is discussed by Brown, *Undoing the Demos*,
    passim, but esp. pp. 220–222. See also Mettler, *The
    Government-Citizen Disconnect*, esp. pp. 148–155, which
    does not explicitly recommend "humanism" but argues
    that anti-government sentiments in America prevent
    citizens from using government to mitigate market-
    based outcomes that presently generate inequality and
    suffering. See also Zuboff, *The Age of Surveillance Capitalism*,

passim, which condemns neoliberalism and argues that its great personal-data-mining companies like Google, Facebook, Amazon, and Microsoft manipulate digital users for profit and thereby destroy their ability to decide for themselves what sort of lives they want to live, separately and together. At p. 513, Zuboff specifically endorses Paine and rejects Burke.

470 To suggest that neoliberals are like barbarians for permitting market-based innovations to undermine long-standing democratic principles and practices may evoke a conservative response that the real barbarians in America today are universities, dominated by liberals who irresponsibly assault long-standing moral truths and social virtues. Two classic examples of this conservative thesis are William Buckley, *God and Man at Yale: The Superstitions of "Academic Freedom"* (orig., 1951; New York: Gateway, 2002), and Allen Bloom, *The Closing of the American Mind* (orig., 1987; New York: Simon and Schuster, 2012). On this point, see Kim Phillips-Fein, "How the Right Learned to Loathe Higher Education," at www.chronicle.com/article/How-the-Right-Learned-to/ 245580.

471 See FDR's Second Inaugural Address at http:// historymatters.gmu.edu/d/5105/.

472 Michaels, *The Trouble with Diversity: How We Learned to Love Identity and Ignore Inequality* (orig., 2006; New York: Picador, 2016). For example, p. 76, "we prefer fighting racism to fighting poverty." Similarly, that American voters may focus on culture rather than economic inequality is discussed in Frank, *What's The Matter with Kansas?*

473 Many economists and other thinkers (1) fear that redistribution would require catastrophic confrontations within society, and therefore (2) prefer that perpetual economic growth will permit everyone to automatically gain at least something so as to avoid feelings of partisan deprivation flowing from zero-sum political decisions. For example, Thomas Byrne Edsall, *The Age*

of Austerity: How Scarcity Will Remake American Politics (New York: Anchor Books, 2012), and Friedman, *The Moral Consequences of Economic Growth*. On the other hand, economist Thomas Piketty insists that his discipline should place "distribution at the heart of economic analysis." See his *Capital in the Twenty-First Century*, pp. 19–21. He is opposed by Mankiw, *Principles of Economics*, p. 5: "When government redistributes income from the rich to the poor, it reduces the reward for working hard; as a result, people work less and produce fewer goods and services. In other words, when the government tries to cut the economic pie into more equal slices, the pie gets smaller." But see Nobelist (economics, 2019), Abhitjit V. Banerjee and Nobelist (economics, 2019) Esther Duflo, *Good Economics for Hard Times* (New York: Public Affairs, 2019), who recommended government intervention to help victims of economic "disruption" – in other words, government promotion of at least some redistribution.

474 Without scholarly elaborations, this is the story told by Zito and Todd, *The Great Revolt*. (See n. 319.)

475 Robert W. McChesney, *Digital Disconnect: How Capitalism is Turning the Internet Against Democracy* (New York: The New Press, 2013), pp. 12–19, *et passim*, regards modern capitalism as an "elephant in the room," and insists that people who write about whether digital technology – including computers, smartphones, the internet, and social media – will help or hinder democracy, should remember always that technology does not stand on its own but is shaped, for better or worse, by the system of ownership that we call neoliberalism or capitalism.

476 On the need for restraint via government regulation, see Tim Wu, *The Curse of Bigness: Antitrust in the New Gilded Age* (New York: Columbia Global Reports, 2018). On the power of private commercial entities to prevent or resist government regulation, see David Rothkopf, *Power, Inc.: The Epic Rivalry Between Big Business and Government – and the Reckoning That Lies Ahead* (New York: Farrar, Straus,

and Giroux, 2012), *passim*. See also Gordon Lafer, *The One Percent Solution: How Corporations Are Remaking America One State at a Time* (Ithaca, NY: Cornell University Press, 2017), which describes the work and influence of nation-wide business lobbies such as the Chamber of Commerce, the National Association of Manufacturers, the National Federation of Independent Business, Americans for Prosperity, the Business Roundtable, the Club for Growth, and the American Legislative Exchange Council. See also Page, Seawright, and Lacombe, *Billionaires and Stealth Politics*, which reports on a study of the political activity of 100 American billionaires and concludes (esp. pp. 126–138) that most of them fund political action by parties, campaigns, candidates, and organizations that oppose redistribution (except upwards, by reducing estate taxes).

477 The likelihood of eventual dictatorial action against the worst environmental downsides of affluence was postulated by William Ophuls, *Ecology and the Politics of Scarcity: A Prologue to a Political Theory of the Steady State* (San Francisco, CA: W. H. Freeman, 1977). The book was updated and republished as William Ophuls and A. Steven Boyan, *Ecology and the Politics of Scarcity Revisited: The Unraveling of the American Dream* (San Francisco, CA: W. H. Freeman, 1992).

478 Sennett, *The Corrosion of Character*.

479 We have noted that so-called "natural markets" are a theoretical fiction, because historians and anthropologists say that only markets shaped by governments (or tribes, or other social entities) have ever existed. If that is so, "intervention" in modern markets may be regarded as adjusting something that government has already contrived rather than treading where politics has never entered. This approach is taken by Baker, *Taking Economics Seriously*, which assumes that using government to promote equity would not be an innovation but merely a revision of official marketplace arrangements that now

maintain a pattern of economic distribution favoring successful, wealthy, and powerful people.

480 See her broadcast from the White House in 1986 inaugurating the"Just Say No" campaign, at www.history.com/speeches/nancy-reagan-introduces-just-say-no-campaign.

481 One can argue that a considerable measure of government intervention and coordination, regulation and services, in the modern and market-based economy, is a *practical* necessity based on historical trends – in transportation, education, housing, health care, internal migration, commerce, and more – rather than a liberal preference flowing from *abstract* ideological sentiments. See John Kenneth Galbraith, *The Good Society: The Humane Agenda* (Boston: Houghton Mifflin, 1996), pp. 14–22.

482 In 2016 Nabisco stopped producing Oreo cookies in Chicago, fired 600 local workers, and moved their jobs to baking facilities in Mexico. See www.chicagotribune.com/business/ct-last-chicago-oreo-0709-biz-20160708-story.html.

483 For liberal criticism of powerful agribusiness entities, see F. William Engdahl, *Seeds of Destruction: The Hidden Agenda of Genetic Manipulation* (Montreal: Global Research, 2007); Frederick Kaufman, *Bet the Farm: How Food Stopped Being Food* (Hoboken, NJ: John Wiley, 2012); and Raj Patel, *Stuffed and Starved: The Hidden Battle for the World Food System* (New York: Melville House, 2012). For a conservative approach to the same conditions, which also criticizes large-scale corporate behavior in this realm, see Austin Frerick, "To Revive Rural America, We Must Fix Our Broken Food System," *The American Conservative* (February 27, 2019), at www.theamericanconservative.com/articles/to-revive-rural-america-we-must-fix-our-broken-food-system/.

484 See "Trump Defends $110B US Arms Sale to Saudi Arabia," in https://thehill.com/homenews/administration/411271-trump-defends-110-billion-us-arms-sale-to-saudi-arabia.

485 An historical point is pertinent here. In the early
eighteenth century, thinkers like Bernard Mandeville, *The
Fable of the Bees: Private Vices, Publick Benefits* (1714), began to
argue that virtuous behavior might not be economically
effective. The general idea was that personal greed is
not admirable but might be morally acceptable because
it gets channeled by economic interactions – say by
Adam Smith's "invisible hand" of the marketplace –
to produce results advantageous to society. That idea
was severely challenged by the Crash of 1929 and the
consequent Great Depression. Nevertheless, after World
War II, neoliberal thinkers revived and expounded the
"publick benefits" thesis for our times, as if the stunning
inequalities in modern society add up to the best of
all possible worlds. Gordon Gekko, played by Michael
Douglas in the 1987 movie *Wall Street*, insisted that "Greed
… is good." Many people who saw *Wall Street* laughed,
perhaps bitterly, at the satire. But Gordon Gekko, in a
way, expressed Milton Friedman's "shareholder value"
theory of corporate governance, which recommends that
CEOs will relentlessly pursue maximum profits. And the
terms of that theory fuel a good deal of respectable talk
in the Age of Populism. On the shareholder value theory
in corporate law and public debate, see David Yosifon,
*Corporate Friction: How Corporate Law Impedes American
Progress and What to Do About It* (New York: Cambridge
University Press, 2018), esp. pp. 60–95. For commentary
on a modern example of literary praise for economic
greed, see Lisa Dugan, *Mean Girl: Ayn Rand and the Culture of
Greed* (Oakland, CA: University of California Press, 2019).
In Marxian terms, which most American thinkers do not
endorse, one might describe the shareholder theory of
value as a capitalist recommendation for business people
to carry their hearts in their purses.

486 Shaw, *The Intelligent Woman's Guide to Socialism and
Capitalism* (New York: Brentano's, 1928), pp. 190–191.
Of course, enforcement of government decisions

is also necessary, because some people will always
bend and stretch to avoid regulation. For example,
see Jack Ewing, *Faster, Higher, Farther: The Inside Story of
the Volkswagen Scandal* (London: Transworld, 2018), on
Volkswagen producing and selling diesel cars designed
to deceive government-mandated pollution tests. If
we think of the Volkswagen case as constituting what
Shaw would have called a "social problem," then
2013 APSA president Mansbridge, "What is Political
Science For?" (see n. 29) observes (in agreement with
Shaw) that problems of social action (she calls them
"collective action problems") can only be solved by an
exercise of what she calls "legitimate coercion" – that
is, by enforcement of serious governmental regulations
enacted politically.

NAME INDEX

SUBJECT INDEX

CPSIA information can be obtained
at www.ICGtesting.com
Printed in the USA
LVHW091145150320
650078LV00003B/1003